To Gina Marie —
with my best

Benjamin Sacco

THE DENTIST OF AUSCHWITZ

THE DENTIST of AUSCHWITZ

A Memoir

BENJAMIN JACOBS

THE UNIVERSITY PRESS OF KENTUCKY

*To my brother, Josek, who by the grace of
God was spared from death in the camps*

To my sister, Pola, my mother, and my father

And to other who were not spared to tell their story

Copyright © 1995 by Benjamin Jacobs

Published by The University Press of Kentucky

Scholarly publisher for the Commonwealth,
serving Bellarmine College, Berea College, Centre
College of Kentucky, Eastern Kentucky University,
The Filson Club, Georgetown College, Kentucky
Historical Society, Kentucky State University,
Morehead State University, Murray State University,
Northern Kentucky University, Transylvania University,
University of Kentucky, University of Louisville,
and Western Kentucky University.

Editorial and Sales Offices: Lexington, Kentucky 40508-4008

Library of Congress Cataloging-in-Publication Data

Jacobs, Benjamin, 1919–
    The dentist of Auschwitz: a memoir / Benjamin Jacobs.
      p.   cm.
    Includes index.
    ISBN 0-8131-1873-5
    1. Jacobs, Benjamin, 1919–   . 2. Holocaust, Jewish (1939-1945)
—Personal Narratives. I. Title
D804.3.J32   1994
940.53' 18' 092—dc20   94-13791

This book is printed on acid-free recycled paper meeting
the requirements of the American National Standard
for Permanence of Paper for Printed Library Materials.

CONTENTS

MAPS AND FIGURES

Maps

Figures

PREFACE

In July 1985 I joined twelve Jewish men and women from the United States on a fact-finding mission behind the Iron Curtain. In the capitals of Poland, Romania, Hungary, and Czechoslovakia we visited a small number of Jews too old to leave for a beginning elsewhere. Most lived in *Altersheims,* homes for the aged supported by Jewish philanthropy. The Jewish life they had once known no longer existed, and anti-Semitism was still widespread. For the Jews, Hitler had won World War II.

When I returned to Boston, I sat back and took stock. I had to confront my obligation, and I began to speak out publicly about how and why nearly an entire people was erased from the face of the earth. In this process the small fragments of memory, fixed in my mind like holographic images, expanded and brought back my experiences in vivid detail.

But life does not always follow a straight road, as I had learned in my youth. One day, during a routine visit to the doctor's office, expecting a clean bill of health, I heard the opposite: "You have throat cancer," I was told. My good friend Dr. Goroll, as devastated as I, insisted that I be operated on the next day.

I imagined the worst. My speaking had become very important, for I had seen its effect on the young, how I had helped them understand the importance of resenting prejudices. Will I still have a voice? I wondered. The thought of becoming mute was overwhelming. I asked the doctors for a prognosis, but doctors are careful; they don't speculate.

Fortunately the tumor was small and, thanks to immediate surgery and weeks of radiation, my voice changed little. But I knew the doctors could not forecast the future. A voice inside kept telling me, "Write—you may not be able to speak for long."

I had to put my experiences on paper, and my work intensified. Comments from others poured in, echoing my own urge to write. This, then, is my story.

Although this book is the result of my recollections, some perhaps still locked in my subconscious, too deep for me to recall, it could not have been written without the valuable assistance I received from many sources. The sheer number precludes my thanking all of them. Nonetheless, I would be remiss not to thank a few.

In developing documentation of Auschwitz III, Fürstengrube, I am indebted to Tadeusz Iwaszko, writer and archivist at the State Museum at Auschwitz. I am grateful to Dr. Dirk Jachomowski of the Ladesarchiv Schleswig-Holstein and to Dr. Marienhöfer of the Bundesarchiv-Militärarchiv in Freiburg, Germany, for documents concerning the *Cap Arcona* disaster on the Baltic Sea. I am particularly grateful to Edith Pfeiffer of the Hamburg-Südamerika Dampfschiffahrts-Gesellschaft and the Hamburg-Amerika line (Hepag) for company records, documents, and the history of the luxury liner *Cap Arcona* and for helping me obtain "top secret" documents concerning the bombing and sinking of the ship. I thank Barbara Helfgot-Hyatt, professor at Boston University and distinguished poet, who from day one encouraged me to write this book. I would also like to thank Ina Friedman, a prolific writer on the subject of the Holocaust, who read the first hundred pages of the manuscript and said to me, "Write. You are bitten with the writer's bug."

Special thanks to Arthur Edelstein and Marge Garfield for their talented revisions of the manuscript. Special thanks to Mark Dane for his valuable time and word processing equipment—for without it I would still be typing this manuscript on a typewriter.

In pursuit of this project, a very special acknowledgment goes to Dr. Karen E. Smith for her valuable advice.

Lastly, I thank my wife, Else, for keeping my spirits up during the more than forty-four years of our marriage. To the rest of my family, to my friends, and to my neighbors, my profoundest apologies for having been a hermit while writing this book.

I have purposely refrained from paving the book with notes and references so as not to trouble the reader who is not interested in research.

The mistakes, errors, and misjudgments are mine and in no way attributable to the people mentioned here, who have contributed so generously.

| 1 |

DEPORTATION

On the morning of May 5, 1941, three ancient trucks labored along a Polish country road, carrying 167 Jews from Dobra, a village in the Warthegau region of Poland, to a destination known only to their captors. It was spring, but the fields, which were full of colorful budding flowers, seemed lifeless on that gloomy morning. The songbirds, whose melodies usually filled the country air in May, were strangely quiet.

This was a dark day in our village. The Jewish Council, by decree of Herr Schweikert, the Nazi governor of the region, had delivered for deportation to a labor camp all Jewish men between the ages of sixteen and sixty, with the exception of one male per family. My father wanted to leave, and I volunteered to go with him, since my older brother was susceptible to ailments. So my brother stayed with my mother and my sister in the ghetto. My father and I were each allowed to take two bundles. My mother insisted that I take the few dental tools I had from my first year of dental training, along with my necessities. Little did I know then that those tools would save my life.

Mother's face was lined with sorrow. Pola, my older sister, bravely held back her tears, and brother Josek promised to live up to his new role as head of the family. We all felt the pain of parting, and I turned my face away from them to find courage.

My parents hadn't often shown affection for each other in public, and certainly not in front of us. But that day, for what was to be the last time, they embraced before us. As we left, Mama reminded all of us not to forget what we had agreed to do. "When this nightmare is over, we will all meet back here," she said, with tears in her eyes.

On the way to the town school, our assembly place, we saw similar scenes. At every doorstep a small drama played out. A young girl cried and wouldn't let her father go, seemingly knowing she would never see him again.

When we arrived at the school yard, SS men were everywhere. From their black uniforms and shiny boots to the skull and crossbones on their caps, they personified malice. Their belt buckles carried the ironic slogan "God with Us." At the center of the yard stood the feared Herr Schweikert, along with Morris Francus, head of the Jewish Council. Two of the ghetto's Jewish policemen were to come with us. Chaim Trzan, formerly a butcher, was perfectly suited for this job. But the other man, Markowicz, seemed out of his league, for he was a simple man with more bark than bite. Dwarfed by the tall SS men was the deputy of Jewish matters for Warthegau, Dr. Neumann. He was burly and middle-aged with snow-white hair and bright blue eyes. His stance spoke all: he was obviously in charge.

The Nazis knew how to pit Jew against Jew. They had created a Jewish Council, the Judenrat, for that purpose. In Dobra, the members of the council were self-styled community leaders with little conscience. With the help of the policemen whom they appointed, they wielded indiscriminate power over us. As difficult as it may have been for them to make the choices that no human should ever have to make, the members of the Judenrat primarily sheltered themselves, their families, and their friends from the privation and discrimination the rest of us had to face. Little did they know that, having sent their people to their deaths, they would in the end fall victim to the same fate.

As Francus read our names aloud, we responded with "Jawohl." At 9:00 A.M. the gates of the school yard opened, and in groups of about fifty-six per truck, we boarded the three trucks. The SS guards jumped on the tailgates for one more check. With this they cast a net around us.

As we picked up speed on the cobbled streets, we saw in a doorway two women watching the approaching trucks. We got closer, and Papa and I recognized Mama and Pola. They timidly covered their yellow Star of David patches and waved to us as we passed. We stared back, our hearts as heavy as the dark clouds above, until they were no longer visible. From this moment on, our family was split apart forever.

So there we were, 167 Jewish men, sixteen to sixty years old, one, two, and in some cases even three from one family, of varied skills, lifestyles, and backgrounds. We were united in the same fate and bound together on a journey as alien to us as the times we were now in. I glanced at my father, and I saw the once-proud head of our family embarrassingly helpless.

Leaning against the side of the truck, I stared at its plume of dark exhaust, believing I saw in it my own black future. To find a bit of solace, I thought back to my childhood days.

| 2 |

A SMALL SHTETL IN POLAND

I was launched into the sea of life in Dobra, a small village of western Poland, on a cold November day in 1919. According to tradition, I was named Berek, after my deceased maternal grandmother, Baila. In retrospect, I see that I was born at the wrong time, in the wrong place, and with the wrong religion to see my youthful dreams fulfilled.

With my brother, Josek, and my sister, Pola, I grew to adulthood in Dobra, where my ancestors, as far as I can tell, had lived ever since Jews settled in Poland. Our family owned a house with two and a half hectares of land that my parents had bought after they married. Ours was a modest house, even by the standard of those days. We had two bedrooms, a dining and living room, and a kitchen. A coal-fired oven, two meters tall, covered with brown ceramic tile, provided heat to our living and dining room in the winter. A black iron cookstove stood in the kitchen. Behind the house, the yard held a straw-roofed barn, two stables, and a small chicken coop. Behind that were several fruit trees. One dwarf tree bore the sweetest yellow cherries, but the sparrows always got them before we did. Plum, pear, and apple trees also flourished there. The seckel pear tree was always the last to bear fruit. On the rest of the land we grew enough rye, wheat, and potatoes to last us for the entire winter season. We worked our farmland, rising every morning at dawn to begin the daily task of plowing, sowing, and reaping crops. We were not rich. In our non-materialistic world we did not have much and did not want much. But we were comfortable and happy.

The only luxury I recall in our house was a colorful Oriental rug under the dining table, which was embroidered with a castle and kings. There in my younger years I lay for hours reading adventure stories or listening to music on my crystal radio set. Our dining and living room walls were covered with family portraits, pictures of men with long gray beards and women in traditional lace dresses—our ancestors.

Papa owned and operated a modest grain business in which we all helped. At the age of ten I carried hundred-kilo sacks of grain on my back from the warehouse to the scale. My father was a simple, hard-working man, good-natured and utterly devoted to his family. He was short—shorter than my mother—and almost totally bald. His face was round, and his cheeks rosy. When he smiled, he expressed a kind nature. I recall that Papa had been very heavy, but once a doctor diagnosed him as having an enlarged heart, he slimmed down. He and his eight brothers and sisters were orphaned when he was only eleven. After that he moved into my maternal grandfather's house, where he met my mother. Although they shared the same last name, Jakubowicz, they were not related. Since Papa had to work at an early age, he did not attend school and barely knew how to read or write. His signature was three crosses, but it was valid everywhere in town. My parents were married in 1912, when Papa was eighteen and Mama was sixteen. My parents rarely argued. Any disharmony that arose resulted from my father's thrift clashing with my mother's generosity. But an argument was as far as it ever got.

Mama was the most progressive Jewish woman in the village, the first to stop wearing the traditional wig. A mild case of diabetes kept her slim. She had dark, wavy hair and was tanned from her outdoor work. She was blessed with a heart of gold, and the poor knew on whose door to knock. The blind man, Iizchak, visited us at least once a week and was assured that he wouldn't leave our house hungry. With a spool of wire and a cane and a bow for a musical instrument, he played songs any trained musician could envy. He imitated all the parts of the orchestra on that ersatz instrument. Mother even gave the wandering gypsies something when they came begging.

We children were never physically disciplined. Denying us meals and keeping us indoors, beyond our patience, was enough. Mama was a parent any growing child would want to have. She had complete authority over the household, although the kitchen was the responsibility of my paternal cousin Toba. We loved both our parents, not out of fear, but for the love and kindness they gave us. We were raised with devotion to Jewish tradition and with a firm belief in God.

My sister, Pola, was two years older than I. She was bright and intelligent and as tall as Mama. She wore her brown hair in a bob over her slightly elongated face. Except for lipstick, she rarely wore makeup. Her hazel eyes, with thick lashes and nicely shaped brows, accented her good looks. My brother, Josek, was six years older than I. After his Bar Mitzvah, he began the study of the Talmud. But the considerable yeshiva rigor soon proved too much for him, and he left the yeshiva and became a dental technician.

The best times of our childhood were the summers, when we went to a tiny cottage my father rented in Linne. It lay in the midst of a forest full of wild berries and mushrooms. In the mornings we set out to explore the small river, abundant with *kielbiki,* a small chublike fish that we would catch in round nets.

One early spring when I was barely seven, Mama gave me a small patch of land the size of the barn. "This is going to be yours," she said. This was my special piece of land, and receiving it was a very proud moment in my young life. Since lots of wildflowers already grew nearby, I planted vegetables in my garden.

Since my mother's mother died before I was born, her father lived with us. He was tall and slender and wore a neatly shaped goatee. He walked erect with a slight forward thrust and a rhythmic motion. He used a cane with a silver handle, not merely for support but as an expression of good taste. He loved all three of us children, but I always felt that he had special affection for me, his youngest grandson. He played a decisive role in shaping my early life. Grandpa was an expert fisherman. On warm days he would take me to the river, and in time I too could land the big ones.

Many summer days, when I came home from heder, I would find Grandpa sitting on a bench, his skullcap on, bent over and reading the Scriptures. Sometimes his eyes closed involuntarily, and he would doze off in the glow of the sun. Hearing me, he would awaken, and his mustache would turn up in a happy smile. In those days people over sixty were considered old. They usually had lined faces and toothless mouths. Our grandpa, though, had all his teeth and still read without glasses.

At times he would wait for me, prepared with two rods, a net, and a bundle under his arm, ready to take me for a fifteen-minute walk from our house, to a small tributary of the Warta River. It was so small it didn't even have a name. As my grandfather raised his trouser legs above his calves and waded into the water, his body looked much thinner. I followed him, and he watched me bait my hook. His arms lifted as he swung the line into wide circles, until the bait fell just where he wanted it. "Slowly, Berele," he would say, "slowly," seeing me wrestle with my line. He knew I could do it right and wouldn't settle for bad casts. I followed closely as the pebbles dug into the soles of my feet. When we fished with a hand net, like one used to catch butterflies, we moved in tandem, pushing the net quietly under the lily pads. "Reach deep, move slowly, step in rhythm," he would say. No catch went to waste. Perch were made into meals, and Mama used the pickerel for gefilte fish.

Grandpa also taught me to play chess. "Chess sharpens the mind," he would say. I knew that in the First World War he had received a citation for bravery from Polish marshal Jozef Piłsudski, but Grandpa never wanted to talk about it.

Anti-Semitism in Poland was already a social disease before Hitler's time. Although other minorities were treated fairly, Jews were made an exception. In the late 1930s in Poland, those who had previously sat on the fence joined Hitler in the Nazi's racial policy. Even though we were born there, we were considered foreigners. For a Jew to be equal in Poland, he had to become a Christian first. While the Polish clergy didn't advocate violence against us, they did not promote brotherly love either. My parents' generation was willing to accept such an oppressed role in Polish society, but my generation found it difficult to live with. We were not Jews first and Poles second. We thought that if we adopted a new way of life and adhered to Polish customs, dress, culture, and language, non-Jews would tolerate us better, but nothing seemed to work. Nothing seemed more astonishing than the lie that the Jews in Poland lived in luxury.

Jews were verbally abused and often beaten in broad daylight. As long as a person was not visibly hurt, the police claimed that they could do nothing about it. The label on Jewish businessmen was *handlarz,* a term suggesting profiteer. Neither my brother nor I wanted to continue our father's business, so we opted for a profession. Little did we know that whatever we became, the deep-rooted bias would persist.

In school our books ignored our history, our culture, and even our existence. The Dobra public school did not have a single Jewish teacher. Because of my given name, Berek, the non-Jews called me spitefully Belis, after the Belis Affair in tsarist Russia, where a Jew by that name had been accused of ritual child killing. I was so embarrassed that before I attended secondary school, I changed my name to the Polish equivalent, Bronek.

In the mid-1930s the Farmers' Union established farm cooperatives in Poland. Their purpose was obvious: to stop Jews from trading in farm products. The cooperative's motto was "We, to Ours, for Ours." This economic squeeze affected all Jewish businesses and, indeed, the entire Jewish population in Poland.

Attempts to set quotas at learning institutions were propagated. Banning shechita, kosher animal slaughter, was another overt act of anti-Semitism. Although Poland was close to war with Germany, Jews were the big enemy. Even the moderates tried to find ways to get rid of us. Taking a cue from the Nazis, the fascists demanded the expatriation of all Jewish people from Poland.

Excessive taxation was another of our dilemmas. Though we paid a parochial tax, Jewish schools and synagogues received no part of the money. I remember hearing Mama plead one day with a tax collector who came with a truck to take our furniture away to wait for Papa. He ignored her and called in his two helpers to take out our furniture. They threw our clean, freshly ironed clothes on the floor and stepped on them. Mama begged them to wait, to no avail. Suddenly lightning flashed, and thunder struck nearby. That shattered my mother's nerves, and she trembled. "The lightning that may have struck someone innocent should have struck you," she said, distressed, as she ran out.

Within weeks a trial against my mother began. She was accused of slandering the state. Twisting her words, the collector said that Mama had said that "the lightning should strike Poland." His helpers supported this callous lie, and the judge convicted Mama and sentenced her to a year in jail. This falsehood created much concern among Jews, not because of the tax man's cheap personal vengeance, but because the state had engaged in an act of overt anti-Semitism.

Jail for my mother was unthinkable, for she would certainly be killed by a patriotic zealot there. Since this was an election year, we hoped that eventually the new government would pardon people sentenced for minor political offenses, so Mama went into hiding, moving regularly from place to place.

Occasionally she dared to come home. On one such night, we heard a fierce knocking on the front door. "Open! Police!" a voice demanded.

"Wait," my grandfather answered them, and he let some time go by.

When he finally opened the door, two police officers pushed in. "Where is Ester?" they asked Grandpa.

"I don't know," Grandpa answered calmly. Appearing unconcerned, he returned to bed, turned over, and seemed to go back to sleep. We knew that it wouldn't be long before they discovered Mother. Each time they were to emerge from searching a room, I closed my eyes in fear that they would have found Mama and handcuffed her. To our surprise, however, they did not. They asked me, then, where my mother was. I bit my lip, and I said, "She is not here." I wondered how well I lied. Nonetheless, they claimed to know that Mama was in the house.

One officer said to Papa: "Look, Wigdor, we know that Ester is here. Where is she?"

Papa told them that they were wrong: "She isn't here," he said matter-of-factly.

They finally left, still shaking their heads in disbelief. We too wondered where Mama was. She couldn't have just vanished into thin air. Then Grandpa asked us to check to see if the policemen were really leaving. Assured that they were, he got out of bed, and we saw where Mama was hidden—in the bed behind her father! A little bit later Papa filled the wagon with hay and buried Mama in it. Then he drove her to a new hiding place. In time, after the elections were over, the hoped-for pardon came. Although Mama had escaped jail, she had served a personal sentence by hiding for more than eight months.

The world depression cast a long shadow over Poland, and it became hard to scratch out a living. To exacerbate matters, Papa had guaranteed bank loans for a German Junker, Herr Heller, and when he went bankrupt Papa had to make good on the loans. Herr Heller coerced Papa into guaranteeing a further loan, with the assurance that he would be repaid with the coming harvest. Papa, trying to rescue himself from his previous loss, agreed. It was a clever deception, for Herr Heller never paid us back and almost bankrupted us. We were deeply in debt, and the vegetables from my garden provided our dinner on many a day. As hard as those years were for us, though, many others in our village were worse off. Knowing a family was in want, those who were better off would help. I remember many times as a child that Mother sent me before the Shabbat with a gift package for the poor.

As grim as the situation got, we had nowhere else to go. The British mandate over Palestine presented great obstacles for our immigration there. The League of Nations debated resettling Jews in Birobidzhan in the Soviet Union or Madagascar. Even though support for Jews in Poland melted, the belief in nazism was not universal. All Christians did not believe in a world built on hatred and deceit, and many went on helping us. My own survival, as the succeeding pages will show, was also due to the help of many kind Christians.

In 1938 Hitler demanded from Poland the Corridor, a narrow strip of land that separated East Prussia from the German mainland. Marshal Edward Rydz-Smigły, who succeeded Piłsudski in 1935, said, "Not one button will we surrender!"

THE BLITZKRIEG

Throughout the summer of 1939 the threat that Germany would invade Poland intensified. Since Dobra was only about 160 kilometers east of Germany, we had good reason to be concerned. My parents, who remembered the First World War, feared war more than the threat from the Germans. Their war experiences hung over them like a bad dream. I was not quite twenty, though, and I was more intrigued by war than scared.

Josek had served two years in the Yellow Cavalry of the Polish army. Consequently, as war hysteria began, he was recalled and moved with his unit to the Polish border. September 1, 1939, came, and the tense waiting ended, for Hitler's armies crossed into Poland and the Second World War began. Many people enlisted, and although it was against my mother's wishes, I also tried to join up. However, the draft age in Poland was twenty-one then. The recruiting officer sent me home. "We'll call you when we need you," he said. Perhaps he already knew that fighting the well-equipped Nazi armies was senseless.

The next day the nearby mental hospital released all its patients, and hundreds of the insane paraded through the village, creating unbelievable scenes. One man mimicked Napoleon Bonaparte and claimed his armies were coming to fight the Germans. Another, marching as if on parade, saluted everything in sight. A pretty young girl, who seemed perfectly normal at first, suddenly burst into a confused tirade. It was pitiful and grotesque to see them all wandering the streets, staring off into the distance. When the Germans arrived, they put them against a wall and executed them.

On September 3 the Nazi armies were just thirty kilometers away. They would soon be marching on the village. Our retreating soldiers vowed to take a stand and fight at the Warta River, the most logical place to resist the

German advance. Our parents remembered a similar situation in the First World War, when our village changed hands several times. We prepared to leave. Just before we left, Josek appeared. "Our battalion," he said, "had only rifles and lances. We were forced into a chaotic retreat."

On Monday, September 4, we decided to leave Dobra. Our truck, an old Peugeot, seemed only to run when we did not need it, so to be safe Papa hitched two horses to a wagon and tied a third to the rear as a spare. After we packed the most essential provisions, clothes and valuables, blankets and bedding, we were ready to leave.

Grandpa refused to come with us. He did not fear German soldiers. "We fought them in the last war. Soldiers are soldiers. They won't harm an old man," he said calmly. And so we left him behind and entered a congested trail of war refugees.

The road was packed with horse-drawn vehicles. Some families even took their cows to provide milk for their children. There were few automobiles, for the army had confiscated them. Our horses were long past their prime, so we walked on foot behind the wagon at each hill. After an hour of slow travel, we heard the sound of approaching airplanes. At first we believed they were Polish. As they came closer, however, we clearly saw that they were not. Their unusual heavy roar and their black cross insignias were enough to tell us that they held the enemy. However fearful we were, we knew that they could see that only civilians were on the road.

When they glided down, we thought it was just to see if we were innocent civilians. We were sure they would not harm us then. Yet to our surprise, they fired at us, creating a mass panic. On the right was the Warta, on the left a field. Only a few trees lined the roadside. We were trapped, with nowhere to run. Since the vehicles followed one another only centimeters apart, every salvo of bullets took a toll. Our three animals rose and whinnied in alarm and tried to tear themselves free of the wagon. After the assault, the Stukas rose up and departed, leaving death and destruction behind. Strewn about were dead and injured people and animals and wrecked wagons. This was my first taste of war. What followed convinced me of the validity of my parents' concerns.

A few kilometers farther on we were spotted by two other German planes. Since there were no Polish airplanes to fight them off, we knew what to expect. We had good reason to be frightened. On the right of the road an embankment ran down to the river. Suddenly an army unit passed us on the left,

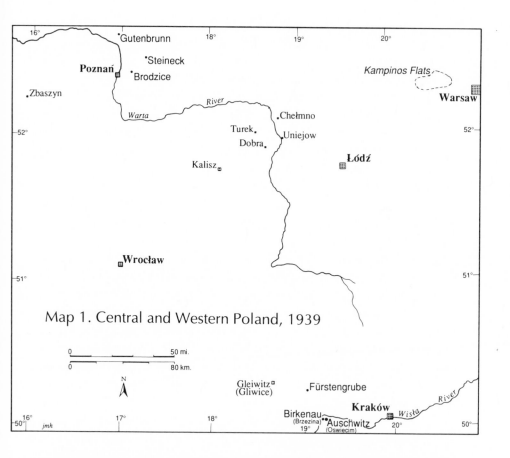

Map 1. Central and Western Poland, 1939

pushing us onto the slippery, grass-covered embankment. Papa jumped down and gripped the horses' reins close to their mouths to steady them. "Out of the way," people shouted, jockeying for space. At that point Mama, Pola, Josek, and I were walking behind the wagon. Suddenly Papa yelled, "Untie the horse in the back!" Just as my brother did, a bomb fell into the river, and an explosion drenched the road. Our wagon was pushed further to the side, and gravity pulled the horses and wagon down into the river. The Warta parted. After a gigantic splash, the water churned, foamed, and sent our belongings and valuables to the bottom of the river. Large waves rolled away in a circle and then dissipated. Only ripples covered our property and the grave of two horses. We had nothing left except what we wore and the horse Josek held on to. The bombers departed, and we were stunned and horrified. People who had seen what had happened streamed by. They were frightened, and everyone just wanted us out of the way.

Papa suggested that we go to his brother's home in Uniejów. "We'll stay there until the war is over," he said.

Uncle Chaim, Papa's older brother, was a very orthodox and extremely pious Jew who often neglected his family. He and his wife and nine children lived on the edge of poverty in a small apartment. Toba, his oldest daughter, had lived with us for years. But in the months before the war she had returned home.

When we arrived at Uncle Chaim's, the apartment was empty. Like most people in Uniejów, they had realized that our army couldn't stop the Germans. They too were probably heading eastward. We could not turn back; we had to go on. Dragging our one horse farther made no sense. We left it grazing in a field, and bedraggled, despondent, and hungry, we left Uniejów.

Outside the town we heard Papa's name being called. It was Mr. Chmielinski. A few years back he had bought Herr Heller's bankrupted estate. My father had had lots of dealings with him since. It was an unexpected miracle. "Wigdor! What are you doing here?" he yelled. "Is that your wife and your children? Come on, we will take you with us," he shouted, unable to stop for us in the traffic.

His tall, spacious wagon, pulled by stalwart Belgian horses, was a stark contrast to our scanty rig. We jogged along next to it long enough for him and his son, Karol, to help us up. Then Papa explained our dilemma. Chmielinski and his wife sat in front. Mama and Papa sat on the same seat facing the rear. The rest of us sat on the bench in the rear with Karol. We are more comfortable now, I thought.

When the traffic thinned out, Chmielinski pulled the wagon off the road so the horses could feed. He hung bags filled with oats on their necks and spread hay on the ground. Then the family shared what they had with us—home-baked bread, butter, and milk—with a hospitality that was easy to accept.

The Polish soldiers that passed us along the road didn't resemble an army anymore. "Where are the Germans?" we asked.

"Keep going, keep going," they replied. Although it was getting dark, we took their advice. Chmielinski set the horses off at a brisk trot. With fewer army vehicles crowding the road, we made better time.

Karol was a good-humored young man of twenty-seven who had been studying at Jagiello University in Kraków. He liked to talk about Marxism, pacifism, and Hitler. The falling dusk and the rhythmic sway of the wagon made me drowsy, and before long I was sound asleep.

It didn't seem that I had slept long when I awoke to a familiar sound. I looked to the west and saw two dots on the horizon. The roar grew louder, and the dots grew bigger, until I could see the much-feared Messerschmitts. Chmielinski turned the wagon into a field that had already been harvested, and we climbed out. People ran, frenzied, slipping, staggering, desperate, but there was no place to hide. The roar was deafening as two bombers, side by side, circled above us. Suddenly I heard the bombs whistle. I dropped to the ground. The explosion sent earth flying, leaving huge craters behind. Terrified by the noise, the horses whinnied and rose up on their hind legs. Although we were civilians and there was nothing military in sight, the Germans kept blasting their machine guns.

Finally, simply because they were out of ammunition, they flew off. I stood up, shaken. My heart was pounding. Above a wrecked wagon and a dead horse hung a bloodied jacket with part of an arm still in it on a telephone pole. We were all scared, and we thanked God that we had survived. There had been wars before but none like this. This wasn't war, people were saying. It was cold-blooded murder. "This is the result of the new terrible weapons," Karol mumbled, shaking his head.

As we continued moving east, the sun rose high. It baked us in an unusual September heat. We came across dozens of dead animals and wrecked vehicles. The smell of carrion was everywhere. I could not shake off my memory of the arm dangling from that telephone pole. After a few kilometers we stopped, and when Papa tried to buy provisions for zlotys, he discovered that what was plentiful just a few days before had all but disappeared. Although our friends' food was almost depleted, they continued to share with us what they had.

We had a few hours' relief from the bombings, but soon the familiar roar reminded us that the Germans ruled the skies. We now knew what to expect, and when the wagon pulled off the road we swiftly ran for cover. I followed my brother into some dry and thorny sage bushes. We flattened ourselves, to be as obscure as possible. The planes came as before. Swooping down, they covered the area with machine-gun fire and dropped bombs. But their guns did the most damage. I checked myself after each salvo to see if I was hit and bleeding.

Not far from us, someone lay slumped over. We went over, and we could see blood trickling from his right temple. A bullet had ended his life. A woman in her middle forties came screaming, "It's Stasiek. My God, it's Stasiek!" Two men were behind her. There was sadness and sorrow and much sympathy, but people were afraid. All knew they could be next and tried to get away. The cries of "Stasiek!" rang in my ears for a long time.

I understood then why my parents had so feared war. It was on this day, in the middle of a Polish field under a sky filled with the rapid fire of airborne machine guns, that I lost the illusion that war was an adventure. As we continued on, we passed Lodz and drove on eastward toward Warsaw. We had decided not to stop before dawn. We knew now that daytime travel was dangerous, and from here on we would move only by night. Living off our benefactors became increasingly embarrassing. Besides, their food was nearly gone. We agreed that we would stop in the next village and again try to buy provisions.

Dark clouds hung in the sky, threatening rain, but as the sun came out they dispersed into another sunny morning. We knew it wouldn't be long until the planes returned. We feared the next bombing, concerned that eventually we would have casualties. But we had to go on. We were near the Kampinoska barrens. The village of Kampinos was dead ahead. We stopped at the first farmhouse. No doubt, a land baron carried weight, and Mr. Chmielinski's status was the reason for the remarkable greeting we received. The exceedingly hospitable peasant allowed us to move not only into his yard but also into his barn. He kept chattering in a dialect that was difficult for us to understand. When he realized that we could hardly follow him, he began gesturing with his hands.

His wife had just milked their cows. She came from the cowshed with their two children—a girl about eight and a boy not over fourteen. They both peeked shyly at us. The plopping of the warm milk in the woman's pail stirred our hunger. Thanks to the bread, butter, eggs, and milk, which we bought from this family, we had our first warm meal since leaving home.

After the long night on the wagon, it was comforting to get down and stretch our legs. But before long the Stukas came again. God, will this never cease? I thought. This time, though, the planes—on their way to Warsaw, no doubt—just passed by.

The next morning we heard that the German troops had been advancing rapidly. Poland could no longer offer them any resistance. What remained of our army could not stop the advance. Rydz-Smigły's bravado, "Not one button will we surrender!" now rang hollow indeed. For us to run any farther east seemed useless. With the farmer's hospitality assured, we decided to stay. The German planes headed toward Warsaw no longer fired upon us. They flew back and forth as if on a regular airline route.

In the next forty-eight hours we heard rumors that the Soviets had declared war on Germany. Great Britain and France were already at war with Germany, but we wondered where they were. Was declaring war just a political ploy? It was no longer a question of whether we would fall into German hands, but when.

| 4 |

GERMAN OCCUPATION

We were homesick and tired of running. We looked forward to the day our flight would end. Kaziek, the farmer's young son, became my daily companion, eager to show me around the village. On September 10, just before noon, we went for a walk. We had gone barely one kilometer when we heard the whine of a motorcycle. It soon became visible at the top of an incline, speeding toward us with a strange-looking soldier in the seat. Its sidecar was empty, and there was a trail of heavy smoke and dust. We were the only people on the road. We were frightened, but it was too late to run.

The motorcycle stopped. The soldier shut the engine off and paused a minute. He then raised his goggles to his forehead and asked if we spoke German.

"Yes," I answered, lowering my eyes in fear.

"Are you afraid?"

"No," I said clearly.

"Are many Polish soldiers here?" he asked me.

"No," I responded.

"Have any gone by today?"

"No," I repeated.

He had seen no one on the road. He asked us where everyone was. "Are the people afraid of us? Tell them that they need not be," he said. Then this soldier reached into his bag and pulled out bars of chocolate and German cigarettes. As he handed them to us, he said, "This is for you," and stared at us both. I was not prepared to see such friendliness or generosity from a German invader and hesitated. He nodded then and repeatedly urged us to accept, and we did. By then several other motorcycles had pulled over to join us. Had these soldiers not been dressed in such strange uniforms, they would have looked like the locals. Many armored vehicles and trucks approached. It was an impressive sight as the soldiers roared away on their motorcycles. We could see why the Germans had won such an easy victory over us. Unlike our army, which moved around on foot and on horseback, theirs was fully motorized.

We ran back to the farm with the news and told everyone how decent the German soldiers were. Everyone knew the Germans had arrived. If this is how they all are, we said, we won't have much to worry about. On the road German troops were steadily passing, singing their glorious odes to the Führer.

We could run no farther. The only choice was to return as quickly as possible to our home. The flow of German tanks and vehicles moving east, however, made that impossible. Furthermore, we heard that the Germans had announced a ban on all civilian travel for the rest of the day.

The next morning we left early, and we traveled all day without incident. On the second day, however, several German officers stood on a hill, watching the streaming refugees. Women and children could pass in silence, while men had to tip their caps in wary respect. As we went by that grandstand review, an officer shouted at us in a belligerent voice, "Look at the Jews! They wanted to escape. Damned Jews, we'll get you now!" Chmielinski saw our faces turn white. He knew the impact this had on us.

"Those bastards!" he said, bristling with outrage. "Someday we'll get even with them." Little did Chmielinski know that two weeks later he would be arrested. Later he would return to his family as a handful of ashes.

With heavy heart, I recalled then what our uncle Shlomo predicted when we had talked about the Germans. He shook his head, saying, "God help us all."

It was dusty and hot when at dusk we drove off the road and stopped for the night under a stand of isolated trees. This attracted others, and we soon had a lot of company. In the rumors of the night we heard that the Soviets had been occupying eastern Poland. That eventually turned out to be true. Those who tried to flee to the Russians were turned back. "Go home," they were told. "Before long we'll come to you." The 1939 "mystery agreement" between Ribbentrop and Molotov became perfectly clear now, but no one believed that those two long-time enemies would stay on good terms for long. Throughout that night, thoughts of the Nazi's ridicule and threats kept me awake. I asked myself the same question over and over: "Are we people of a lesser god?"

Thanks to the Chmielinskis' kindness and generosity, we arrived home safely. Although nothing had changed in our house, the Nazis had nevertheless made their authority felt in the village. On the second day of their occupation, the Germans, at random, hung ten men on the gallows, while the rest of the people had to stand by and witness it. Their aim was to discourage any resistance. One of those executed was my best friend, Szymon Trzaskala.

On September 27 Warsaw fell. In a way we were happy the war was over, or so we thought. Annexing the Corridor and Warthegau was one of the Nazis' first territorial grabs in Poland. Otherwise, except for food shortages, little changed initially. To win the Polish people's cooperation in repressing the Jews, Radio Warsaw fed outrageous lies to them. Someone once said, "Blatant falsehood, if repeated often, eventually seems to be the truth." So it was.

Before long Polish publications, as well as Jewish ones, were shut down. The eight-page tabloid that appeared in their place was filled with nothing more than bulletins and stories about the persecution of Germans in Poland before the war. It was the Germans' attempt to justify their occupation. When all our radios were confiscated, we knew only what the Germans told us. The rest of the world became a remote place.

Hans Frank became the governor of Warthegau, and Herr Schweikert was to be our county's administrator. They quickly enacted a number of directives that restricted Jewish freedom. The rules were sometimes so murky that anything that wasn't explicitly allowed for us we had to assume was forbidden.

The last time our family was together for a celebration was in December 1939. It was during Hanukkah, the miracle of lights. But suddenly the sky reddened. It seemed as if the whole town was afire. Terrified, we learned that the Germans were burning down the Jewish synagogue and its two adjoining prayer houses and destroying the Torahs. The village Jews were devastated. The orthodox Jews rent their garments and sat shivah in mourning. Each subsequent December reminded me of this, our last and saddest holiday together.

Each day the governor imposed more restrictions on us. Only six people were allowed to attend funerals, although ten were needed for a prayer service. A new curfew barred us from the streets between 7:00 P.M. and 8:00 A.M., and it was so strictly enforced that some Jews were shot. We were limited in what we could buy and where we could buy it. Since our avenues to the farmers were cut, even those of us with money couldn't buy much with it. Our few non-Jewish friends, those who were still willing to help us, were prohibited from doing so. Soon all Jewish homes had to display the Star of David, and all Jews six years of age and older had to wear it. Not sparing us another insult, the German word for Jew, *Jude,* in Hebrew-style letters had to appear inside the star.

Our own emblem was to be our badge of shame. Then our use of the sidewalks was forbidden, forcing us to walk in the gutter. The Germans amused themselves by driving their vehicles at us. Bearded Jews became their prime targets. They cut or plucked the beards or set them on fire. All our gold and silver was ordered confiscated, and withholding any was punishable by death. Physical brutality now occurred daily.

One December night we woke to a violent pounding on the door and an order to open it. At first we didn't answer, hoping the intruders would leave. They threatened to break down the door. Because males were primary targets, Mama went to the door. "Who are you? What do you want from us?"

"Open!" they repeated, pounding. "Weapons inspection." We knew the inspection claim was just a thin excuse, but refusing to open the door would bring more wrath. Mama unlocked the door and let in what seemed to be four German postal employees. Mama looked relieved. "Jews?" one asked. Mama didn't answer.

While three of them went roaming around the house, the fourth asked Mama where our guns were. She shook her head. "There are no guns in our house," she answered.

Nearby in the foyer, where Grandpa slept, one asked him the same question. "Where are your guns?" The man peeked under the bed and found my dental instruments in a small box. A triumphant smile widened on his face as he lifted it up and shouted, "Was ist da drin?"

"Those are my grandson's dental tools," Grandpa answered.

"Dental tools?" he blurted in disgust and slammed the box into Grandpa's face. As my instruments scattered, my grandfather shrieked.

In the meantime, another one of them had been cursing my father. "You Jews are the cause of all evil. You wanted this war, and you'll have to pay for it."

My father, his face white, protested quietly. "See for yourself. We have no weapons." But his words fell on deaf ears. Even a confession from him wouldn't have changed their minds. They were here for one purpose, to castigate and beat up Jews.

The man then hit Papa in the head with his bayonet. When I saw blood dripping down my father's face, I thought he had been killed. Another German kept shooting bullets into our furniture and mirrors. The third slapped my brother in the face. Then he turned to me. "Auch Jude?" he bellowed, as if to assure me that I also deserved a beating. Terrified, I pushed my body into a corner, dropped to the floor, and pulled my knees up to my chest. I covered my face, hoping to escape the worst.

"Leave him alone. Don't you see he is not quite there?" I heard another say to him. I did not escape entirely. He landed his boot on my behind, kicking me a few times. Otherwise he let me alone.

Then they left. The nightmare was over. Josek's nose was broken, Papa's forehead required several stitches, and Grandpa lay bloodied in the foyer. Pola tended to Grandpa. Mama kept placing wet towels on Papa's head and muttering, "They were just plain post office workers." She sighed. This was too unthinkable and too cruel. In spite of my twenty years, I was still too naive to understand that people could carry so much hatred for others. Then I thought of the golem story, which dates back to the Bible and the Talmud and has been retold throughout the centuries: In a mystical rite, invoking the Divine Name, a wise man gave artificial life to a human body made of clay or wood. This soulless body was then ordered to do tasks blindly. The golem was the perfect metaphor and offered an answer to my questions. "Who are we? What have we done? Why are we so despised?" I asked myself. That night something changed my theory of humanity forever. I realized that our lives had been irreparably altered.

One woman in the village admitted that she had heard Germans asking where Jews lived. "Someone must have pointed you out," she said.

In Poland, the Volksdeutsche, people of German descent living outside Germany, seemed to have sold their souls to the Führer. The best example was our long-time neighbors and friends, the Marxes. Mrs. Marx now defended the Nazis in whatever they did. She didn't even come to see us after that night. From that time on we lived in fear. Each time we heard someone outside at night, we wondered if Germans were coming to terrorize us again. This was not the first nor was it the last time that Jewish homes were invaded at night and people were beaten. The fear of that night terror became our steady companion. Killing Jews was now permitted and even encouraged.

The *Racias* (roundups) followed. Jews were gathered and ordered to do demeaning labor. One day Pola was seized and taken to the German army barracks. There she was made to clean privies. "It's a pity that a pretty girl like you has to be Jewish," one soldier wisecracked, as the others laughed. Pola came home trembling. "I would rather die," she said, "than go through this again."

Pola and I decided to escape into the Soviet-occupied part of Poland. Although our parents weren't in favor of this, they recognized that, in circumstances like these, everyone had to make a personal decision. It was late December, almost New Year's, when we left. It was cold enough for a heavy snowfall that morning, but no snow had fallen. We removed our yellow patches from our clothes and hoped to pass for non-Jews. To be less conspicuous, we took only necessities. After exchanging farewells with the rest of our family, we left. The air was raw. A white frost blanket covered the fields, and the streams were frozen. We trekked through the forests on our fateful odyssey.

Four hours later we reached the train station. It was the end of the first leg of our journey. We had several hundred kilometers to go. Pola, a light-haired brunette with non-Semitic features, had no difficulty buying the tickets to a town near the Russian border. Then we sat and waited for the train to arrive. We spotted more Jews who had the same intention in the waiting area. We didn't talk to anyone for fear of being recognized. When the train finally arrived and we thought we had made it, we were stunned to hear an announcement: Jews were restricted from using the train. All others could board it. Somehow the SS men knew that Jews were among the travelers.

A dozen of us who remained on the platform looked on as the train chugged away and slowly disappeared. Then two SS men collected our papers and stamped a *J* on them. Before returning them to us, they issued an angry warning. "Whoever tries to use the trains again will be shot." Our plans ruined, we felt crushed. We had little choice but to return home.

Although our family shared our disappointment, they were happy to have us back. Papa, as always, found a silver lining. "Whatever happens to us, we'll at least be together," he said. Then he added a contention he had often used. "Things are never eaten as hot as they're cooked!"

A few weeks later one of my sister's friends returned disappointed from the Soviet-occupied part of Poland. He warned us not to go there. "The Russians have been rounding up the Jews that came over and deporting them to labor camps in Siberia," he said. We could not imagine why the Soviets were also our enemies. It shattered our idea about Jews being seen as equal to others under communism.

Because my grandfather was constantly harassed in the street about his beard, he stopped going out. Removed from his friends, he grew weak. One morning we were shocked to find him in a deep sleep from which he never awoke. My idol was dead. We knew that Grandpa had died because he lost his will to live. I understood that with him gone, my life would never be the same. The procession to the cemetery consisted of only the family, as others were forbidden to attend. All the mirrors in our house were covered, and we sat shivah for a week. Friends, at risk to themselves, came to make up the ten-man prayer service. I overheard them saying that they envied my grandfather for his peaceful death.

A few days later Mother and I took a back road to the other side of the village. Halfway there, I noticed a former classmate of mine coming toward us. Like many of the others of German ancestry, he too had joined the Nazis. He wore a brown shirt with a red *Hakenkreuz* (swastika) armband. Presenting himself as a German, he sought to demonstrate his faithfulness to the Führer. Coming upon us, he pushed my mother, and she fell to the ground.

I was shocked. I searched his face. "Otto, why are you doing this?" I demanded, outraged. In his eyes I saw sinister cruelty and mercilessness. The schoolmate of yesterday was a foe today.

Then he began to use the common Nazi hate rhetoric. "You Jew swine, you pests, you war criminals."

I could see that he knew who we were, but he showed no remorse. He left us, still mumbling with enmity. My blood pounded in my temples. I thought that I should have ripped the swastika off his arm, but I was paralyzed, as if I had no command over my limbs. Pale and humiliated, Mama could not stop trembling, but fortunately she was not hurt. I could not comfort her. I had not defended her, and I felt a deep guilt. This incident convinced me how quickly people's minds could be poisoned. This was a bad year, and the next one might be worse.

THE GHETTO IN DOBRA

Greed for Jewish booty lured many followers to Hitler. Little by little, without pretense or restraint, the Nazis had taken our homes, our possessions, our hope, and our pride. And though each downward spiral seemed to take us to the lowest state imaginable, we were to learn that this abyss had no bottom.

In the spring of 1940 we were ordered out of our house. We were the only Jewish family in the vicinity. Everything of ours—business, house, and land—was given to Anders, a Volksdeutscher who was a former worker of ours. His only credential was his heritage. The Judenrat then assigned us an attic room across the street in what was once a school. We were allowed to take one armful of possessions. Pola sneaked across to our house once more and rescued a few of her favorite books. Unsuited to running any business, Anders closed its doors shortly afterward. Nothing caused my mother more pain than looking down on her home, which now seemed so alien.

The third-floor attic room, once used for storage, became our living quarters. Pola, Josek, and I slept on straw pallets on the floor. Mama and Papa had two cots. We hung blankets to create privacy.

We continued to observe the Shabbat. Each Friday evening Mama lit candles and recited the prayer. Papa, acting as if not much had changed, kept saying, "Nothing is lost. It's all only temporary. When the war is over we'll move back to our house, and everything will be as before."

At the end of March 1940 the birds returned. Nature was taking its course early that year. On one sunny day, as I stood in the school yard, five Germans in army uniforms rounded the corner of the school. This was odd, I thought. What could they want? No one except the former caretaker and ourselves lived in the schoolhouse. As the Germans walked toward me, a corporal, their leader, sternly asked if I was Bronek Jakubowicz.

"Yes," I said.

"You are under arrest."

I thought surely that it was a mistake. "Are you sure that you want me?" I asked. "Why? What have I done?"

"You'll find out later. Come with us."

Although I knew it was unmistakable, I still couldn't understand why they were arresting me, or why they needed five soldiers to do it. Mama and Pola had heard the commotion. They came down to the yard and, startled, gasped. "Why are you arresting my son? What do you want of him?" Mama asked.

"He is coming with us," one soldier bellowed, ordering me to move.

"Wait, let me at least bring down his jacket," my mother pleaded.

"He won't need it. He is going to be shot," the corporal grumbled back at her. Mama nearly fainted. She covered her face, as my sister held on to her.

I followed them out of the yard, one soldier on each side, two behind, and the corporal ahead of us. That aroused the neighbors, and they came out and looked. I had lived in this village since I was born, and nearly everyone knew me. They couldn't understand why I had been arrested and was being led away by five soldiers. In spite of my fear, I held my head high like a character in a Shakespearean play. It was a long way. I was led to the other end of the village, into the army headquarters and Schweikert's residence. In the yard, against a barracks wall, soldiers with rifles in hand guarded four other men. The corporal waved to me to join them.

Then I recognized on my right Wigdor Celnik, a friend of my sister's. Next to him stood Jan Kozlowski, a Pole of questionable character from Dobra. He had been jailed several times. "One would do well not to have anything to do with him," I had heard people say. The third, Pavel, I knew only by name. The fourth was a stranger. I thought Celnik might be there because of his having once been a representative of the Bund, a Jewish socialist labor organization. Was I arrested because of my membership in the Zionist youth organization Hashomer Haklal Hazoni?* I had not known anyone arrested for that offense before.

I asked Wigdor why he was arrested. "What did they say to you?" he whispered back.

---

*During the interwar period, Jews living in Poland, especially my generation, were attracted by the Zionist ideology, Herzel's "Judenstaat," the idea that one should not wait for

"I heard them saying that I'd be shot."

"Me too," he replied.

Suddenly one of the guards yelled at us, "Shut up!" as he cocked his gun. I wasn't ready to die. Why was I here? Was it God's will, as people sometimes say? If this is my fate, I thought, what can I do to make the agony of dying easier? I tried to convince myself that I had lived what was to be my life. After all, no one lives forever. I tried hard to persuade myself, but that didn't make much sense, and it wasn't very consoling, but it was the best I could do. All of us were puzzled. Without knowing why we were there, we exchanged worried looks. Even passing soldiers asked their comrades who we were and why we were under arrest. The guards didn't know either.

After two hours a sergeant came over and ordered us to follow him. We went a few hundred meters down the road and came upon odd-looking rigs—three shallow carts with huge wheels that had six Belgian horses hitched to them. We were ordered to board. The sergeant and guards followed. As we left the army compound and headed out of the village, I spurred my courage and asked the sergeant where he was taking us. He did not answer. He seemed surprised that I had asked him. Wigdor Celnik, who was on the same wagon, looked at me as if to say, "Did you expect him to tell you?" Discouraged, I asked nothing further.

After a while we veered off the road into a gravel pit. Why did they bring us here? I wondered. A gravel pit that is constantly dug in would hardly be suitable for a burial place. The sergeant then got off and ordered us to fill the wagons with gravel. That still did not make sense. After a couple of minutes the sergeant looked around carefully. He whispered to me, "You will not be shot." Then he uttered the name of a dentist in Dobra, Krusche.

I only knew Krusche by name. I knew that he had come to Dobra a couple of years before. He was the only dentist in the village. People did not say bad things about him. "He is a cross between a decent Pole and a decadent German," I had heard. When the Germans came to Dobra, he quickly rose to prominence in the Nazi aristocracy.

I was overcome by a sensation of having been born all over again. I passed the news to Celnik, and he relayed it to the others. We began fill the wagons

---

the Creator to send a Messiah to return his people to the homeland but should advance that conviction by working for a homeland in Palestine.

with fury, as if to avow our usefulness to our adjudicators, thanking them for saving our lives.

At the first opportunity I asked the sergeant what Krusche had to do with my arrest. "I can't tell you here," he said uneasily. "Give me the address where I can find you, and I'll come to see you." I gave him directions to the school, and he promised to come.

We filled the carts with gravel in record time. By five o'clock, after ten loads, the gravel had piled up in the yard of the army compound. Without indicating to any one of us the reason for our arrests, the Germans released us.

I thanked God over and over and quickly disappeared from their sight. Once on the road, I ran as fast as I could. When I reached home, out of breath, Mama's face lit up. Seeing me, her agony was replaced by joy. She had already been to the Jewish councillors, I learned, begging them to find out why I was arrested and pleading with them to intervene. In contrast, Papa believed it had been a mistake all along. A few days later I heard that Kozlowski was arrested once more. No one ever saw him or heard from him again. The rumor was that he died in some camp.

At dusk I wondered if the sergeant would keep his word. After a while I saw someone resembling him coming down our street, checking house numbers. When he saw me, he came up close and whispered, "I have to be very careful." He quickly entered the school with me. When I introduced him to my family, he gave his name as Sergeant Sprengle. He begged us not to tell anyone he had come into our room. Then he told me that because of Krusche's complaint, Schweikert had ordered my arrest. Krusche insisted I had practiced dentistry here, depriving him of his income. All this, of course, was a lie. Few Poles were conscious of dental care, and most were too poor to spare the money for it. Even after losing their natural teeth, they didn't see the need to get false ones.

Before long Sergeant Sprengle developed a friendship with us and came to see us almost every day. At first we were cautious of him, but in time we learned to trust him. He seemed to lack the anti-Semitic venom that characterized most Nazis. One had to wonder about him as a member of a superior race. Sprengle was an odd young man. Of medium height, he had very short legs, almost to the point of abnormality. His typically German light hair was in a military crew cut that looked as stubby as a badger's bristles. The tanned reddish skin over his square jawbones made his face look as if it were cut out of a redwood log. Seeing him, one couldn't escape the thought that he might be trapped in a role that didn't fit him.

Sometimes he brought us German newspapers. Of course they were full of the usual anti-Semitic propaganda, which portrayed us as devil-faced Lucifers and as disease-spreading, unsociable villains of society. Two things we never talked about were nazism and politics. The sergeant often warned us to leave. "We won't do you much harm, but those who follow us will make your life very difficult," he muttered.

When the Germans invaded France in May 1940, they made light of the Maginot Line, calling it a picket fence. A few days later we read that France had surrendered and Hitler had celebrated the victory in Paris. Shortly after that Sprengle's company was transferred west. By then we were so fond of him that we genuinely missed him. Although he promised to write, we never heard from him again. As the first German troops were replaced with new ones, more discriminatory laws were piled on our backs. Jews had been barred from associating with any other race. The Aryans shall be spared the impurity of Jewish blood, the laws said.

By the summer of 1940 the vise around us tightened even more. The Nazis decided to clear Dobra's slums and create a ghetto there. Some of the poor Jews who had lived there for years could only keep one room. They had to give the rest to other families. We had to move out of the school and were given a room with a dirt floor. We came to realize that even our cramped quarters had had advantages. By then our home was just a distant memory.

The ghetto rations were our only source of food, and hunger became the number one enemy. Butter, milk, sugar, and flour were almost never available. Even though we were ready to part with anything to win another day of life, those who came to trade with us, masquerading as do-gooders, did so mostly for personal gain. Because we had fewer and fewer tradable goods, in time the merchants stopped coming.

Each morning all Jewish men, and sometimes women, had to report for arduous and demeaning chores. I'll never forget the strain of kneeling on the side of the road and breaking down large stones with a heavy hammer for road construction.

In the meantime the Nazis rolled through Europe with unparalleled ease. To the west they were in France, Belgium, and the Netherlands. In the north they were in Norway. To the southeast, Italy, Yugoslavia, Greece, Romania,

Hungary, and Bulgaria were under their control. In North Africa, General Rommel was near El Alamein. The Nazis seemed to extend their influence to the entire world. It seemed unlikely that Great Britain and the Soviet Union were a match for Hitler's armies. In their speeches, Hitler, Himmler, and Goebbels used harsher, more venomous anti-Jewish rhetoric. For the Germans to fail was unthinkable.

Deprived of hope and broken in spirit, we waited for a miracle that we never really expected. Our biggest dilemma was that our people would not believe what was about to happen. We defied conventional wisdom. At each new Nazi anti-Jewish action, people commonly thought, That's as far as they'll go! What else can they do to us? But we were living in a world that didn't make sense, and what we thought to be inconceivable happened. Escape from a Warthegau ghetto held extraordinary risks. Even if we were successful, where would we go? We had to accept whatever our fate had in store for us.

Suddenly the tires screeched, and the truck swerved to avoid a cow crossing the road. I opened my eyes. I was on the truck, and my father was staring at me, reading my expression.

A while later the truck pulled off the road and stopped on a grassy embankment. The guard yelled, "Get off, everyone, and relieve yourselves in the woods, but be back in five minutes." The guards now formed a cordon around us. "If one of you escapes, all of you will pay for it." We knew it wasn't an idle threat.

There was a dense forest on the side where the trucks had stopped and a green meadow with red poppies across the road. When I went into the forest, the trees were so dense that they repelled nearly all light. Pervasive in the near dark was the scent of spruce. Twigs snapped under my feet. After relieving myself, I returned to the truck. I found Dr. Neumann's eyes fixed on me.

"You there, come here," he snapped at me. I wondered why, of all of us, he would call me, so I didn't respond. But when I once more heard his command, I turned. "I am calling you," he said.

Though I knew that being singled out by a Nazi often meant nothing good, I had no choice but to go. I rushed over to him and stopped at a distance of two meters, as Nazi protocol required. Don't show him you're afraid, I thought. "Jawohl," I said loud and clear. He asked my name and age. When I answered, he asked me what I did before the war. "I was in dental training," I answered him obligingly.

"Report to me when we get to camp," he ordered.

I managed to reply a second time, "Jawohl," and returned to the truck. My father had heard it all and saw that I was worried. Papa, always the optimist, urged me to forget all about it. "By the time we get there, he'll have forgotten about you," Papa said.

We drove past a pious woman kneeling in front of a Black Madonna icon, with her kerchief pulled over her face. These statues were quite common along Polish roads. A while later we came to Turek, the county seat. More trucks like ours waited in the square. They carried Jews from Kłodawa, Kutno, Golina, and Turek itself. Thirty minutes later the whole convoy pulled out in an northerly direction. "This means that we are going to Poznan," Papa said. He had traveled here often, and he knew the roads well.

Outside Turek the road widened, and the trucks began to clatter along at a faster pace. The sun arched overhead, bathing the fields and the people who toiled in them in warmth. Most of the peasants stood up and stared at the convoy of strangers being herded past. The two Waffen SS guards on our truck stood stone-faced and rarely spoke. After a three-hour journey, we turned onto a gravel road. The bouncing of the truck made resting against the sideboard uncomfortable. Big clouds of dust, loosened by the tires, enveloped our clothes and faces. Gravel banged against the fenders constantly.

As the sun made its slow descent, the vehicles approached what seemed to be a typical two-story schoolhouse. Near it were three wooden barracks. All this was surrounded by a three-meter wire mesh fence topped with barbed wire strung on cane-shaped posts. Except for these structures, there was nothing but fields. This must be our new home, I thought.

| 6 |

STEINECK

The lead vehicle stopped at the entrance. Several SS men with German shepherds at their sides stood, awaiting us. Dr. Neumann handed one a list of our names. They spoke briefly, and one SS man grabbed a bullhorn. "You have been brought to Steineck labor camp, where you'll learn how to work." Then he lowered his bullhorn and scanned our faces on the trucks, as if to say, "Are there any questions to be asked?" If there were any, who would have dared? He moved and paused at every truck, repeating his decree, making sure no one missed it.

Then our guards lowered the tailgates and pushed the human cargo down with their rifle butts. "Down quickly, all down," they shouted.

We grabbed our bags and jumped off the trucks in panic. Two SS men at the gate funneled us inside like ranch cattle being readied for branding. Chaos erupted as the first group of men reached the gate. Two SS men standing on either side whipped us at random as we passed them. Given leash, the dogs picked up the cue and lurched at our arms and legs. Those of us who staggered were their special targets. I saw what was going on and froze. If Papa and I were to avoid being battered, I thought, we'd have to slip by as the men lifted their whips. With my suitcases in one hand and my box of instruments dangling from my shoulder, I held on to my father. I hung back and waited just long enough. When the whips rose, we dove past like sprinters. I escaped injury, but my father was not so lucky. He ended up with a laceration on his scalp.

Once inside the camp, we ran up some stairs, through a pair of swinging doors, and down the corridor of the schoolhouse. On the right were windows overlooking the yard; the rooms were on the left. "All to Room 4," yelled Chaim, the policeman who came with us.

On three walls of the room were rows of bunks, mere shelves stacked atop each other. On them lay straw pallets with gray blankets and pillows. Most bunks were already occupied. The greeting we received had fueled fear. Chaos prevailed, as most of us were unable to find bunks. Finally Papa and I spotted two empty bunks on the lowest level. Little did we know they were the least desirable. The bunks were so tightly spaced that we had to kneel on the floor and slide in. Our baggage we piled up against the wall by the window. With my box of instruments under my pillow, I felt as if I had arrived not just at a labor camp, but in another world. I knew that here I had to learn life all over again.

More people came. They milled back and forth between rooms, unable to find a place. Amid the tumult, someone yelled, "Attention!" The SS man who had so succinctly instructed us at the gate entered Room 4, followed by Chaim.

"Here all of you will work. You must salute when you see people in uniform. When spoken to, you must stand at attention, chest out, head up, shoulders back, hands at your trouser seams. The first of you who sees one of us enter the room must call everyone to attention. All inmates must be in their bunks by eight. The light must be out a half hour later. Wake-up is at 4:00 A.M. You'll get an hour to be ready for work. Saturday and Sunday are free. Tomorrow your clothes will be deloused, your hair shorn. You'll get your work assignments on Monday!" He turned to leave. Then he stopped, as if he had forgotten the most important announcement: "Anyone contemplating an escape, better not try!" Then he turned and walked out, followed by the policeman. He left us frightened and pondering the consequences of any disobedience.

Fifteen minutes later a whistle blared. "Quick! Quick! Everyone out to the yard for a roll call!" Then we learned another lesson. No one walked in Steineck. With Papa at my side, I rushed back through the same corridor toward the exit. An SS man, his dog at his side, awaited us. Using the same maneuver as before, I escaped a lashing. But this time the German shepherd buried his fangs in my thigh and shook his snout from side to side. When I freed myself, my pants were torn, and blood was running down my thigh. My leg hurt as if a dozen nails had been driven into it. I wanted to check my leg further, but I knew the roll call took precedence. I followed everyone else to the yard.

Early in 1941, long before the Wannsee conference at which the Nazis made killing Jews an official policy, Alfred Rosenberg, the Nazi Reichminister for occupied Warthegau, proposed labor camps for the Jews living in the region. In a widely reported speech at Poznan University, he said, "The Jews will have to pay with blood for the twenty-five years of suffering they have inflicted on the Germans and Poles here." Like Rosenberg's other proposals, this one received unanimous acceptance. In May 1941 the first *Judenarbeitslager* was established in the Sport-Stadium in Poznan. One thousand Jewish men were brought there from the Lodz ghetto. The second labor camp was Steineck.

The Kommandant from the Stadium camp directed our roll call. He had come here to set up Steineck. After we were ordered into rows of five, we had to count, one after another, until the guards were satisfied that all of us were present. After being released, I finally went to the washroom. Here a thirteen-meter pipe dripped water into a trough beneath it.

The washroom was a perplexing sight, an affront to dignity. A long, half-cylindrical cement object with pipes above it ran along two walls. Several shut-off valves were visible. The toilet was an unfinished plank of wood over a twenty-meter-long pit. Those using it who had diarrhea wound up with feces on their clothes. I cleaned my wound, washed off the blood around the two rows of teeth marks on my thigh, cleaned my underwear and pants, and left.

Papa had been waiting for me in the room, his head still hurting. The bell rang, announcing that it was time for our first food ration. The line extended twice around the corridor. After waiting for twenty minutes, we each received a "pica," a wedge of bread weighing less than a fifth of a kilo, and something resembling coffee. The only element the dark liquid had in common with real coffee was its color. Bitter it was, and impossible to drink without sweetener. The bread wasn't any better. It was old and stale and tasted of oats. "If this is a sample of our food here, we'll starve to death," someone remarked. Eating it seemed revolting at first. This food was not fit for animals, much less for humans. But in time, to stave off starvation, we all ate it.

The cook was a round-faced inmate by the name of Rachmiel. "Tomorrow," he promised, "we'll also get margarine and marmalade."

When the bell rang in the morning, Papa had to nudge me awake. That morning we got the promised margarine. The cook hastily dispensed a spoonful of marmalade and slapped it on the "pica" of bread. It dripped off even before we turned around. Then came a call: "Eintreten!" Once again we counted off: "Eins, zwei, drei, vier." Then we were ordered to undress and put our clothes in one pile for delousing. Barbers, most of whom had never cut hair before, clipped off our hair from head to toe. We became an unsightly spectacle to those passing the camp.

At noon, after searching in the piles, we found our clothes. They now had a strong odor of naphtha. Then we got an anemic mixture of turnips and potatoes as our midday ration. Though at first it turned our stomach, hunger eventually won over, and we ate it. In the afternoon there was another roll call, this one for the purpose of inspection. The SS men seemed to have a special interest in shirts and jackets that were totally buttoned. Five lashes were administered to those whose clothes were not fully buttoned, and the same punishment was meted out for leaving a shoelace untied.

Then came an exhibition of our marching, with which they were most displeased. The first lesson in marching "Nazi style" followed. The younger of us could adapt to it, but to my father and his peers, goose stepping was as strange as could be. And how could they expect Reb Yankev, a scholar who had lived according to God's Law, to raise his legs and pound the ground, as goose stepping required? Just walking in line was strange to him, and he became the most abused. The soldiers made him fall down and drag himself on his elbows. Then he was ordered to get up and to repeat this. They ordered him to run until he broke down and collapsed. In the end, seeing his state of severe exhaustion and his inability to comprehend their commands, they whipped him mercilessly.

"Du Scheiss Jude" was the beginning of their standard curse, and accusations blaming us for all the world's ills followed. Did they really believe that? Or was it a self-imposed justification? In any case, they enjoyed their roles. Although by now their castigation of us was familiar, the charges were hard to accept. I never understood what we had done to earn these allegations. Once dismissed, we sat down in groups, on the grass near the fence. Relaxing in the sunshine offered a bit of a physical and emotional boost. But the intellectuals, without respect or purpose, found it hard to defy their fate.

Today, we were reminded, was Shabbat. Even without a place of worship in the ghetto, we had still come together to pray. Here Shabbat was just another day. "It seems that all gods have been replaced by one, Adolf Hitler, and losing ours, we lost most," someone in the group remarked.

To this, Reb Yankev couldn't remain silent. "The Lord won't let us suffer," he predicted. "Thou alone wilt be exalted, and thou wilt reign over all in unity," he prayed.

A strange quiet followed. It seemed as if everyone's thoughts questioned this wisdom. A few minutes passed, and my father, as if in an afterthought, made the most optimistic remark. "It's only a matter of months," he said. This reminded me how much Mama must be missing him. They depended so much on each other, especially in a time of crisis.

I looked at David Kot, a good friend of mine. At home our two families had been very close. I had spent many days at his house, and he at ours. His once heavy head of hair and the brave and alert look in his black eyes were gone. What's more, our careless and happy adolescent life had been cut short, and the intimacy we once enjoyed was no longer there. A sudden ring of the bell announced the time for evening's rations.

Sunday morning I woke amazingly early. Everything—the whistles, the whips, and the barking of the dogs—already seemed routine. After the roll call, the Kommandant asked doctors, cooks, and tailors to come forward. There were no doctors among us, but more than enough cooks and tailors. As an alternative, he picked Goldstein, a barber from Dobra, to be in charge of the first aid room. It only stocked a few bandages, some iodine, and aspirin.

Rachmiel got four more as kitchen help. So many envied this job that people battled for it. In addition to offering extra food, the kitchen was always warm, and the work wasn't exhausting. A camp tailor and four inmates to serve as extra police were also selected. The rest of that Sunday was free. When the bells called lights out, it was still daylight. In our bunks, however, we saw only unfinished wood. The nights were still cool, but the combined body heat of eighty or more inmates in our room was enough to make one sweat. I watched my father as he pulled himself into his bunk, careful to avoid splinters.

In the beginning our camp was big news in the area. On Sunday the peasants would stroll by to find out who we were and why we were there. Although this region was known for its intense dislike of Jews, the local people, hearing that our identity was our only crime, showed genuine outrage. When an SS man saw some peasants at the fence, he admonished them to leave at once and never come back.

It was unusually warm for the middle of May. On Monday, our first workday, the bells rang at 4:00 A.M. It was dark when we assembled in the yard. The Kommandant from the Stadium camp and Dr. Neumann were in the center, surrounded by several SS men and a few of our policemen. I hoped that, as Papa had predicted, by now Neumann had forgotten about me. He did not, however, and after four hundred inmates, including my father and me, were separated from the rest, I suddenly heard, "Dentist, report to Dr. Neumann."

An electric shock went through me. I didn't know what to do. I feared to respond, and at the same time I also feared not to. Every second seemed like an hour. When I was called again, I still hesitated. "You have no choice," Papa said. "You have to go."

I made my way through the line, then ran forward, stopped, and clicked my heels two meters in front of him. "Dr. Neumann, Bronek Jakubowicz reports to you as ordered," I said brightly.

He scanned me from top to bottom and then motioned me to his side. "Wait here," he said.

I turned and found myself standing in a row with the SS and all the Nazi dignitaries. When I raised my eyes, a thousand fellow inmates looked at me, puzzled about why I was called there. I wanted to be with them. This was not my place. I had not chosen to be here. The remaining men were soon arranged in groups. Then Neumann pointed at the first four hundred and said to me, "Dentist, you'll be their Kolonnenführer." Thereupon he chose a Kolonnen-führer for each group.

As we were led out, I saw many men wearing black, the color of the Gestapo, waiting for us at the gate. Dr. Neumann handed one of them a list of our names, and they took charge of us, ordering us to march out. On the road they began to prod us to walk in military rhythm. "Eins, zwei, drei, vier," they repeated.

I left last and walked in the last row, without any idea what they expected of me. It was shortly before daylight, and I could see that despite the color of their uniforms, our commanders were neither Gestapo nor SS. Their coats lacked the Gestapo insignias and had no lapels. Their faces looked modest and unassuming. That made me curious about who they were.

The man in the black uniform who walked behind me carried a briefcase. I dropped back a bit and walked beside him. I wanted to say something, to be-gin to talk to him, but my words got stuck in my mouth. He hardly looked at me. I saw a weathered sign on a post, indicating that the road led toward Poznan. Finally I dared to ask him whether we were going to Poznan. A few agonizing moments passed, and he didn't answer me. I was about to repeat my question when he spoke up. "We were advised not to fraternize with our prisoners." Then after a while he added, "We are going to the Hoch und Tiefbaugesellschaft, to Brodzice." Though he spoke German, I was sure that he wasn't a German. I guessed that he was either a Volksdeutscher or a Pole.

"What is Hoch und Tiefbaugesellschaft?" I asked him, to keep the conversation going.

"They are building a railroad here," he answered. After that our conversation took a more normal course. We still had an hour to march, he said, meaning that we would have a four-hour walk to and from work. As we left the main road, the sun began to clear away the morning haze. We then marched around a crescent lake, our shoes pounding and raising clouds of dust. Soon barracks became visible. "This is it," the man said, pointing at them.

The first building was clearly for offices. The second looked like a kitchen and hall, and the third had picks, shovels, and wheelbarrows in front. This was the toolshed. One guard insisted that we approach the workplace respectably. "One, two, three, four, left," he prompted. But he had to settle for the sound of tra-tra and ta-ta.

The guard I had talked with seemed to be in command. He handed some papers to the guard at the gate, who scanned them briefly and then asked the first, in Polish, how many we were. "Four hundred seven," he squeezed out.

Then the second guard turned and asked the people around him, only this time in German, how many inmates they each needed. "Fifty," "forty," "thirty-five," they answered.

He assigned them as many of us as they asked for, and each led a group away from the yard. Twenty of us, I among them, remained standing. To our left I saw a couple of cauldrons resting on a hearth. A woman about thirty years old was standing at the kitchen door. "Mr. Witczak, don't forget, I need three men," she called.

He pointed at the nearest three and told her to take them. Then she reminded him that she needed two more people to fetch water for her. He pointed at me and the man next to me and grunted, "You two work with Stasia." And with that he turned and led away the remaining inmates.

The woman Stasia equipped her three kitchen helpers with knives and buckets of potatoes. Then she handed the two of us four pails. "Take these," she said in a friendly voice. Pointing in the direction of a forest, she continued, "You'll find a spring in these woods. Follow this road, and you'll come to a small path." She was at a loss to explain the trail further, so she signaled the guard. "What is your name, mister?"

"Tadeusz, but everyone calls me Tadek," he said.

"Tadek, can you show them the spring?" He was also puzzled. Stasia pointed out a few markers, but he shook his head. Stasia, with good intentions, gave us two shoulder-carriers. "Here, they will make it easier."

By this time the three potato peelers were hard at work. I saw how clumsily David Moszkowicz, a Jewish elder from Dobra and a confidant of Mayor Muszynski's, handled the potatoes. This was, no doubt, a first for him, and every so often the knife slipped out of his hand. This didn't escape Stasia. She took the potato and showed him her skills, how to roll it around the knife.

With our pails dangling from the chains, we followed our guard, Tadek. The man chosen to go with me was taller than I, and I had to take three steps for each two of his to keep up with him. Indifferent, hardly raising his eyes, he walked ahead of me. I asked him what his name was. "Marek," he answered. Marek, I judged, was about thirty-five. He had the intelligent look of a city lawyer. Seeing him in his well-tailored gray trousers, herringbone jacket, and red tie, without the water pails, one would think he was on the way to court. His kind face drew me to him. I liked him from the first moment on.

As the pails bounced at our knees, we silently followed Tadek's instructions. The smell of freshly cut grass tickled my senses. In many homes in rural Poland, water was supplied this way, by professional water carriers. Their carrying devices were made from logs and designed to contour to the shoulders. The length of the chains could be adjusted by knotting them in the middle. To us, however, the carriers were so uncomfortable that after the first try, we preferred to carry the pails in our hands. The trauma of the last three days had had a deeply dehumanizing effect on us. I felt all the more trapped.

The thick brush in the inner forest slowed us down. The path led us over bumps covered with slippery moss. Rotted trees and roots were everywhere we stepped. Finally we had to jump over a small stream, and then we found the spring. The spring water was pristine and cold and seemed to be bubbling out of the earth. Mosquitoes and other little insects swirled in a screen of dew that hung over the water. The look of the water invited us to sample it, and it was pure and delightfully refreshing. Because of the spring's shallow basin, we took some time to fill the pails. I asked the guard, speaking Polish, if he had been here before. "No," he said.

I continued probing. "How long have you been in this service?"

"I just started doing this last Wednesday."

"What kind of service is this?" Marek dared to ask.

"It was organized by Germans just recently, to guard all kinds of installations."

"Including camps?" Marek continued.

"Yes. Mostly Jewish," he disclosed. Then we knew that our guards were Poles. The pails were as full as we could get them, and we returned to camp.

Stasia waited for us at the open hearth. The peeled potatoes received a good washing, and we went back for more water. Tadek was anxious to be with his comrades, and he asked if we could find our way without him. "Yes!" we replied in chorus, eager to be alone. As we entered the forest, we realized that this was the first time we had been unguarded.

Marek Lewinski, I then learned, was an electrical engineer from Koło, a town less than fifty kilometers from Dobra. He was handsome, nearly two meters tall, and slender. He had an olive complexion, a straight forehead, and a slightly elongated nose. He had been seized in a Racia. The Nazis took no heed of his being the only male in the family. He and the other men of Koło were loaded on trucks and brought to join our transport. He never got to say good-bye to his wife and two children. The bitterness of his ordeal lay on his face. As he talked, his eyes glued to the ground, I sensed anger and condemnation of Koło's Judenrat.

We were soon at the clearing. We put the pails on the slimy soil surrounding the water pit and sat down on a large rock. The peace and serenity we found in being alone brought a discharge of emotions. We were glad to have this opportunity to unburden ourselves of the rage accumulated in the last few days. Our new helplessness and despair, buried in our hearts for the last week, forced tears, and we both sat and cried.

About fifteen minutes later, at about a quarter to eight, we heard voices in the distance. As the sound grew, we heard young girls singing a gentle, popular Polish school graduation song. The singing dried our eyes, but suddenly the song stopped, and the cheer and beauty of it faded. As the silence persisted, that minute of softness seemed just a dream. I closed my eyes. It was difficult for me to let go. Suddenly I heard movement in the bushes, and raising my eyes, I saw another pair of eyes staring at me. The bushes soon parted, and before us, in the bright sunshine, five young girls emerged. We could not believe our eyes, but they were real.

"Dzień dobry" (Good morning). I greeted them quickly so they would not fear us.

"Dzień dobry," they answered in unison. The five neatly dressed young girls with bundles under their arms radiated happiness. "Who are you?" they asked.

"We are Jews. My name is Bronek Jakubowicz. I am from Dobra. My friend Marek is from Koło."

"What are you doing here?"

"We are at a camp called Steineck. Today is our first day at work at the Hoch und Tiefbaugesellschaft."

"In Brodzice?" one of them asked.

"Yes."

They were Jadzia, Halina, Kazia, Anka, and Zosia. Schoolmates before the war, they were all from Poznan, and they worked on a nearby plantation. Poznan, a city the Germans claimed, was the home of very few Jewish people. When the Nazis entered the city, it quickly became *Judenfrei* (free of Jews). When we told the girls about conditions in our ghettos, they were outraged. They were also shocked to learn about the conditions in camp. "All this just because you are Jews?" they asked. "Why? Why?" This was the question we never stopped asking ourselves. There was no end to their curiosity. They wanted to know why we were hairless. One stared at me, stretched her hand out, and said, "I am Zosia Zasina. I can't believe the Germans can be so horrible." What a lovely name, I thought. "You must be hungry. Here, take this," she said, giving us her lunch.

It was embarrassing. I refused to accept. I wasn't quite ready to forgo the normal gentlemanly response. "I can't take it, Zosia," I responded, her name rolling off my tongue softly.

"Please take it. Share it with your father," she pressed. Hearing my father mentioned, I knew I should accept.

As if to comply with Zosia's lead, the others left their food as well. "Please, please," they pleaded, "give it to the others." We thanked them warmly. "We'll stop by tomorrow at the same time," they said as they left. We watched as they disappeared into the thick forest with tears in their eyes.

Carrying the food bundles with us would give our secret away, so we buried them. Lest our guard come looking for us, we filled the pails and swiftly started back to the camp. I walked ahead on the narrow path. I was filled with excitement and longing for the next day. I saw Tadek coming toward us. I wasn't sure how he would react if he found out about what had just happened. "We lost our way for a while," I said. He accepted that, and we returned to a more impatient Stasia.

"Where have you been so long?" she queried.

"Oh, we strayed a bit, but we are sure of our way now," I said, hoping we wouldn't lose their trust and could continue bringing water by ourselves.

The guards, preferring to sit in the shade talking, smoking cigarettes, or playing cards, weren't anxious to have to escort us. Stasia gave a short speech on how poorly the potato peelers did. She had to check each potato, to remove what she called eyes. I wanted to explain that until today they knew little about the art of potato peeling, but instead I just said, "In time you'll see, they'll do better." For a moment it sounded like the old Nazi claim that Jews were lazy.

Returning again to the spring, I was still occupied with the thought of what had happened earlier. Zosia's beautiful face pushed all others aside. I was moved by her generosity, kindness, and genuine concern. The food they left us was irresistible: tempting fresh bread, ham, kielbasa, cookies, and fruits. We ate more than our share there, and the rest we concealed in our pockets to take to the others. Stasia did not want any more water, so we waited for the midday break.

At noon work halted. As the foreman brought the inmates in front of the kitchen, out came the casseroles, pots, and saucepans. The foremen, supervisors, technicians, and engineers ate in the mess hall. Stasia prepared their food with particular reverence. She lunched with Mr. Witczak after everyone left. I saw that after just a half day of work my father looked worn. When I asked him whether the work was too difficult, he said, "No, I am strong. I can do it."

Schmerele, an Austrian foreman in whose detachment Papa worked, quickly got a reputation for being a terrorizing bully. He demanded that every shovel be full each time it was lifted. At forty-seven, with a heart condition, my father wasn't the person to lift fourteen-kilo shovelfuls of dirt all day. I gave Papa part of the things Marek and I had brought from the forest. I didn't say where the food came from, and he didn't ask.

The soup at Brodzice did not smell as foul as the camp slop. Although its main ingredients were potatoes and turnips, it contained slivers of horse meat.

We scraped up every morsel. After the meal, Marek and I went back for more water. Our comrades headed back to work in the marshes. Witczak later ordered me to find out how many inmates each foreman had on each site, so only Marek was left to provide Stasia with dishwater.

Most earthmoving in those days, especially in Poland, was done with pick and shovel. As I proceeded through the site, I saw how hard our inmates worked digging and lifting the stringy soil, loading it on wheelbarrows, and pushing them hundreds of meters, for a new rail bed. Most of the foremen were more humane than Schmerele. As the inmates' strength diminished, their attitude also changed. After I counted the inmates, I wanted to report to Witczak. His office curtains were drawn, so I knocked on the door. He opened it and took my notes without saying a word. I quickly learned that he wasn't a man to waste words.

Although Hoch und Tiefbaugesellschaft was strictly a German concern, the three Poles—Witczak, Kmiec, and Basiak—ran this part of the project. Kmiec and Basiak were of the Polish intelligentsia, while Witczak was not of the gentry. Kmiec and Basiak often expressed their disgust for Germany's treatment of us, but I never knew Witczak's opinion.

At four in the afternoon work ceased. On the way back to Steineck, guards tried to teach us to march in rhythm. They would yell, "One, two, three, four! What do people say when they see you looking like wobbling ducks?" To us, exhausted, tired slaves, it mattered little what people said. How could one expect Cantor Pinkus and other scholars, who had lived so long in a world where goose stepping didn't exist, to march? They had spent most of their lives in Talmud study and in teaching spiritual enrichment. In time the guards became convinced we were too fatigued and accepted our marching in the only way we knew how.

When we finally arrived back in camp, the yard became a beehive of activity. Inmates were trying to attend to their personal cares all at the same time. Many brothers, fathers, and sons were assigned to different groups, and changes were nearly impossible. When we returned, those already in camp surrounded us to talk about their work. We were all doing the same thing: laying rails.

That night I lay thinking of Zosia. In the dark I saw her face. At 4:00 A.M. I was so deeply asleep that even the sharp school bells couldn't awaken me. It was my father's tugging that brought me to my feet.

The inmates' strength was waning, and we had to find ways to substitute our meager camp rations of coffee substitute, mortar bread, and fake marmalade. We had all heard the aphorism "Necessity is the mother of invention." We flattened the ends of spoon handles with rocks, to make a knife-and-spoon combination.

After breakfast rations our group assembled, and we went to the gate, where Tadek, the chief guard, took charge of us. It was only our second day of work, and already life had become a routine. The sky looked threatening, but no rain fell. The thought of Papa still working under Schmerele nagged at me. I had to try and get him out of there soon.

We reached the construction barracks a little before seven. Stasia, Witczak, and his foremen waited. The shovels, picks, and wheelbarrows were outside the shed. After Tadek's report, inmates were ordered to follow their foremen. "If your foreman isn't present," said Witczak, "go to your site and begin where you left off yesterday."

Stasia left Marek and me at the barracks and escorted her three helpers to the potatoes and knives. Marek and I left for the spring, without a guard. It was only a few minutes after seven, too early to expect the girls. Close to nine, we had just filled our pails for the second time when we heard them coming. "Good day," they cheerfully said, reaching the spring.

"Good day," we answered.

That day lacked the curiosity and spontaneity of the day before. We even talked about the weather. Only Zosia seemed to have retained a gentle fascination for us. I thought she looked as if she wanted to say something. Jadzia broke the ice. "We had few Jewish students in school," she said. Kazia and Halina agreed.

"I had a music teacher, Mr. Kaplan, who gave me private piano lessons. I think he was half Jewish. I liked him a lot," Zosia said. "He and his wife were already old when the war began. I don't know what became of them."

"You said that you are married and have two children," Kazia queried Marek.

"Yes, my son is nine, and my daughter is three. Next week will be her birthday," he replied. From his breast pocket he pulled out a brown leather billfold with his initials in gold and showed them a picture of his wife and children. Like any proud father, he watched their faces as the postcard-sized picture was passed around.

"What an attractive wife you have, and what beautiful children," they said. "Can they write to you?" one asked.

"They are still allowed to send mail from the ghetto, but we won't receive it," answered Marek.

The girls looked at each other, amazed. "What harm is there in your having contact with your families?" Kazia asked. "If you'd like to write to them," she said, "a letter or a postcard, we'll be happy to send it out for you."

"How gracious of you," Marek responded in impeccable Polish. His good manners were not those of a water carrier. He thanked them and gratefully accepted their offer.

I seized the opportunity and asked if I too could send a letter to my relatives. Halina quickly agreed, and so did Zosia. "Gladly," they said.

We reminded ourselves that our delayed return might bring someone to look for us, and Stasia surely would miss the water. Since it was way past eight, the girls too were expected at work. A large box rested at Zosia's side, a collective endeavor, I thought. Discreetly, lest she embarrass us, she pointed to the box. "We brought it for you." Knowing that such a gift would not deprive them, we accepted it. As they were leaving, Zosia turned to me. "Bronek, can you come here at lunchtime? We are free between twelve and one. Can you come?"

"I think so," I answered. A certain warm feeling touched me inside. Was she interested in me? Then they left us, taking with them their vitality, the vitality of freedom.

We hid the food, picked up the pails, and left. On our return Witczak was walking around impatiently. I soon learned, though, that this was his habit. He never stood still. Seeming to be in a hurry always, he walked fast while talking to people behind him. As we approached him, he signaled me to follow him.

"Yes, Herr Obermeister," I said, following close behind. He didn't answer.

We passed the toolshed and the administrators' dining room and entered an office. No one was there. Witczak pointed to a desk at the yard window. On it, surveyor's manuals and books were stacked against the wall. He picked up a ledger. "From now on you'll keep a daily record of the people you bring," he said. "You'll also enter their time of arrival and the number of hours each worked. As you probably know, we pay the camp for what you do." This was news to me. From an open drawer he took out a list, apparently the one Tadek had given him. "Use this desk," he said, fidgeting as he left.

"Yes, Mr. Witczak," I said, but it was too late for him to hear it. He was on his way to the sites.

A stuffy, pinesap aroma permeated the air. Except for the three desks and chairs and one drafting table, which were all well worn, the office was bare. I opened the door and found Marek waiting outside. In the two days we had worked together, I had liked being with him and had learned a lot from his experiences. At times we sat and listened to the sound of water rushing at the spring, thinking of the magical moment when the girls had unexpectedly come upon us. Will I get to see Zosia again? I wondered. "Mr. Witczak wants me in the office," I said to Marek.

He was disappointed. As I began to work at my new job, Witczak's remark to me, "We pay for your work," rang in my ears. I never thought that the Nazis would be selling people's suffering. To hear that they were selling our labor was shocking. I opened the ledger and began to enter the names of the foremen alphabetically, along with the inmates assigned to them and the hours worked each day. Certain names on the list were of people from Dobra. I thought of our common past.

Shortly thereafter Stasia came in, her face beaming. She indicated her influence at the camp. "You know, when Mr. Witczak said he'd like to have someone to help him in the office, I suggested you," she said. "Mr. Witczak is a good man," she continued, making sure I got the intent of her comment. "I think you are nice, Bronek, and even though he may not show it, he too likes you. In his position he has to be careful."

I said I understood and thanked her politely. Tadek walked by, poked his head in, and asked what I was doing there. When I said I was working for Witczak, Tadek's look took on a new measure of respect. "I understand," he said approvingly. Basiak, followed by Kmiec, arrived at the office, and both seemed surprised to find me there. Working with these two gave me an opportunity to get to know them. Even if for different reasons, hatred for Germany was something we had in common. That the Poles hated Germany was a long-standing historical reality, and the latest German occupation brought renewed antipathy. Both men seemed friendly.

At noon Marek waited. "I'll be working with Witczak from now on," I said. When I suggested that he get someone to replace me, he said that he could handle it by himself. The box the girls brought was still where we had left it.

If I wanted to find Zosia, it was time for me to go. Inconspicuously I moved to the rear of the barracks. From there I crossed over a small mound. Then I couldn't be seen from the yard. I walked the rest of the way with long strides. Zosia was sitting on a stump. She got up, and we touched hands in greeting.

"You made it," she said warmly.

"How could you doubt that I would?" I replied.

Neither of us knew where to begin. She looked at me the way other girls my age once did. Could she possibly have a romantic interest in me? Sitting there, I tried to think of what to say. I could have said I was glad to see her. "Being here is courageous of you," I finally ended up saying.

She began to tell me about her life. She lived in Poznan. Her father was a bookkeeper, her mother a homemaker. She was an only child. When the schools reopened, she said, she wanted to get her *matura* (high school diploma). She loved playing the piano, gardening, reading, and seeing the American movies that had by that time disappeared from the Polish screen. When I had gone to school in Kalisz, the family of one of my friends had owned the Apollo cinema. Together we often picked up reels of film from the railroad station. We were free to view them as often as we liked. Zosia and I compared movies we remembered seeing and talked about our favorite actors and actresses. Then it was time to end our meeting. Zosia knew that I wouldn't be able to meet her in the morning. We agreed to meet at lunch the next day.

When I returned to the camp, most of the inmates were still there. No one except Marek knew where I had been. He thought it was dangerous for me to be away at that time.

"Where were you?" asked Stasia. She had something for me to eat. I didn't expect this. With my fellow inmates eating from the kettles, how could I, in their presence, have different food? I thanked her but said, "I'll eat with my comrades." In time, however, hunger won out, and I occasionally accepted her leftovers.

Papa also worried when he did not see me in the yard at noon. I saw that my father's strength was depleting quickly. His foreman, Schmerele, was certainly the woe he was made out to be. I didn't like Papa's situation at all. I had always known that our roles would change in time, but I had not realized it would be so soon. "How is Schmerele?" I asked Papa.

"Good," he said. "He yells a lot, but he isn't treating me worse than anyone else."

"What does that mean, Papa?"

"Sometimes he gets angry, because he thinks we don't try, but he isn't really as bad as he seems."

My father wasn't one to complain, especially to me. It was just his second day there, but his usually pink-colored cheeks had turned purple, his eyes had deepened and had dark rings, and he was walking much more weakly than before. I was concerned and decided to do something. I knew that my new job brought me some influence. Kmiec and Basiak regarded me as part of their team, but I was most at ease with Stasia. I decided to ask her if she could use my father's help in the kitchen.

The foremen made their voices heard. "Return to work!" they yelled in chorus. Marek went to the spring, and I to the office. There I found Basiak at the drafting table. Although he was past forty, his light complexion and thick blond hair made him appear much younger. He had a small, shapely nose and delicate Slavic features that complimented his good looks. His tempered disposition made him easy to talk to. A small wedding picture of him and his wife, Cesia, sat on his desk and faced him squarely as he sat working. He was recently married and childless. He promised to take me to his home someday, but it never happened. I envied him. I wasn't much different from him, so why was I subjected to all this discrimination? Does my darker hair make me an *Unmensch* (nonhuman)? At four the whistles dutifully announced the end to our workday. What remained of the contents of the food box—some bread and a bit of cheese—Marek handed out. Before a line formed, it was all gone.

It was obvious that no one could survive on our rations. What the girls brought could not help many of us. In time I realized that my having been placed in a position that gave me an advantage carried with it rejection by the other inmates. Although I had seen the small recessed house with the sign "Piekarnia" (bakery) before, that day returning from the work camp it especially captured my interest. Would the baker possibly sell us bread? I wondered. We could find out. I remembered what Tadek had hinted to me, saying, "There must be many rich among you."

I drew up a plan, and I wanted to share it with Marek. When I told him to come by my room later, he sensed that it was important. I didn't have to wait long. "Did you notice that bakery on our way?" I said. He looked at me curiously.

"If Tadek will let us go in, on our way to work, one of us could see if the baker would sell us some bread."

"And who is going to pay for it?" Marek asked.

"All of us, according to our means."

"If it worked," he said, "it would be really good."

"OK. I'll ask Tadek as soon as we leave the camp tomorrow."

"What about the rest of the guards?"

"If Tadek allows it, I don't think they'll say no," I reasoned. "You'll go in to talk to the baker?" We decided to act but not to reveal our plan to anyone then, not even my father. We hadn't received much more food in the ghetto, but there we didn't do the hard work that Steineck demanded. Calories in particular were the prerequisite for endurance.

After our evening soup, which I still couldn't swallow easily, I slid into my bunk, covered myself, and fell asleep. The dutiful bells too soon announced time to rise, and the hectic chase began instantly. In the next hour we had to wash, dress, be at the kitchen in time for rations, eat, and then report for roll call before going to work. On the road I decided to take my chances. Thinking of the many times that Tadek had let Marek go to the spring by himself, I thought he had every reason to trust us.

"Would you let Marek go into the bakery for a few minutes?" I asked, promising to make it up to him.

Reluctantly Tadek agreed. "Make sure he returns quickly," he said.

It was a tense moment before Marek came back with two round loaves of bread under his arms, each the size of a bicycle wheel. The aroma of fresh baked bread followed him. "He will sell us as much bread as we want," Marek said triumphantly. "Beginning next week he'll bake twenty extra for us every day."

Except for the money, all elements of our undertaking were in place. What bread Marek brought was quickly ripped to pieces. Of course it wasn't enough, and inmates began to grumble. Someone said, "Tomorrow I'll also go in."

I feared this might lead to chaos and destroy our endeavor. I asked the man not to go and told him that our plans were to organize for everyone. Anyway, we had a few days to work it out. We knew that it was necessary to gamble in order to survive. What was safe, and how far we could go, remained open to question. At noon that day I went to meet Zosia. Our conversation was light. There was no mention of camp, Nazis, or politics. We had a more normal boy-girl relationship now. Zosia was my heroine, and she excited me. When I asked her if she had a boyfriend, she said no.

Zosia took the note I had written to my family and promised to send it at the first opportunity. In this letter I did not mention Steineck's harsh conditions. I assured my mother that Zosia could be trusted as an intermediary.

When we parted I kissed Zosia's forehead and cheeks. She made me feel warm inside, and I looked forward to seeing her as often as possible. When I returned to the camp, all the inmates were back at work. Unnoticed, I passed the dining barracks. Not a soul was in the office. Stasia, however, knew of my absence. No sooner was I back than she came with a plate of food. Eating scraps reminded me of our new place in this bizarre social disorder, but it was difficult to go hungry and be proud at the same time.

"Don't let the Germans see you away from the construction site. Some, as you know, hate Jews," she said protectively. Stasia loved playing this role. I learned that one couldn't hide things from her for too long. It was far better to have her on your side. I decided to take Stasia into my confidence.

"Stasia, I've met a girl from the garden nursery whom I like," I said. Her eyes narrowed as she grinned at me. Looking me in the face, with her colorful *kupka* (kerchief) riding up her forehead, she gave me a triumphant smile, as if to affirm that her suspicions had been correct.

"I knew there was something like that. Be careful. You know we are not allowed to fraternize with you. I don't mean you, but with all of you." She stopped and thought for a minute. "Some of our people don't like Jews because they opposed Christianity. I know, Bronek, that all early Christians were Jews. And our religion was founded by one coming from Jews. To me, Bronek, even if they aren't Christian, they are still people," she philosophized.

Stasia regarded me differently once she could express her enmity for the German occupation. She knew I wasn't bound by secrecy alone but by what an inmate could allow himself to say. Thus I also became her confidant and heard a lot of company gossip. She too had her secrets, for she was having an affair with Witczak.

Each day Papa's face grew thinner and more sallow, and I knew I had to get him transferred as quickly as possible. The next day at noon, Papa waited for me at the office. Although everyone had always thought I resembled my mother, Stasia saw the resemblance between me and Papa. Later I asked her if she couldn't use one more hand around the kitchen. "Is it your father you have in mind?"

"Yes," I said.

"Who is his foreman?"

"He works for Schmerele."

"For Schmerele?" she repeated, surprised. "He is an unpredictable son of a bitch. They all are," she added. On that occasion she made it known that she was still unhappy with the potato peelers. I promised to talk once more to our people. By the end of the day she had worked it out so that Papa could start on Monday.

"As for Mr. Witczak, don't worry. I will take care of it," she said. My father took the news with great happiness, although neither good nor bad impacted him very much then. He had a strange kind of spiritual dignity. As the youngest in the family, I was at the center of his life. Nearly illiterate himself, he was proud of his son's scholastic progress. For the first time, that day I had the feeling I was doing something to help my father.

It was Thursday, and I had to tell Tadek that we wanted to pick things up from the bakery daily. It was then that I began to hear that he and the other guards liked the class ring I wore. "The baker promised to bake some extra breads for us. Will you let us pick them up?" I asked Tadek.

"Hmm," he grumbled. It wasn't yes or no.

I took the ring off my finger. "Tadek, I don't have much use here for this. I'd like to give it to you."

He glanced at me and at the ring. "You don't have to do this." He hesitated and then finally agreed. "But if someone gets caught, I don't know anything."

"It's still dark at that hour. No one will catch us. And if they do, I guarantee you'll not be involved," I said. Little could I guarantee, but we could move on with our plans. Still, we were taking chances. I felt that someday something might go wrong, and eventually it did. But that was much later, so until then we had a source for badly needed extra food.

Marek collected enough zlotys for the week. The rest, I thought, should be relatively easy to find.

In only a week at Steineck, so much had happened.

7

ZOSIA

Zosia and I met every day. She became more than an acquaintance
to me. Our attraction was real, and we both knew it. One day she and her work
clothes smelled of exotic flowers. She came close to me in her modest way,
her thick brown hair rolling around her face in the warm breeze. Her satin skin
glistened with light. Her delicate smile had a sensual expression. I drew her
close. She put her hands around my waist. I embraced her and gently caressed
her face. Our lips touched. The scent of her skin and the softness of her lips
sent my heart racing. Suddenly I felt my lost sexuality steering me. We kissed,
separated, then kissed again. I desired her, and she wanted me. We sat and
looked at one another on a moss-covered tree stump, knowing our relationship
had to climax, but not here and not now. Leaving her on that day was particularly hard. In parting, Zosia hinted in a timid way that perhaps on Monday we
could meet closer to the garden nursery. We kissed in an unrestrained passionate embrace. For a young Jew, a camp inmate, to be loved and to be in love
on a spring day—what a priceless feeling.

I recalled that while I was a student at the Jewish gymnasium in Kalisz, my
cousin Josek, who was ten years older than I, wanted me to experience sex. The
prostitute was a very attractive young girl. I remember my fascination with her
craft and my regret that she sold her body for money. I spent all my time with
her in an attempt to reform her. In the end I left without touching her.

When I returned to the office, Stasia squinted at me. She was curious, and
it wasn't long before I admitted that I had been with Zosia. "Be careful,
Bronek," she reminded me in her motherly way.

Returning to camp after our first work week, we were told that our camp
Kommandant had arrived. When I entered the corridor, I saw him coming out
of the first aid room, with a policeman trotting behind. The Kommandant was

about two meters tall, around forty-five years old, and overweight. His square jaw made him look brutish. Across his bulging stomach, covered by a well-tailored black SS uniform, was a stub-nosed handgun held in place by a thin leather belt and holster. Riding britches and shiny boots completed his uniform. His SS cap showed that his Nazi rank was Scharführer, or group leader. Ironically, his last name was Krusche, the same as that of the infamous dentist in Dobra. He had a cold and distant look. In the first days he made new assignments and named the Stubenältester (room wardens) for each room. He stressed strict obedience with a fiery arrogance typical of the SS.

There was no doubt about who was running the camp now. From this time on, once a week we got gray, blue-striped undergarments, which were permeated by a strong smell of disinfectant. On Saturday afternoon, Krusche came, followed by our policeman, to check his flock. That year we had a warmer than usual spring. Patches of green grass sprouted near the fences, and once a bird flew into the wires, fluttered its wings, and dropped to the ground. The bird tried to get up but did not succeed. I wondered, Is this an omen?

A debate erupted. Someone said, "Why are we always the scapegoats?"

"As we have done many times before, we will also survive this, Amulek (devil)," said Reb Moishe, who sat next to him. "Eventually all people have to live by God's Law."

"Did God really think men would live by his laws?" asked another.

"Yes," the rebbe said. He then recited: "I'll make thee a great nation, and I'll bless thee and curse him who cursed thee."

Then another prisoner interrupted. "Why were we driven out of our homeland and dispersed throughout the world? Why are we made into contemptible slaves? Why are we the focal point of hate at all times?"

Reb Moishe answered with calm dignity. "Losing faith and losing the belief in God run counter to our principles, counter to our Halakah." He had such a strong belief in what he said that it was hard for him to listen to the others. He ended the discussion, saying, "Our belief in God and hope is our only salvation." My belief was not as clear as his.

"Wars don't last forever," Papa remarked. "Once this is over we'll all celebrate victory over this amulek." No one mentioned resisting. We all seemed to be resigned to whatever fate had in store for us.

Organizing was the term we used for the simple thefts that kept us alive. To go on, we had to find ways to supplement our meager rations. That involved danger. It meant testing how far we could venture. On weekdays my group looked forward to the fresh bread we got from the bakery. Sundays always brought curiosity seekers to the fence. Most outsiders were sympathetic at first, but as the camps multiplied the novelty wore off.

Based on the news that filtered into the camp, a quick end to the war did not seem possible. One had to separate the probable from the desirable. Some lies were easily spotted, and others were speculative. We heard of Germany's resounding successes. Europe was at Hitler's mercy. The mere mention of his name made nations tremble. His newest successes were in North Africa. It was common talk that the Nazis would invade Russia. There was little hope that the other European countries would stop them. Only the United States, we thought, could deliver the Nazis a decisive blow. But we did not believe it would really happen. Freedom seemed far away.

That night I dreamed I was with Zosia in a strange park. Everything was alive as we walked close to each other. She had her arm around my waist and her head on my shoulder.

Monday, after a dismal start, the sky brightened, and we faced another warm day. Unlike the first weekend, this one had passed uneventfully. Marek told me he had gotten enough money for a week's worth of bread. As we approached the bakery, he and three other inmates ran ahead. "Be careful. If you see anyone in uniform, leave the sacks in the field," I cautioned them. We watched with suspense as they disappeared into the bakery.

It went without a hitch. The smell of fresh-baked bread made the thought of eating it irresistible. It was pure drama that morning as the oven-fresh bread passed down the line. Some cut it with their improvised knives, and others just ripped it apart. Fresh bread was always my favorite. This reminded me of Sunday mornings at home, when Mama would serve cake or challah for breakfast. I would quietly swap this with kids in the neighborhood for plain bread.

At noon I easily found the new meeting place that Zosia and I had arranged. It was the same distance for me and safer from discovery than the spring. It was a secluded area on low ground. On one side we were surrounded by tall spruce trees, and on the other wheat swayed back and forth. We talked briefly about my life in Dobra.

The next day I arrived early. I watched as Zosia gracefully came into sight, wearing a Krakowianka, a dress of hand-sewn lace in rainbow colors, typical of Kraków culture. The flaring skirt accentuated her small waist. Her white blouse was stitched with colorful silk threads. Her peach-colored small breasts were slightly exposed in the square-shaped décolleté. Her sparkling eyes radiated Polish beauty. The sun shone on her face. I was filled with desire, and as I clasped her hand I could feel her tremble. We walked into the wheat field. Finally our romantic urges won. I put my hands around her waist. She leaned slightly on me. As I lowered her slowly toward the ground, I saw anticipation in her eyes. The idea of lovemaking electrified me. Blood flamed in my temples, and my heart pounded. When we began kissing and then stopped, our lips could not bear the separation. If there is such a thing as dying of passion, I was close to it. Her breasts swelled, rising and falling rapidly. "Oh, Bronek," she repeated, as I thrust myself on her. The feel of her body increased my sensations, and I was in paradise. These were emotions I had not known before. Ecstasy brought tears to my eyes, followed by a pleasant feeling of exhaustion. Looking up at the bright sky, I realized what value she had brought into my dubious life. "I love you, Zosia," I said for the first time. She looked into my eyes and kissed me sweetly. I knew that she loved me too. But we each had to return to our jobs, she to the garden and I to the office.

On my way back I realized how risky this relationship had become and what danger it presented. According to Nazi theory, sex between races was the ultimate sin. If we were caught, it could cost us both our lives. Despite this, I knew that from now on we could not go on just being friends. We wanted something more, and so our lives were entwined in a most dangerous love affair. This was something I had best keep a secret.

Zosia, now our postal intermediary, received a package from my mother. She brought it promptly to me. Papa and I knew that whatever Mama and Pola had sent us, they could not spare. We asked them in our next letter not to send their small rations and not to worry. Between our share of bread from the bakery, Zosia's gifts, and the occasional leftovers from Stasia, neither Papa nor I suffered hunger. The work at the kitchen was more suited to Papa's strength. Also, I had been able to keep an eye on him.

Walking to and from work, we noticed the movement to the east of many German armored vehicles and tanks. It wasn't long before we learned of the Nazi invasion of the Soviet Union. For a while that news lifted our spirits because we hoped that the Soviets would bring the Germans' appetite for world domination to an end. To keep the German war machine moving and their blitzkrieg against their former friend and ally in high gear, we were driven to work harder to complete the railway eastward. In the meantime, the Nazis were achieving one victory after another. Though most of us believed the Soviets would be victorious, the Nazis grabbed a good part of Russia on their first assault.

The fields of rye and wheat that we passed on our daily marches swayed as their stalks arched under the weight of heavy kernels. A field of potato plants was a lush shade of green. On the edges of streams and marshes were thousands of irises and marigolds. Frogs croaked in the green algae. Our sixth Sunday in Steineck had arrived. Before noon, a young boy came running up to me, almost out of breath. He looked around to make sure he would not be heard. "Someone at the fence is asking for you," he whispered. I followed him, and once we were near the fence he forgot all caution. "Right there," he pointed. "The girl and the man asked for you by name."

When I walked closer, I saw Zosia standing beside an older man. Her skin shone through her lace blouse. She wore a pink skirt. My fellow inmates were curious about who they were. Zosia had obviously not known that visiting an inmate in Steineck was *verboten* (forbidden). "My father wanted to meet you," she said, and he nodded.

"Zosia has told me so much about you," he said, looking at me through the squares of the fence. His voice sounded friendly. He was visibly moved.

"Zosia," I said apologetically, almost being impolite, "I forgot to tell you that we are not allowed visitors. If a guard were to see us, we might be in for trouble."

I wasn't sure what her father knew about us. But in coming here, he demonstrated that he approved of her helping me. At the risk of sounding ungrateful, I did not say anything further. While they looked at me, I remembered visiting the zoo. Now I was the one inside the fence.

"I have a letter for you," Zosia said. She had the letter and a package under her arm.

So far the guards hadn't noticed us. We only exchanged a few more words, and then Mr. Zasina, sensing that all wasn't right, said, "We should leave now."

There was enough space under the fence for the package and the letter to slip through. Zosia passed both of them to me. In a low tone, she and her father said good-bye, and then they left. As they walked off, I became concerned about what the pious brethren thought of my companionship with a shiksa, a girl who was not of the Jewish faith. With the letter and package carefully concealed, I returned to Papa in the room.

Papa read Mama's letter several times. The news was bad. He, the eternal optimist, was now concerned about the harassment and brutality that had spiraled in the ghetto. Even so, our receiving mail from home reminded us that even though we were divided, we were still a family.

The sun rose earlier every day, and soon we arrived at the longest day of the year. After wake-up, shoes pounded on the floors, as more than a thousand inmates hurried to shave and wash and prepare for work. Then followed the endless hours of standing in line for our rations and the all-important *Zahlappell* (roll call count) that one never dared missing.

On the way to work, we saw that the night's heavy rains had weighed down young willow branches. They swayed in the light wind like drunkards. The huge acacia trees bore balloon-sized blossoms. Freshened by the rain and the sun-warmed air, they released a flood of perfume. Farm dogs, though they had seen us come and go for weeks, still barked as we passed.

We encountered increasing difficulty in buying bread. The baker had continually increased his prices, and it was almost impossible to collect enough money for the food. Besides, now the guards also wanted their palms greased. But no matter what, we had to go on helping each other.

The next time Zosia and I met, I explained my strange behavior on Sunday. Suddenly I noticed something crawling up my sleeve. It was a body louse. I hoped she had not seen it. I excused myself and went to examine my clothes. There were more. I recalled that my grandfather had once told me he was a similar predicament in a trench during the First World War. They buried their clothes in the soil, he said, leaving a small piece out. Deprived of oxygen, the vermin would crawl out and sit on the piece of garment, and from there they could easily be shaken off. I tried it, but it didn't work. Always conscious of the ugly pests, I felt them crawling on me everywhere. I feared that if Witczak, Basiak, or Kmiec noticed the blight, I would not be allowed to work in the office. A ghastly awareness kept me from eating that evening. The turnip soup tasted so foul that I vowed that if I survived I would never eat turnips again. These schoolrooms weren't built to house eighty people. On warm nights the stench of our bodies was overpowering. No matter how much I tried to force myself to sleep, the bugs wouldn't let me. This seemed to be a new form of Nazi cruelty, as if to assert the claim "Jews are social vermin." At times all this seemed like a bad dream. I thought that someday I would wake up, and everything would be the way it used to be.

The next evening I saw my father picking the lice off our blankets. He thought the best way to get rid of them was with naphtha. I went into the first aid room to ask for some.

This was the first time that I had gone to the first aid station. The room was spacious and had a cabinet, two chairs, a table, a bench, and a stool. In the glass cabinet were aspirin, bandages, and a few bottles with iodine and the like. Goldstein, our first aid attendant, had the same remedies for all ailments: aspirin and bitter-tasting Baldrian drops. When I asked him if he had any naphtha to get rid of our lice and fleas, he laughed. "We do not have naphtha, and even if we did, you could not get rid of them. Every room is infested with them," he said.

Goldstein knew that I had been a dental student before the war. A few days later, on a Saturday afternoon, he came looking for me. Could I help an inmate suffering pain from a toothache? he wondered. I followed him into the first aid room. The man, about thirty-five years old, had a handkerchief tied around his swollen right cheek. There was nothing in Goldstein's cabinet that I could use to help him. I thought of the box under my pillow. When I returned with my tools, I looked into his mouth. I could see a fistula beside his second upper molar. I disinfected my scalpel over a flame and cut through the fistula, letting the pus drain out. My first operation was a success. From then on, Goldstein called me regularly. After work I spent many hours helping fellow inmates in the first aid room. By then, because of the lack of vitamins, especially vitamin C, most inmates suffered from bleeding gums. All I could do was dab iodine on the diseased gums, for temporary relief. In time everyone called me Dentist.

Eventually the day came when I had to attempt to extract a tooth. I winced at confronting it, but there was no one except me to do it. We had no novocaine. I had no choice. I quivered, my hands shook, and sweat ran down my forehead, fogging my eyes. I had to wipe them constantly. When I grasped the tooth with an angle forceps, Goldstein gripped the inmate's head to keep it still. But the molar crumbled and broke off, leaving all three roots in the gingiva. Shaking, I reached in and tried to pry out each root separately, using levers. The poor man cringed and yelped, yet he held on and let me do it. After a half hour of torture, I succeeded in extracting two of the three roots. By then we both had had enough. Luckily his gums healed, and the remaining root did not bother him. Extracting a decayed molar without novocaine gave me confidence in the future. I knew that I could do it again, even with my rudimentary skills and no anesthesia.

The bugs now multiplied much faster than we could kill them. My greatest concern was for them not to be seen on me by the people working in the office. When they gnawed, I discreetly scratched through my clothes, but that led to more itching and pain. Sometimes I could not stand it and had to leave the office. One day I saw them crawling on my sleeve. Kmiec was next to me. I held my breath in fear that he might have noticed. I walked out and went to a secluded spot, and there I again tried the technique my grandfather had told me he had used. I undressed, buried my clothes, and waited. My skin looked as though it had been pricked by a thousand needles. There were handfuls of lice in my armpits and my crotch. I waited, but as before, the method didn't work for me. These were not the same lice. They were not the lice of the First World War. Nearly impervious, they could only be killed with a hard fingernail. I killed as many as my time allowed and then returned to work. To go on killing them was useless. I knew that once I was in camp they would infest me again.

To avoid embarrassment, I was seeing Zosia less frequently. One day when she insisted on knowing why, I told her, adding that she should decide to stop seeing me. "Bronek," she interrupted, "this is not going to change our relationship." She came to see me as before.

The bugs were determined. The more we killed, the faster they seemed to multiply. They now were able to change colors. On the blankets they were gray, and on our bodies they disguised themselves in the color of their hosts' flesh. Shaking them off our clothes only freed space for new colonies. Finally one day, in desperation, we burned all the straw that filled our pallets and pillows and slept on the bare wooden planks. The people of Heine, Kant, and Goethe were degrading us to a life in lice pits. Even now, so many years later, remembering this still brings shivers to my spine.

On a hot unbearable night with a bright full moon, I noticed that my father had left his bunk. I waited a while. When he didn't return, I went to look for him. He wasn't in the washroom or in the yard. I went back to the room, hoping he had returned in the meantime. I was startled, for he wasn't back. This was unusual for Papa. I went back to the facilities building and saw him sitting in the back facing the fence. Being there at night was extremely dangerous. I walked in the shadow of the building so as not to be noticed by a guard and whispered, "Papa, is that you?" Hearing my voice, he rose. "Papa, what are you doing here? This is a very dangerous place at this hour. Is anything wrong, Papa?" I asked.

On the way back to our barracks, he said, "Oh, I just couldn't sleep." Back in the room I saw that his eyes were red, and I knew then that he had been crying. It suddenly occurred to me how hollow this sounded. So many things were wrong. It was wrong for us to be there. It was wrong for them to make us into slaves. That and more was wrong! I never found out why my father had sat out in the moonlight weeping. My father's generation of Jews believed that they were at the mercy of their fate, without rights or the capacity to change. It saddened me to see this once-proud man cleaning floors, peeling potatoes, and washing dishes.

We Jews weren't alone in hating the Nazis. One day when I came into the office, Basiak was standing by the window. "Those bastards," he gasped. "They took away my sister to work for them as a slave in Germany."

By then Tadek had my ring, and the other guards also had to be paid, as our bread-buying project continued. Most of us had found ways to communicate with our families. The news from the ghetto wasn't encouraging to anyone. In each letter new victims were mentioned. With Zosia's help and Stasia's leftovers, Steineck was still bearable for my father and me, but a sudden incident of deception changed our lives.

8

KRUSCHE

By the end of August the warm weather had come to an end. One day when we returned to camp, Chaim looked at me uneasily and said, "Krusche wants to see you, in the first aid room."

"Why?" I asked. "What does he want me for?"

"He just wants to see you," he repeated. His face showed concern, and I was sure that he was hiding something. No one was called to Krusche without a reason. I thought that Chaim knew more.

"What does he want of me?" I asked again, frightened. He looked around and then whispered that Krusche knew about our bakery ventures. I grasped my predicament, and immediately fear shot down my spine. "Who told him? How did he find out?" These were the big questions that troubled me.

"I think one of your group told him." I couldn't believe it. One of us? Why? "I think it was Baran," he mumbled. I was stunned. Feivel Baran, a respected man from one of the most outstanding families in Dobra? The student of the acclaimed Gerer Rabbi Yeshiva? I could hardly believe that he could squeal on his fellow prisoners. With Krusche waiting, Chaim urged me to come, and I followed him.

When we entered the first aid room, the raffish German stood, feet apart, whip in hand, with Cheetah, the fierce German shepherd, at his side. Krusche's face, never pleasant with its cramped lips, now looked full of violence. "Herr Lagerführer, Bronek Jakubowicz obediently reports as ordered," I announced myself, expecting the worst. His heartless eyes speared me and made me believe I was standing before a tribunal of one. I had good reason to be frightened.

With his eyes riveted on me, he tied Cheetah to a chair. Then he came within centimeters of my face. I could smell his foul breath and feel his blazing anger, and in his guttural German he yelled: "Du Schweinehund, which guard let you go to the bakery and buy bread? Which one?"

I cringed. I had to gather enough courage to lie. I knew I couldn't name Tadek. "Herr Lagerführer, we did not buy any bread. People left it for us on the road," I mumbled.

He was convinced that I was lying, and his voice rose and became loud and threatening. I realized that he was mostly interested in the guard who had allowed us to leave the group. "You damned Jews, all you know is lying. I know you bought bread. Who permitted you to go into the bakery?" This time he struck my face with his gloves. "Tell me who let you leave!" He was furious. I saw that it was too late for me to admit having bought bread.

My heart pounded. Cold sweat ran down my spine. I had given Tadek my word not to give him away, and I had to stick to it. Besides, I thought, what I might say wouldn't matter now. Krusche would punish me just the same. I bit my lips, dug my fingernails deep into the palms of my hands until it hurt, and repeated the lie. "Herr Lagerführer, the only bread we had outside was what people left for us on the road."

But nothing would dissuade him, and he came violently at me again. This time I was sure he would kill me. He tore at me, hitting both sides of my face with his gloves. My head bobbed like a Ping-Pong ball. Cheetah barked and foamed at the mouth, trying to get close and grab me. I was lucky that Chaim held her back, or she'd have torn me apart. Though my courage was waning, I kept telling myself, "Don't give in." It seemed that my persistent lie obsessed Krusche, and he was intent on punishing me rather than trying to get at the truth. Blood splattered from my mouth and nose onto my clothing and the floor. My stomach cramped. Will it ever end? I wondered.

Krusche picked up his leather-covered wire whip and handed it to Chaim. The real torture was about to begin. Krusche ordered me to lean over a chair and lower my pants, and then he ordered Chaim to dole out twenty-five lashes on my naked behind. I knew that Chaim wanted desperately not to have to do it. Chaim's whip came down hard, but not hard enough for Krusche's liking. Krusche took the whip and landed three very slow and deliberate blows on my rear. "This is how you do it," he said, and he made Chaim begin all over again. This time I was ordered to do the counting.

One, two, three . . . I sensed when the whip rose and gritted my teeth until it landed. "One at a time," Krusche said. "Slowly. Let him suffer." The time of waiting between the blows doubled my pain. I bit my lips until they bled.

And so it went on, seemingly forever. The last number I remembered counting was fifteen. I heard Krusche rumbling, "Slower. Harder." At that point I
thought life had left me, and I remembered nothing further.

By the time I realized I was still alive, I was on the corridor floor, still only
half conscious, with my hands on my belly, doubled over with pain. I saw Papa
and a few other inmates leaning over me, staring. I felt numb. Slowly I grew
conscious and remembered what had happened. Papa and some others tried to
help me to my feet. I got up, staggering. Blood was dripping from my mouth
and nose. Papa ordered me to tilt my head back until the bleeding stopped. He
shared all of my anguish. When they got me to the washroom, I saw Krusche's
fingerprints on my face. Because of my bludgeoned behind, I walked with my
legs wide apart, trying to keep my clothes from brushing against my flesh. The
most persistent and excruciating pain, however, was in my stomach.

Then I returned to the room and slid into my bunk. I pondered, wondering whether there was really a God, as I was taught to believe. I wallowed on
the bunk. I thought about Feivel. Something must have gone wrong with his
mind. How could he, also an inmate here, turn on his brothers? Perhaps he
wanted to ingratiate himself with Krusche? These and other questions raced
through my head.

It was the first time Krusche had punished any of us so brutally. As the
night continued and the throbbing in my stomach didn't subside, I wondered,
Will I have to live with this pain from now on? The pain did not stop then and
has not ever since.

Streaks of dawn found their way through our dirty windows, smearing the
floor in colors. When the bells rang, I was already in the washroom, wiping
my face and putting cold water on my behind. As my group assembled, I saw
Krusche talking to Chaim. Chaim was his most-trusted policeman, and
Krusche passed most of his orders concerning us through him. Then I saw
Chaim go to the gate and call the head guard, Tadek. They returned and
stopped before Krusche. Tadek saluted him with "Heil Hitler."

"This is a Jew swine!" Krusche shouted to Tadek, pointing at me. "Did
you know that he has been leaving the group to buy bread?"

I wondered how Tadek would respond. "I don't know anything about that,
Herr Hauptscharführer," he answered.

Krusche didn't ask him anything further. My misdeed was then far more
important to him, and pointing again at me, he said, "He will be replaced as
group leader at once."

"Jawohl," Tadek said obediently.

"One of these days I'll hang him," Krusche said. This brought silence. "Does anyone in this group speak German?" he asked. At first no one responded, but when Chaim repeated it, his nephew, Chaskel, raised his arm and stepped forward. I knew Chaskel well. He barely knew Polish, and the German he spoke was just a broken Yiddish. As Chaskel took my place, I went to stand in line next to my father. Krusche then instructed Tadek to tell the foreman that I was to work at the hardest possible job, so that I might perish. An obedient "Jawohl" from the guard followed.

Krusche, of course, knew that I worked in the office. When we finally left, he gritted his teeth. Four hundred pairs of feet stomped through the gate, and a ribbon of men moved out. It was hard for me to keep up, walking with my legs wide apart. Getting bread from the bakery was now a dead issue.

Krusche's threat terrified me. I knew if he wanted to he could hang me at any time. It was the norm for the Nazis to use hanging as an example, to warn others; they had hanged my friend Szymon, in Dobra. I walked out of the camp dejected, disgraced, and fearful.

Later on Chaskel came and apologized. He said he was "sorry." After all, someone had to take my place. He said he hoped I bore him no ill will. I knew my relatively easy life in Steineck was over. What was the future? What would happen to me in Brodzice?

When we arrived at the workplace, Tadek told Witczak what had happened. Sensing some unusual conversation, Stasia opened the kitchen door and listened. Tadek then dutifully said to Witczak that he ought to send me to the hardest job at the site. I agonized on hearing it, but Witczak turned to the foremen. Shrugging his shoulders, he said, "OK. Take your men, and let's go to work." I wasn't sure where I was to go. I did not think that returning to the office was my right, under these circumstances. But when I went to the shed, Witczak called me back. He ordered me to go to the office and do what I had done all along. Tadek once more reminded him of his orders from the Kommandant. "Yes, yes," Witczak retorted. "I know." Before Tadek could argue with him further, he was gone.

I knew that Witczak didn't like to be told what to do, but defying an SS man put him, in my mind, in a different category. I feared that Witczak's refusal to follow Krusche's orders would anger Krusche even more. It reminded me that often when two people quarrel, the bystander gets the blame. Though they hated the Germans, the three Poles ran the project for them as if it had been their own. They must have known their diligence helped the Nazis. Perhaps we all did.

When I told Stasia how all this had come about, she said, "It was dumb of you to take such a risk. You know the Germans." Then, with a look of patronage, she added, "Mr. Witczak said that the Kommandant is not running this company. We decide where people work here." With this she walked out, holding her head triumphantly. I was grateful. There were certainly others who could do this work as well as I could.

When I asked Feivel why he had squealed, he turned away, mumbled something inaudible, and left me like a hunted fox. I still couldn't figure him out. Had madness gained the upper hand with him? Perhaps hunger, hard work, isolation, and fear had jostled his mind. It was hard to believe how he, once a decent human being, could undergo such a change. The favors he may have expected in return from Krusche never materialized. When Kmiec and Basiak learned what had happened, they also were determined to keep me in the office. At this point my fate was in their hands.

At noon I left to meet Zosia. Along the way I stopped in the wheat field and dabbed tincture of iodine on my wounds. In the sunlight, I could see how bug-eaten my naked body was. I dressed and went to the edge of the forest. Seeing my battered face, Zosia wanted to know what had happened. I explained. I felt so humiliated and hurt that our meeting that day didn't last very long. Romance was the farthest thing from my mind.

Tadek had not come near me much all day. But on the return to camp that afternoon, we spoke. He knew I had kept my word to him and did not tell Krusche about his involvement in getting the bread. He was still my friend, as he would prove later on. That evening Chaim told me that what he did to me hurt him as well—but he had no choice. I knew that under the new laws we had to live by, if he had disobeyed Krusche, he would have in the end also landed on the chair.

When I fell asleep that night, I had a strange feeling. I saw myself on the gallows, and I woke up in a sweat. I wasn't willing to see Krusche make good on his threat. Life was still too precious to lose it here, in this godforsaken place. The next day Zosia said that she thought I ought to escape. The question was, Where would I go? Returning to the ghetto was out. Besides, I could not leave my father.

My bruised face turned colors. One eye was purple and half shut. My stomach throbbed as if I had a screwdriver turning inside my guts. When I ate something, the ache subsided for a while, only to return with more vengeance. My two terms of biology in school were of no help in diagnosing myself. I felt as if I were returning to a nightmare each day as I came back to Steineck.

I feared being caught by Krusche in the first aid room. But when Goldstein called me, I had to go. The place felt like a torture chamber, and I left as quickly as I could. At roll calls I hid behind my father to escape Krusche's stare. Our guards were now extra cautious when we passed the forbidden bakery every morning. I wondered if the bakers knew why we weren't buying bread from them anymore.

Tadek let me know that Krusche, hearing his orders were not obeyed, had reminded the guards that his orders concerning me must be followed. When we got to Brodzice, Witczak was irritated by that order. "We don't take orders from your Lagerführer," he said with finality. I went to the office, uneasy about what the future held for me. I didn't like my role in this power struggle. I remembered an old saying: "In a two-man fight for power, the innocent are most often hurt."

Shortly before noon I went over the hill in back of the barracks and undressed. My underwear was bloody and crawling with pests. Once more I tried the experiment. I covered my clothes with soil and waited for the bugs to appear. But as before, it didn't work. I returned to picking off as many as I could and killing them one by one.

The next day we got a note from Pola:

> We are happy you found someone as kind as Zosia. Our condition has worsened. We get only a kilo of bread each day and soup. Josek no longer has to report each day to the labor office. He works steadily at cleaning the army barracks. With the help of our friends, our former neighbors, we still manage. But that is not true for most here in the ghetto. Young and old are dying of hunger every day. I wish I had better news for you.
>
> How are you, and Papa? Please write.

It had been raining for days. Our clothes, now threadbare, were drenched and foul-smelling. I continued to dread the return to camp and Krusche. What if he asked me where I now worked? What if he found out his orders had been ignored? For a Pole to thumb his nose at a Nazi officer was unprecedented. This time, I thought, Witczak had dared too much.

When the bell rang early each morning, I opened my eyes. Then, shunning the reality of another miserable day, I closed them again. Papa tugged on my blanket, and I knew I had to get up.

With Krusche present at roll calls, tension grew. We had to count, yelling our names aloud over and over again. Whoever failed to shout was in for a lash or two. One morning Krusche asked Tadek where I was working. Tadek said that despite his reminding Witczak, I was still working in the office. Krusche was furious. Gnashing his teeth, he pointed his index finger at Tadek and bellowed, "I'll be out there. Tell them I'll be out there today. Understood?"

"Jawohl, Herr Lagerführer," Tadek dutifully answered. I was now in the middle of a conflict between Krusche and Witczak. I knew I would be the loser in the end. When I told Witczak about Krusche's intention, he seemed unworried. I also told Basiak that I would go to work elsewhere to avoid controversy. But he also said no. Kmiec was annoyed as well. "That son of a bitch," he said. "We don't interfere in his affairs. Once and for all he has to learn not to interfere in ours."

Stasia, who listened to it all, had a helpful word. "Bronek, you see, they like you. You are different."

"Stasia, it is because you know me that you feel this way," I said. "All inmates are like me." Nevertheless, I was grateful that Witczak had stood up to a Nazi in defense of me, a Jew.

Halfway through the morning I noticed that a car drove up to the office and stopped. Krusche got out with two SS corporals in tow. Kmiec went out to greet them, and Witczak joined them shortly. At first they spoke casually and went to inspect the work sites. Half an hour later they returned. Krusche and his two companions got in their Mercedes and left. Witczak and Kmiec returned to work, without saying anything to me. Later I saw Witczak with Stasia. I knew she would know what had happened. When she came into the office, her face beamed. She looked as if she had good news. "Did you hear," she said to me in a whisper, "what Witczak told your Kommandant?"

"No, Stasia. What did he tell him?"

"You'd have loved hearing it, Bronek." Her admiration for Witczak was obvious. "This Kommandant of yours hates you," she muttered. I agreed. Who knew this better than I? "But, you know, Witczak isn't afraid of him!" Now her face took on an expression of strength.

"What happened?" I urged her on.

"Krusche insisted we put you to hard work here, but we, I mean Mr. Witczak, doesn't care what he wants. Witczak told Krusche that we know what's best for the company and he will keep you working right here in the office." Though I couldn't know what the final outcome of this would be, I admired what Witczak had done. I continued on my job and had the benefits that came with it. The most important one, of course, was that I could go on seeing Zosia.

I know I lived a life of double standards—while I dreaded being in camp, going to Brodzice each day was a relief. In the meantime, my face, partly black from Krusche's beating, now turned green and yellow. The sores in my mouth had healed, but the pain in my stomach grew worse.

An unexplained magical love drew me to Zosia. Her love returned a lot of what had been so abruptly taken from me. I saw her now as often as I could. The next time we met was a cool day. She was wearing a thin dress, and as we sat down, she began to shiver. Then the sun broke through and warmed our small hideout. I looked at her. She was exactly the girl I had dreamed I would find someday. At that time, when I could no longer think of myself as being human, she made my life worthwhile. We remained sitting there, watching swallows swooping effortlessly, catching insects in the air. We could have stayed together for hours.

Witczak broke his habit of never seeming too friendly to me. He sat down and asked me where I was from, why I was in camp, and other such questions. But he didn't say anything about the conversation he had had with Krusche about me, nor did I ask him about it. At the end of our talk, he ordered me to check with each foreman, to see if all inmates recorded at our camp were at work.

It was heartbreaking to see some of our people standing ankle-deep in mud, lifting fourteen-kilo shovelfuls of dirt onto the wheelbarrows. The skin on their hands was calloused and cracked. Some even had open wounds. When I told Basiak about it, despite his sympathy, he said that as long as the camp sent them, they had better be put to work. On our way home, clouds grew thicker, and suddenly it began to rain heavily.

At the food line inmates milled around, trying to barter cigarettes at the kitchen window for anything edible. The cigarettes were discarded butts rolled in plain paper. Usually the policemen and the cooks were their best customers.

Once I saw an inmate picking up a thrown-away cigarette butt. Seeing this, the foreman stepped on it and squashed it. Ahead of me in the line was David Kot, a friend of mine. "Take the ladle down to the bottom, please," he said. He passed by me mumbling disappointedly. There wasn't a single potato in his soup. We were a sorry lot, looking like the unsociable creatures portrayed in propaganda. Some days, the sight of my body filled me with disgust. I was sickened seeing what the bugs had done to me, and sometimes I even felt them crawling inside me.

It was October 1941, a month after the second anniversary of the Blitzkrieg, which Hitler claimed would catapult the Third Reich into a thousand-year reign. We were resigned to Churchill's prediction: "This will be a long war." Our hopes for a quick ending to our misery looked very dim. We were distressed by a new rumor that special Nazi units were killing entire Jewish communities. My father would not believe it. It seemed so outrageous that those who feared it refused to believe it. One day I saw Papa chanting quietly. It was the holiest day of the year, Yom Kippur. It was inconceivable not to fast or worship on the day of atonement. Yet here, this most solemn day passed like any other.

As we went to work that Yom Kippur, I recalled a particular incident when my brother and two friends of his were once seen in a restaurant on this holiday. At the next services in the Temple, our unduly pious rabbi insisted that, in the eyes of God, that crime disgraced the entire community. All of us, he said, must pray to the Almighty for forgiveness.

If God is really for us, why is all this happening? Has he decided that we do not deserve better? I wasn't sure of many things I once was told to believe. I questioned God and my faith in him. Did he really exist? I knew that my father would never agree with my thoughts. He would never waver from his beliefs.

Each day my stomach pain became more intense. This did not escape Zosia's notice. She advised me to tell our camp doctor. "We don't have a doctor in camp," I replied. After a minute of silence, she said that she had an idea. She would go to a doctor and make my symptoms hers. Whatever he prescribed for her as medication she would bring to me.

One morning Marek wanted me to come along with him to the spring. I knew something was on his mind. We were hardly halfway there when he stopped. "Don't tell anybody," he cautioned. "I am going to escape from here."

It shouldn't have surprised me. I knew he was extremely depressed. Those who were less affluent at home adapted to life in the camp better than he and others like him. For them the degradation was unbearably hard. Though I knew the risk he was taking, I could not and would not try to change his mind.

"Marek, watch out. Don't get caught," I warned.

He looked at me, and I saw his determination. He told me that as soon as he brought enough water to last Stasia through the day, he would make a run for it. At about two o'clock he peeked in the office window and waved good-bye to me. I went out, we shook hands for the last time, and I wished him good luck. Then I saw him slip over the hill. As he was the first one to flee from Steineck, I had no idea of the consequences of his action on the rest of us.

No one noticed that he had gone during the day, and by the time we left Brodzice, the guards could only report him missing in camp. The following morning Krusche asked who knew of Marek's escape beforehand. He got silence in return. Then he threatened us all. "If anyone escapes again, you will all be responsible for it. For each one that escapes, I'll hang ten of you," he said. A few days later he claimed that Marek had been caught and executed, though it couldn't be confirmed. I hoped that by some miracle he had made it back to his family and that Krusche had told us a lie.

The weather was deteriorating, and dusk nudged itself in earlier each day. All that remained of the once-burgeoning wheat and rye fields were short, dry, stubby roots. The cycle completed, they too withered and died. I remembered that after our potatoes were put in the cellar at home, we kids still found some under the bushes. We would then gather dry twigs and build a fire and bake them. Even Mama's kitchen-cooked potatoes could not compete with our cookout.

Cold, drizzly weather had arrived. Most of our clothing was just layers of tatters, and our shoes had long since fallen apart. Just getting to work was a struggle. Some inmates made it through the day by sheer force of will. One day a fellow inmate collapsed from weakness. I was told that the foreman just left him there, because he didn't want to disrupt the others' work. When we finally brought him into the camp, no miracle could save him. On his skin feasted thousands of bugs. Paradoxically, I thought, their feast would end soon. He died before dawn. Scenes like this would become common. Many died soon afterward, but his death, the first one, was the most shocking.

Zosia said that when she described "her" discomforts to the doctor, he diagnosed a duodenal ulcer. She brought me belladonna, a powdery antacid, Papaverine pills, and a liquid acid-neutralizer. It is not a cure, the doctor told her, but it should make her discomfort more bearable. The antacid helped my heartburn, but the Papaverine seemed to dry my mouth.

The landscape was changing with the seasons. Trees were bare, and winds whirled around with fury. Though malnutrition and hard work had already taken its toll, the winter cold would be even more devastating. It was November 11, Poland's independence day, when two of our inmates collapsed at work. No one could help them, and no one could even try. Their lives simply ended. This happened so often that we now carried stretchers to work with us all the time. A new term, *Mussulman,* was born, probably because of the ashen color of the faces of these inmates who were "on the way out." Their eyes deep in the sockets reminded us of desert people. While no one could tell who would survive, the next victim could often be predicted. Yet everyone was sent out to work every day. The sick wobbled and staggered to make it to work, and some never came back alive.

As the tragedy of knowing we were on a path to disaster grew, our senses dulled, and indifference set in. The will to go on ran up against our painful helplessness. Nobody felt much bereavement at the sight of fellow inmates dying. Mayer Siskind, just twenty-seven, was next. What I once believed—that needing our work, they would keep us alive—was obviously not their plan. In six months, of the 167 who had come here from our village, more than twenty were dead. The Nazis soon found it necessary to replenish the dead in our camp with new slaves. A transport of a hundred Jews from Konin, a nearby town, was delivered to us. Although Konin was only eighty kilometers from Steineck, these arrivals had not known that Steineck existed. At first their fresh look and decent clothes set them apart, but after a few weeks they blended in with the rest.

Winter dropped its first load of snow, but nothing would deter Kommandant Krusche from sending everyone out to work. After New Year's more Jews arrived, this time from Lodz. They told us a horrifying story about a village called Chełmno. The Nazis, they said, had a better method to kill Jews. They had new vehicles that diverted the engine exhaust into the truck body. Under the guise of resettlement, the people were driven away and killed on the

road. The bodies were taken to Chełmno, which boasted the largest crematorium in the area, with a capacity to burn five hundred bodies per day. Because
this act was so outrageous and diabolical, Rumkowski, the elder of Lodz, inquired if it was done on higher orders or by local Nazi zealots. The answer
from Berlin came that it was official policy and that many such places were
soon to follow. Because Chełmno was only about sixty-five kilometers from
Dobra, this news rekindled our worse fears about the ghetto and the well-
being of my mother, Josek, and Pola.

On one gray raw day, returning from work, I saw an inverted U-shaped
structure with large hooks standing in the reporting area. It was unmistakably
a gallows. I turned pale. Having failed to have me worked to death, I thought,
Krusche was now determined to make good on his threat. He was going to
hang me. Once we were dismissed after roll call, I asked Chaim what the gallows meant. It surprised him too, he said, when he saw it being erected. That
evening I could not take my mind off dying. When I finally fell asleep, I saw
myself, hands tied behind me, being led to the gallows. I tried to run away, but
wherever I turned, SS men were in my way, stopping me. Finally the nightmare ended when I woke up choking. This must have awakened my father as
well, for he looked frightened. Each time I saw the heinous device, shivers
went down my spine.

One time I came upon Moniek, whom I knew from Dobra. Although he
was my age, he looked like an old man. His flesh looked bug-eaten and his veins
as if they were filled with water. When he buttoned his shirt, he could
barely move his fingers. He was a Mussulman. I took him to the infirmary,
where Goldstein asked him if he was sick. No one ever wanted to admit to being sick, fearing the worst. Work was the best recipe for staying alive. Since
Moniek had no injury or discernible ailment, Goldstein couldn't let him stay.
Those were the rules, he said. Thus, without being sick, Moniek went to work
and was later brought back on a stretcher. He died the following day. There
was no one to mourn him, no one to say a prayer for his soul. Starvation happened to so many that it soon became our number one killer.

In observing a man's manner of walking and seeing the color of his skin
and lips, I could tell the onset of a Mussulman. As I later saw, other labor
camps, while more pernicious and more destructive, had better sanitary facilities. Some even offered periodic clothes changes and shoes to inmates, and
most had inmate doctors and even small infirmaries.

The author's beloved grandfather, Hersh Yankow Jakubowicz, in 1937. Harassed for his beard, he died of self-imposed isolation in 1941.

The Jakubowicz family in summer 1934. Standing, left to right: Berek's father (Awigdor), mother (Ester), brother (Josek), and cousin (Toba). Seated: his sister (Pola) and fifteen-year-old Berek.

Left: Awigdor Jakubowicz, Berek's father, a grain merchant, about 1929. He was killed by a Kapo at Fürstengrube in 1944.

Below: (left to right) Josek, Pola, Berek, and Uncle Schlomo in 1934, on one of Schlomo's annual visits to Dobra.

Pola in 1940. She preferred to die with her mother in Chelmno rather than face tyranny at a concentration camp.

Berek in 1941, only months before his deportation to one of the first labor camps near Posnań.

Members of the Dobra Zionist organization, about 1933. In the first row, holding up a sign, are Berek (third from right) and David Kot (third from left); Josek is second from right. Pola is third from the right in the second row. Except for Berek and Josek, only one other person from this group survived the war.

(Above) A cynical sign at Auschwitz: "You have arrived at Auschwitz, a German concentration camp. It is not a sanitorium. You may survive only a few weeks here, three months at best. The only way out of here is the chimney. And if it is not to your liking, go to the fence and end it now." A photograph of this sign now hangs in the Auschwitz Museum. A 1985 photo by the author.

Left: The death block at Auschwitz, where Berek was quarantined for three weeks. A 1985 photo by the author.

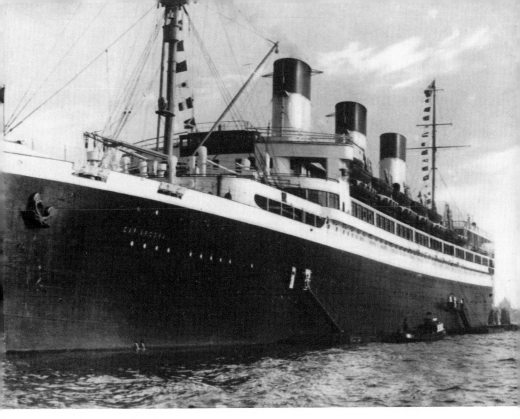

Above, the luxury liner *Cap Arcona* in its heyday. On May 3, 1945, the *Cap Arcona* and the *Thielbek* were bombed and sunk by the RAF in Lübeck Bay. Berek was one of 15,000 prisoners on three ships; only 1,600 survived. From Joachim Völfer, *Cap Arcona: Biographie eines Shiffes* (Herford: Koehlers Verlagsgesellschaft, 1977).

Below, the *Cap Arcona* on May 3, 1945, sinking in the Bay of Lübeck.

Berek's cousin Aaron Pacierkowski, at age five, with his parents in 1945. He survived three years of "Hell on earth" in the Lodz ghetto by hiding in his father's horse-driven hearse.

Mendele (center) at thirteen, the youngest inmate in Fürstengrube, with two other survivors of the *Cap Arcona* sinking: on his right, an unidentified Kapo; on his left, former camp elder Otto Breiten.

Above: Berek in Lüdenscheid, Westphalia, shortly after surviving the inferno in Lübeck Bay in May 1945. He wears the German naval uniform Mendele had found for him.

Above: One year after the *Cap Arcona* disaster, survivors march to place a wreath in memory of their perished comrades.

In 1985, Benjamin Jacobs places flowers at the Timmendorf Memorial for victims of the *Cap Arcona* and *Thielbek* sinkings. The plaque at right indicates that inmates from thirteen nations died in the disaster.

Above: "Pamietamy"—"We remember." Benjamin Jacobs at the Chelmno Memorial honoring the death of his mother, sister, and 360,000 other murdered Jews in Chelmno, where eighty-two children from Lidice, Czechoslovakia, were also killed. Their ashes lie in the nearby forest.

Below: In 1985, forty years after war's end, Benjamin Jacobs visits with former Polish neighbors in Dobra.

The winter of 1942 was a bitterly cold one. Except for the spruce and pine, every tree was bare. The roads were covered with snow; streams and lakes lay under layers of ice. At work, the earth had to be chopped before, in lumps, it was loaded onto the wheelbarrows. For the first time we heard about a camp called Auschwitz. In Auschwitz, we heard, the SS put older men, women, and children to death as soon as they were brought in. No normal brain could absorb this, and many of us were not even willing to listen. We insisted that the story couldn't be true.

By the middle of March a rumor spread in camp that a hundred inmates were to be transferred out of Steineck, but no one knew where they would be sent. This should be our opportunity to get out of here, I thought. My father agreed. Chaim, usually well informed about things like these, didn't know more than what was rumored. I asked him, if it should turn out to be true, if he would arrange for Papa and me to be on the list. He wasn't sure what Krusche would say, but remembering well the Kommandant's threat, he promised to try. In a few days it became official. On Saturday one hundred men were to leave Steineck. I just wanted to leave, wherever we went.

Stasia disagreed. "Bronek," she warned me, "as long as you stay here, I will help you."

Witczak, Basiak, and Kmiec were probably the reasons why Krusche had not strung me up on the gallows. The thought of leaving Zosia weighed heavily against my decision as well. I knew that if I were to leave Steineck I would lose her. When we met again, Zosia wore a flowered kerchief tied loosely around her neck. It flapped in the early spring breeze. Her eyes were the smoky color of a wintry sky. We sat on a moss-covered rock. I looked at her and was heartbroken at the thought of leaving her. She meant so much to me. And now it all might come to an end, and I would never see her again.

When she heard of our plans, she turned sad. "Where will you be? How will I find you?" she asked. We talked a long while, assuring ourselves we would be together after this was all over. We hugged and kissed until we had to leave. Then she held my hand as we walked together for the last time.

"Remember, Zosia, if you don't see me on Monday, we were able to leave Steineck. I will never forget you," I said. "I will always love you, Zosia."

"Send me a note to let me know where you are," she pleaded. I promised I would. I left and walked sadly up the hill to the office, knowing that, if we left, part of me would always belong to her.

At day's end I thanked Stasia, Witczak, and the other kind people in the office. "I might be back on Monday," I remarked casually. "But I will always be grateful to you."

We had little to take with us. I went to the first aid room, packed my dental instruments back into my box, said good-bye to Goldstein, and returned to Papa. All night long I lay awake. I feared what Krusche might do if he saw me leaving. Yet I knew that I had to take this chance. I feared that Krusche had not yet given in to Witczak. My future in Steineck was unpredictable.

On Saturday we were awakened a half hour earlier than usual. Chaim told me that Papa's name and mine were on the list. Since it was still dark, there was a good chance that Krusche would not detect me, I thought. As we came to the yard, Krusche, his dog, his whip, and his helpers were there. Papa and I went to the back of the line. I froze at each of Krusche's stares in our direction. I feared that if he spotted me he would make me stay. Then what would happen to Papa? Could he survive without me? When I looked at the inmates in our line, I noticed that nearly all were Mussulmen. Chaim, no doubt, was instructed by Krusche to get rid of them, the least productive. We wondered whether we really were going to another camp. Yet I waited anxiously for the order to march. Finally Chaim shouted, asking for one more roll count. He did this often because he knew it appealed to the Kommandant.

Finally we heard "Forward march!" We were out of Krusche's domain.

| 9 |

GUTENBRUNN

My heart beat heavily when we passed Krusche at the gate. I had hoped never to see him again, and my wish was being granted. Yet I equally regretted leaving the people from Dobra, among whom we had lived all our lives. I knew that that chapter of my life was closed forever.

As the morning slowly brightened, I could see David Kot, Reb Moishe, Hershel Sztein, Josef Glicensztein, and a few others waiting to leave. Two of the SS men and some of the guards I knew, including Tadek, were at our side. Tadek told me we were going to Gutenbrunn, a camp like Steineck, but larger. This was a relief. "I will stay there with you," Tadek added. Tadek was a decent guard, and since I had kept my word, he trusted me. "Gutenbrunn is twenty-five kilometers away, and part of the same railway project," he said. This good news spread quickly.

It was finally day. The crowing of a rooster and the barking of a dog were the only sounds on the road as we passed a lonely farm. In front of us I saw Rachmiel, the cook, and Leibel, a jovial man who had often hauled grain for us in Dobra. I pictured the pasture near Leibel's house. Back when I was five years old, he would grab me in fun, and to be sure I wouldn't escape, he took my clothes away. Though I knew it was a joke, I did not like to be teased. I would beg him to give me back my clothes, and eventually he would let me go.

We reached a paved road, and walking became easier. We passed many Black Madonna statues. The sun appeared, and we knew we were going north. After we passed a sandy flat and a bare bluff, we saw a group of brick buildings. One was a small grocery. A few hungry chickens followed a farmer who was raking away the remnants of winter. Women holding half-naked youngsters appeared, silently staring at us. The villages in this region were all similar, indistinct places, nameless blurs along the road. But one farmer greeted us with "Heil Hitler!"

"Heil Hitler!" the SS men and some of the guards returned the salute. "Heil Hitler!" a passing bicyclist chimed in. All these "Heil Hitlers" had a bitter ring in our ears.

Outside the village were windmills. Further on we came to a dam, and beyond it were several barracks that housed Polish women. The barracks were unfenced. These people did not live as pariahs.

A few kilometers beyond, the SS men led us off the road for a rest. Later, at the next fork in the road, we turned right. Just ahead were some heavy cement buildings with a fortlike tower in the center. Coming closer, we saw four huge buildings set in a square, with a gate and tower in front, typical of the traditional German Junkers' and Polish counts' farm estates. These people ruled the farming industry in Poland, and the peasants held them in reverence.

We stopped at the entrance facing two armed sentries. Unlike the flimsy wire gate in Steineck, this one was of solid oak and joined two twenty-meter-long concrete buildings. Each building contained several small windows with iron bars strung across them. A rusty sign above the gate read "Gutenbrunn."

The SS men led us inside. Surrounded by the four massive buildings, the yard was dark. We had come to a farm. These buildings were once stables. At the far end of the yard I saw a gallows. It looked much like the one I had been lucky enough to escape. Here we seemed to be cut off from the rest of the world. In the center of the yard were two SS men surrounded by camp police. They were obviously expecting us.

One man dwarfed them all. He was very tall and had stern, catlike eyes. He looked at us with disgust. "What have we got here?" he asked. "A bunch of Mussulmen?" Because he wore civilian clothes without an inmate's patch, we did not know who or what he was. We were convinced he was a German. He was over two meters tall, had a square jaw, rosy cheeks, and large protruding lips. He wore black riding britches that were tucked into an officer's shiny boots. He wore a brown shirt and a beige sweater, and a woolen scarf was wrapped around his neck. His strange-looking hat could have been from the French Foreign Legion. As he strode about, surveying us with contempt, he slapped his billy club against his boots. The loud boom echoed off the concrete buildings. As he called for the camp police, he kept taunting us as a disorganized bunch. Intimidated by the cruel giant, we stared at him and then at one another. He was a real mystery to us. "This is Gutenbrunn, you lazy Ost-Juden." This was his name for Jews who were born east of Germany. "You mother-fucking bastards. You will have to earn your keep here."

The SS men just stood by. They didn't need to intimidate us, since this giant was doing their job for them. Then our new boss divided us into three groups and ordered his policemen to lead us into three different blocks. As we left, he handed out a slap here and a curse there. When he saw the box I carried, he slapped it with his club and asked me what I had inside.

I looked at his glowering face. "Those are my dental tools."

"What!" he said, as if he didn't understand what I had said. "Dental tools?" he repeated. "Who allowed you to bring them here?"

"I brought them here because they were helpful in Steineck," I countered. He looked at me sharply but said nothing further. A young policeman, Menashe, took charge of my group. At a safe distance, I asked him who the man was.

"He is an inmate from Hamburg, the Lagerältester here," he said. Then, realizing he had omitted the most pertinent point, he added, "He's a Jew like all of us."

This was mystifying. I had never heard the term *Lagerältester,* and I had certainly never heard of a Jew who was so powerful in a labor camp. It was hard to understand how he could have gotten all this authority. And even more important, how could he treat his fellow Jews in such a cold and callous manner? "What's his name?" I asked.

"Kurt Goldberg," Menashe answered.

Each camp building seemed thirty meters long and about twelve meters wide. Inside each were eight rows of four-tier bunks, capable of housing eight hundred inmates. On the thick cement walls were rings that once held cattle in place as they were milked. Our new home was a stable, now housing human beasts of burden. The floors were hard clay, the kind that kept the cold inside. "Even on warm days," we were told, "the temperature never goes above thirteen degrees Celsius."

What light entered the room came through windows of iron bars, augmented by an occasional light bulb that hung listlessly from the high ceiling. There was just enough light so that we could see the bunks. This time Papa and I were determined to find bunks higher up from the floor. Someone helped us to find two spaces at the very top. The inmates were already back from work. Most were from Lodz, now called Litzmannstadt by the Germans. There were Jews from Germany, Holland, and Austria here. While most of us from Steineck were craftsmen and merchants from small villages, the other inmates here were more worldly. I met intellectuals, authors, and lawyers. But like the world outside, there were also a number of common thugs. It was a multilingual camp, and if one of us spoke in Yiddish, we could expect a reply in a dialect of German.

Kurt Goldberg was twenty-four. He was the product of a mixed marriage and felt more German than Jewish. In 1933 he had joined the Hitler Youth, but later the Nürnberg laws reclassified him as a Jew, and he was expelled from the "Aryan" organization. Nevertheless, he was convinced that he deserved better, and he took out the anger and frustration of his misfortune by intimidating his fellow Jews. His boldness and his command of the German language made him a perfect tool for the malevolent Nazi system. He once admitted that if his mother had lied and claimed he was fathered by an Aryan, he would be free of this Jewish stigma. His special contempt, however, was reserved for Polish Jews. He claimed that the "Ost-Juden" were responsible for his dilemma. Among the many diabolical characters anointed in that era, he will always remain the most enigmatic to me. Ultimately he fell from Nazi favor and died.

Gutenbrunn had begun to operate as a camp four months before we arrived. In quick succession other camps had cropped up all around Poznan: Eichenwalde, Lenzingen, Antoninek, Fort Radziwill. By the time we got to Gutenbrunn, eighteen hundred inmates, all Jews, were already inside the walls. The guards were Poles, just as they were at Steineck. Our food rations were identical: a "pica" of bread, morning and night, and soup twice a day. Yet Gutenbrunn was in many ways different. It had better facilities, including showers and an infirmary. The camp doctor was Seidel, an Austrian. He supervised a hospital with twelve beds. The bunks were roomier, with fresh straw on each with a pillow and pallet. But not even this brought an end to the bugs, although taking periodic showers and delousing our clothes brought some relief.

While on the surface it would seem that life was better here, it wasn't. In our block, a boy barely twelve years old drew my attention. He was the youngest person I had seen so far in camp. His name was Mendel, but everyone called him by the diminutive, Mendele. He had been arrested in Lodz for smuggling food into the ghetto. He had claimed to be sixteen and was believed. This landed him in Gutenbrunn. With a round face and bright smiling eyes, he was pleasant to look at. He had a typical Lodz Yiddish accent and was a compulsive talker. He knew how to stay alive in Gutenbrunn by doing whatever was required to survive. Neither a hard worker nor lazy, Mendele was camp smart. Even though he was a malingerer and a goldbricker, the foremen generally liked him. He knew how to make them believe he worked hard, by wiping his forehead when they watched him. He stopped his work as soon as they walked away. Gifted with the knowledge of how to con everyone, he knew how to organize and outsmart inmates twice his age. While others got punished for an offense, Mendele, who committed the same offense, got away with only a warning. He was no stranger to anyone he thought he could profit from. The ghetto life had equipped him with a strong survival instinct. He was a product of the new order. Yet one could not help but like him.

We could not see outside the camp grounds, for Gutenbrunn's four tall buildings and enclosing walls blocked out the world. Sometimes it seemed as if this was all that was left of the universe.

We had been in the block less than an hour when we were called to the *Appellplatz* (mustering ground) again. The SS men were gone, leaving us to Goldberg and his policemen. Goldberg barked out orders in a cruel tone as he continued to demean us with insults. The police obediently assisted him with their own abuse. We were told that on Monday all of us were going to work in the Herdecke Kommando, a newly formed group. Even though we knew that everyone's usual work was constructing railroad tracks, we didn't have the foggiest idea what the Herdecke Kommando was. Our experience with rail construction nonetheless must be valuable to Gutenbrunn, we thought. Unlike the prisoners already here, the one hundred from Steineck had by now worked nearly a year on this railroad. Perhaps that was the reason we were brought here.

The monotony of the food continued. Our meals consisted of a square of margarine and a spoonful of marmalade, and at noon and in the evening we also got a ladleful of turnip soup. The staple crop here was turnips. Getting food here took us twice the time it did in Steineck. They needed kitchen help badly. As in Steineck, the policemen here were not short of food, German cigarettes, or alcohol. When we returned to our bunks, I learned that Goldberg had been asking where the dentist was. Soon I could hear him yelling from the far end of the building. When he saw me, he came over and asked me which bunk was mine. I didn't know what to say. But this time he acted more rational, and his voice was much calmer. Soon I learned why. He was to take the bunk next to mine. I was surprised that a powerful man like him didn't have a better place to sleep. I was perplexed and puzzled at why he picked a bunk next to mine. Was he targeting me for mischief? Though there was no homosexuality in Steineck that I knew of, this was Gutenbrunn, a different camp. Now that I knew Goldberg was a prisoner, I decided to disregard his authority and treat him like anyone else. I knew the situation required me to be careful, though. I could not object to his bringing his personal things and leaving them on the bunk next to mine. He came late that evening, long after curfew. Neither my father nor I were yet asleep. He noticed our uneasiness, then uttered a few words to me, turned, and fell asleep. Though I was never at ease with him next to me, I didn't fear him any longer. A couple of weeks later he decided to move to another bunk. In time we developed a smoother relationship, and he even went out of his way to help me.

Monday at six in the morning policemen came into the block and began hitting the bunks with their billy clubs and shouting, "Aufstehen!" The usual rush began. Standing in the food line, I began the silent debate. Shall I eat my pica all at once or save part for later? In the confusion of the first morning, a young inmate's bowl of soup spilled to the ground. Tears ran down his cheeks, for he knew he would go hungry that day.

"Eintreten! Step in line!" the policemen yelled, herding us into rows of five. Soon we learned how the Herdecke Kommando got its name. Herdecke was then the engineer in charge of building this section of the railroad. He was German, like all the foremen here. My father and I were assigned to haul split stones in wheelbarrows up to the rail beds. Pushing them on the sandy soil was hard enough, but doing it uphill was definitely beyond my father's strength. Yet he couldn't let on, for that would brand him a work shirker, and that was a dangerous image to have in camp. In a few days our arms and shoulders had become so sore that we could hardly lift them. Fortunately, Herdecke noticed it on one of his inspections, and Papa was moved to raking, where he could take short breaks. We were able to return to the camp at noon for soup. Since we no longer had Zosia's food packages or Stasia's scraps, we relied solely on what we got in camp.

Although I was unable to contact Zosia, one day she came. I was told that she was at the kitchen gate asking for me. This gate was open all day for the trucks that delivered food. I wondered how she had found me. "I heard where you were from the people in Brodzice. I had no trouble finding the camp," she said. By now nearly all the inmates knew that I had a relationship with a shiksa. The attention we got made us both uncomfortable. When the sentries at the gate were gone, we casually walked outside. I discovered that we could have a certain amount of privacy here. I embraced her, and we kissed. I was delighted to see her again.

First she was concerned about the quantity of medication I still had. Then we talked a while about Gutenbrunn and our work. As usual, she had brought some food for us. After we said good-bye I watched as she disappeared into the distance. I wondered if we would ever have the freedom we had at Steineck. I returned with Zosia's package, and for the first time Papa and I had real bread in Gutenbrunn. My father must have known about Zosia, although he had never met her and I never spoke with him about her.

The inmates in Gutenbrunn did not have any dental care. Since Goldberg knew about my instruments and my dental work in Steineck, I decided to ask him if I could help when needed here. He listened, and then he sent me to speak with Dr. Seidel, whom I had not yet met. I went after work. The first aid room was full of inmates suffering from a variety of ailments. A large number of them had swollen legs, with huge ankles, and I wondered why. Dr. Seidel said it was edema. He told me that to still hunger, some inmates drank more water than their systems could handle, and the excess settled in their legs. "The slightest scratch or abrasion will not heal. The wound becomes infected, and that has disastrous consequences for them," he said. "The cure is rest and proper nourishment." Those luxuries were not available to us. Some of the sick begged the doctor for a day or two off, hoping to recuperate, but he could not grant their wishes.

Dr. Seidel was in his early forties, small of stature with narrow shoulders and a slightly sunken chest. He was a quiet, well-mannered man. He spoke with a squeaky voice. When he looked at me, his eyes seemed to pierce right through me. He was direct and quite sure of what he said. He seemed constantly to chew on something. His standard advice was "Let those wounds dry, and they'll heal by themselves." At first I thought his remedies were the result of having few medical supplies. Later I learned he actually believed this to be good therapy, and it was often so.

Because a lot of inmates were waiting, I wanted to leave and return another time. But when he heard that Kurt Goldberg had sent me to see him, he waved me into the next room. I explained who I was and why I had come. He listened carefully. I told him that I could come after work and help if a dentist was needed. He promptly agreed. "You could keep your things in one of these two hatches," he said, pointing at them.

I had few tools or medications: three extraction forceps, a couple of scalpels, some explorers and excavators, a chisel, two scalers, a dozen pulp-canal reamers. Some of my drills were useless without a drilling machine. I left them all in the infirmary. The inmates most frequently complained about painful and bleeding gums. Without proper equipment for sterilization, I had to disinfect my instruments over an alcohol flame.

At the next roll call Goldberg announced that a dentist would be available for the inmates in the infirmary every day after work and on weekends. By now I had experience extracting teeth. Gutenbrunn held nearly double the inmates that Steineck had had, and some days I extracted as many as half a dozen teeth. Once when Goldberg came into the first aid room with the Kommandant, he proudly pointed at me, as if I had been his discovery, and said, "Herr Lagerführer, we now have a dentist. He is one of those who came from Steineck. He has instruments. He comes here after his regular work on the Baustelle." That idea appealed to the Nazi.

On Sunday afternoon, when it was quiet in the stable, I heard Reb Moishe pounding his chest in prayer. "He is perfect and dealeth truly with the pure in heart. And all believe that his work is perfect." In the pits of existence, he still believed deeply in the Divine. I could hear the church bells ringing outside. Birds flew in formation in and out of our "fortress" with ease. I wished that I could share their freedom.

Like clockwork, as soon as the kitchen window opened, inmates formed lines stretching hundreds of meters into the yard. Rachmiel, wearing a chef's hat with an apron draping over his bulging belly, looked on as we stood there craving his foul-tasting soup, which in a normal world would have been scorned by dogs. But to us a bite of bread and a spoonful of soup had immeasurable value. To understand what hunger can do to the mind, one has to go hungry for a long time. Hunger gnaws at the insides like a worm. The desire to eat something is so great that one is ready to do anything. Rumors that inmates ate grass to stay alive in Gutenbrunn are true. Retaining a vestige of pride in the face of such hunger was very difficult. This was especially true for my friend, David Kot, who had been pampered with cookies and milk at home. Once a rugged fellow, he was losing strength and looked thinner every day.

The latest letter from home was most disturbing. We could no longer deceive ourselves but had to expect the worst. "Except for a few older men and some still protected by the Judenrat, most have been deported from the ghetto.

The outlook for our survival here much longer is bleak. We know that our lives will soon end," Pola wrote. She corroborated the news from recently arrived inmates: "All the ghettos in Warthegau will soon be empty... while the people are told that they're being resettled, they are killed in the newest, most barbaric way, by the exhaust of the very vehicle they're transported in."

One morning as we were about to leave for work, Herdecke came to the camp and asked Goldberg for additional workers. At the same time he asked for someone who could do office work. Goldberg must have remembered that I had said that I worked in an office in Steineck, because he ordered me to report to Herdecke. My string of good luck was continuing.

Not every German at the camps was an unscrupulous, virulent anti-Semite. Although Herdecke was a member of the Nazi party, he did not totally believe in their racial policies. While I worked for him, on more than one occasion I heard him voicing displeasure with Hitler's senseless war. He never mistreated any of us, and he ordered the Germans under him to do likewise. That was a quality that wasn't often found among Nazis in camp.

Herdecke's field office, where he put me to work, was a tiny hut with barely enough room for a drafting table, desk, chair, and file cabinet. When he was there the hut was crowded, but that only happened when he came to brew coffee for himself with an electric immersion heater that he called a *Tauchsieder*. My work consisted mostly of making hand reproductions of technical blueprints and collecting construction data from the foremen.

One day as I stirred my soup in camp, fishing hopelessly for bits of potato, a sudden turmoil erupted. I saw an inmate being dragged by a guard. He was yelling and begging to be let go. Apparently the inmate had been helping to unload a truck and was caught stuffing potatoes in his pockets. This "crime" had been punished before with a heavy beating by our policemen, but this time a sentry hauled the inmate to the guardhouse and did not release him. We did not see him for the rest of the day. Though I no longer recall his name, I did know him. Given the opportunity, many of us would have done as he did, so we were anxious to learn what his fate would be.

Two days later, when we returned from work, we were marched to the gallows. Our hearts were heavy. We knew something was wrong. Could it be that they were going to hang a man for stealing a few potatoes? Soon our fears were confirmed. Surrounded by three black-uniformed Gestapo men, the inmate was marched with his hands tied behind his back to the gallows, where a sign was placed on his chest heralding his crime. His jacket hung loosely, as if he had shrunk in those two days. He was pale, his eyes bulging. "What have they done to him?" we whispered. Then one of the Gestapo ordered him to stand on a chair below a dangling noose. Next they tied up his legs and slung the noose over his neck. The Gestapo man read his sentence aloud: "For the act of sabotage, Reichsführer Himmler sentences you to death by hanging on the gallows." A green-uniformed Waffen SS man jerked the chair from under the inmate's feet. His body dropped, and his feet swung back and forth. Then his neck snapped, pitching his head to one side. We looked at each other with astonishment. This was a new low for us. Outrage welled up in my throat. I thought the fate of all of us was hanging on those ropes. I felt like yelling "Murderers!" The ground seemed to shake under my feet. It was as if I were a witness to a medieval horror. There was a strange silence. Then Dr. Seidel examined the inmate and pronounced him dead. Two first aid people removed his body and laid it at the side of the building.

I saw firsthand the hanged man. On his neck were deep rope burns. An enlarged blue tongue hung out of his mouth. Urine and feces fouled his dead body. I asked God if he was ever hungry. Later, as we stood in line for our evening ration, I had a fleeting thought: How can we go on as if nothing has happened?

Penalties for petty crimes stiffened. Almost anything that wasn't explicitly allowed became a crime. Sometimes simple allegations of a planned escape were sufficient to cause a hanging. The victim was often blamed for being caught. We now risked execution at every turn, but prisoners continued taking risks, for the alternative was starvation. In time we witnessed more such horrors, and Thursday became a regular execution day in Gutenbrunn. When more than eight hangings were scheduled for a day, there was a double shift at the gallows. On one day eleven prisoners, not all from Gutenbrunn, were executed. After they were declared dead, we removed them. On one occasion, as if by a miracle, suddenly one man began breathing. For a moment I thought they would let him live. But when one of the Gestapo noticed his chest moving up and down, he walked over and shot him point-blank in the head. This was hard to shake off. Someone protested, muttering, "The Geneva Convention forbids double punishment." But who could stop them?

Another ugly incident would puzzle me for many years to come. On one Sunday afternoon, as I walked in the yard, two Gestapo came through the kitchen door into the camp and ordered a policeman to drive a hook into a door frame. Then, in extraordinary secrecy, they executed a pretty young girl who had come with them in their car. Afterward, they put her body into the trunk and left. Since on Sundays the Kommandant and many guards did not come to the camp, few people ever knew what had happened.

The price paid in human life in Gutenbrunn wasn't only on the gallows. Here, as in Steineck, more inmates died from malnutrition and from exhaustion. Those who lay in the infirmary talked to one another. They could no longer contain their misery. "We gave in to slavery, and we labor for them to see an end to this, but if it goes on much longer, none of us will survive," one said. "Why did we allow them to bring us here?"

"What was our alternative? If we hadn't come in peace, they would have taken us with violence, and we still would have ended up where we are," said another.

"Why does the world remain so indifferent to this? Don't they know what is happening?" the first said.

"They probably don't," said the other.

"They must know," the first insisted. "They just don't care."

"Red Cross people know what is going on." I was called away and heard only fragments of their continuing discussion. They said they feared that because the Germans rendered us worthless parasites, the rest of the world didn't see us any differently. They spoke as if a sense of abandonment had taken hold of them, as if they thought that the world had given up on us.

Among the newest group of Jews to arrive was a journalist from Leipzig named Richard Grimm. I met him on the tracks. He told me that he deplored the Goldberg reception. He was a clever, courageous, and physically imposing man with broad shoulders. Like Goldberg, he spoke fluent German. Unfamiliar with camp strategy, he was cautious. He worked hard, probing and asking questions. After he learned the camp rules, he went on the offensive against Goldberg. With a recent change in Kommandants, Grimm saw an opportunity to undermine Goldberg's authority. That gave Goldberg much to worry about.

The clever and courageous Leipziger journalist quickly attracted the new Kommandant's attention. More mature than Goldberg, with superior intelligence, Grimm was appointed to a newly created position as camp administrator. No one knew exactly what his responsibilities were, but his post made him an insider. Since it brought him into constant contact with the SS

Kommandant, he developed a power base and often challenged Goldberg's authority. There was bickering and posturing as the two vied for the favor of the SS. Goldberg complained about Grimm, and Grimm openly criticized Goldberg. It became clear that only one of them could be the top Jewish inmate in the camp. The Kommandant preferred Grimm's bright, decisive approach to Goldberg's impetuous brashness, and Grimm became the camp's Lagerältester. Richard Grimm was now the main player, and although Kurt Goldberg still hung on as head of the police, at long last his rule was over.

In October 1942 the weather turned foul. The clothes we had worn all these long months turned to rags, and our shoes had long ago fallen apart. Some tied string around the fragments of their shoes. How much we wanted to delay winter's coming! At work the prisoners did everything to stay warm; they flung their arms about and stamped their feet to warm their freezing limbs. Some even traded their soup for newspapers or empty cement bags to tie around their bodies. Herdecke now spent more time in the hut keeping warm and drinking coffee. I noticed loads of wood scraps lying around, and a plan developed. I knew that for Herdecke to agree, my argument would have to be based on an increase in productivity. Each time I was ready to bring up my proposal, he left.

One day I stopped him before he could leave the hut. "Mr. Herdecke, our people are losing much of their strength just keeping warm. I think if we give them a chance to warm up at intervals, they will be more productive. I wonder if you could allow them a break at midmorning. We have enough wood scraps to keep a fire going, and we could even brew coffee, as we did in Steineck."

He raised his eyes from his blueprints and looked at me with a distant gaze. A few moments passed, and when I thought he would say no, he agreed. I could see that I had stirred his humanity. "Yes," he said, "but where do you want to build the fire?" I told him about Stasia's field kitchen, and he agreed to the idea and offered to bring us some ersatz coffee. A few days later I called on my father to gather wood, start a fire, and brew the coffee. It could not have come at a better time, for Papa was beginning to take on the look of a Mussulman. He set up a kiln of bricks, and within a couple of days the half hour coffee break was a reality. This simple work break may have saved many lives that winter. Thereafter, everyone called Papa the Coffee Man.

It was refreshing to encounter a decent Nazi like Herdecke.

Good will is mighty contagious. He set an example for his foremen, and they too became more reasonable. Herdecke was condemning his Führer in front of me more often now. He told me he had joined the party to hold on to his engineering career. But he felt that the Führer was leading his people to disaster. Regardless of what he thought, I couldn't afford to discuss that subject.

My father also began to bake potatoes for inmates who managed to steal them. In return, he could keep a share for himself. Relieved from hard work and with a bit more sustenance, Papa slowly regained his rosy cheeks. Thanks to Grimm's influence on the Kommandant, our medical barracks was enlarged, allowing us to keep more of the sick inmates in bed. Papa and I also moved into a new barracks, which was built to house new arrivals. I stopped working for Herdecke so that I could remain in the infirmary full time.

It was a long trip on foot for Zosia to visit me, yet she came at least once a month to bring some food, supply me with medication, and deliver letters from Pola and Mama. One Saturday she handed me two of their letters. I thought this was very unusual, since the letters were postmarked only two days apart. When I returned to the barracks, Papa opened one, and I the other. The first letter told of the ongoing deportations. The second, however, was even more disturbing. My brother, Josek, had been arrested and deported, and Mama and Pola didn't know his whereabouts. Even his exemption, issued to him by a captain in the German army, wasn't of any merit. It was a severe blow to Mother. "No matter what," wrote Pola, "I am not leaving Mama." Papa looked at me, and with a deep sigh he intoned, "God asks us not to question his will." His voice began to quiver with enormous pain. We both knew that Pola and Mama were now in true danger. In my mind I was at home with them. I went to the infirmary, my heart in a vise.

Before long Goldberg lost all of his authority and had to resign himself to Grimm's rule. His once unrestrained, cocky demeanor disappeared as he sank into isolation. Grimm was unscrupulously fair. One of the benefits of his rule was that he called for mandatory bed rest on Sunday afternoons between the hours of two and four. In moments of hope, quite foreign to this place, the remembrance of passionate lyrics to an old Jewish melody prompted the inmates to compose "The Song of Gutenbrunn," following the form of a then-popular Yiddish song, "Americzke Ganiv," about the underworld in America. The refrain of the slow, morose melody was repeated:

> Gutenbrunn, here from morning 'til night we toil
> For a reward of stale bread and turnip soup.
> As Jews we have no right to complain.
> And if we do, who will listen?

After each refrain, inmates would spontaneously add their own lyrics, such as:

> Work, work, work, 'til freedom comes.
> Then life will be good again.
> But as for now we don't complain.
> And if we do, who will listen?

Yet another inmate broke in and sang:

> What is the use, what will they do?
> The fate is ours to bear.
> Don't grieve, don't be bitter.
> And if we do, who will listen?

These and similar verses could be heard each Sunday afternoon.

For a while it seemed that the war had come to a standstill, as if all of the territories the Nazis had won would forever remain theirs. But one day some welcome news arrived. We learned that the United States had declared war on the Axis in December. It was now January 1943, and Tadek told me of the newly formed Jewish labor camps nearby.

Though it was still winter, we were graced with rather pleasant weather one Saturday when Zosia came. This visit was especially welcome, as I hadn't seen her in many weeks. Under her coat she wore a simple but attractive polka dot dress. In the absence of the sentries at the little gate, I went out, and we walked down the road. By now the guards knew me as the dentist, and at worst they'd only call out to me and ask me to return. We kept on the road until we came to a small forest, which we entered.

We strolled through the forest a while, and then we stopped. I looked into her sparkling eyes, took her in my arms, and kissed her. She put her arms around me and gave in to my advances. As we kissed, she rested her head on my shoulder, and our passions rose. We couldn't resist our desires. I lowered her onto the snow, and we made love for the first time in Gutenbrunn. Suddenly we heard voices coming toward us. I sensed trouble. I looked around and didn't know where to hide. As we saw four men coming directly toward us, we tried to act casual. They stopped in front of us. One, the youngest, who was about my age, looked at me with a hostile expression, which told me that we were in for more trouble than I had first thought.

"What are you doing here?" he bristled.

Zosia broke in and answered, "He is my friend, and I came to visit him."

Paying no attention to Zosia's words, he turned back to me and barked, "We know that you're a fucking Jew from the camp. We watched you two go into the woods. And you," he said, pointing to Zosia, "you should be ashamed of yourself, mixing with Jews. A Polish girl whoring with a Jew is disgraceful."

We were at their mercy. He grabbed me by my shirt and punched me in the face several times. He then shoved me into the hands of one of his comrades, who slapped me and threw me back to him. I was thrown to the ground and kicked as I tried to get up. Zosia was crying and pleading, "Why are you doing this? Why are you hurting him? He hasn't done a thing to you." She begged in vain, as the other two bullies grabbed her and dragged her away from me.

Each time I tried to get up, they kicked me as if I were a soccer ball. I thought they would never stop. "Why are you beating me?" I pleaded. Throughout my ordeal, I kept thinking of the consequences of being taken to the guardhouse. I thought I was finished.

Their rage and anger eventually subsided. They had had enough, and they left. My nightmare was over, and I was fortunate that they had not taken me to the guardhouse, where anything could have been done to me. My head spun, and my face burned. My clothes were bloody, the insides of my cheeks were cut, and some of my teeth felt loose. I tried to move my jaw. Though it hurt a lot, it wasn't fractured. Zosia was aghast, seeing the cuts on my face. Though my body hurt from the pounding it had received, the deepest pain came from within, as stomach cramps doubled me over, repeating the agony I had felt after Krusche's beating in Steineck. Zosia knew how ashamed I felt.

"They're just a bunch of hoodlums. They don't know what they're doing," she consoled me. Zosia helped me to clean off my clothes. I wanted to get back to the camp as quickly as possible. She left me my medication and a bundle she had brought with her. Draped in shame and anger, I kissed her good-bye.

At the edge of the woods I carefully scanned the road to the camp. Seeing it was safe, I walked the short distance back to the kitchen gate. Once I was in the yard, I could easily mingle with the other inmates. It was now half past two. The soup ration had long ago been distributed, but the perpetual optimists still monitored the kitchen window in case some seconds might be given out. I left the bread and medicine package under Papa's blanket. I went to wash my face and rinse my mouth. I hoped that in time some of my wobbling teeth would tighten.

This winter didn't turn out to be as bitterly cold as the previous one, but our clothes, now in tatters, were no match for it. The attrition rate among those handling the icy rails was considerable. Though I no longer worked for Herdecke, our detachment still had the half hour breaks, and my father was still in charge of brewing the coffee.

One day at the beginning of April, Mendele followed me as I crossed the yard. "Did you hear what is going on in Warsaw?" he asked. Mendele often told strange stories, some barely half true. But what he said sounded so terrible that I decided to listen. "The Germans are transporting men, women, and children from the ghetto to a camp called Treblinka, and there's where they're killing them," he said.

"Mendele, you are spinning some tale again," I said.

In a wild rage he repeated the story. "I swear to God, it's the truth," he countered. This sounded serious, so I asked him who told him in the first place. "A Pole from the underground," he said. This was the first such mass extermination that we had heard of. Much later I learned that nearly three hundred thousand people were killed there. By inspiring a mixture of terror and reverence, the Nazis shaped us into well-disciplined slaves willing to work for them just to continue living. But when they couldn't kill us fast enough with forced labor, they came up with ideas like Chełmno and Treblinka.

As the workers completed one section of rail, they were moved further away from the camp. This added three to five kilometers of walking per day to their toil. Because of more frequent casualties, Dr. Seidel wanted us to patrol the sites at least an hour each day for sick and injured. I was the first volunteer. With bandages, cotton, and a bottle of iodine, I went each morning to the work site.

On a Sunday in late April, when Zosia came, she had a letter from the ghetto. My premonition was right. The news was grave. Reading just the first sentence, I froze. My mother and sister had been murdered.

10

THE MURDER OF MY FAMILY

When I finished reading the letter I closed my eyes and stood paralyzed. Zosia sensed that something terrible had happened in the ghetto. She asked me what it was. I could not answer her. When she asked me if it was my mother and sister, I nodded my head. She looked at me and saw that I was in no condition to talk. She left me quietly.

I felt ill with stomach cramps. Walking back to the camp I read the letter again, hoping that it wasn't so. But over and over the words spelled out worse than we had expected:

> When you receive this letter, Mama and I will no longer be alive. Though we were told that we are going to be resettled, we know where they are taking us—Chełmno—and no one has ever come back from there. We are the last in the ghetto, only two hundred of us left. It really doesn't matter anymore. We have had enough of this shameful life. Should you ever see Josek, let him know about us. Don't write anymore, as we will no longer be here. We hope that you, Papa, and Josek still have a chance to survive. Love to Papa and you, Berek. Pola.

Mama added two lines of good-bye to Papa and me. "Perhaps we'll all meet in another world," she wrote.

It was devastating. I couldn't breathe. My legs buckled and refused to carry me. I remembered Mama and Pola on the day of Papa's and my deportation. I remembered Mama's forlorn look and Pola, poised and fighting back her tears. I looked at the letter, and the outrageous crime stared me in the face. Their long suffering was ended. They had endured the ghetto for more than two years for naught. I raised my eyes and looked up, transfixed, to the heavens. I asked God why, but only silver rings swirled in front of my eyes. I had been raised to revere him. Now he had failed me.

I weighed the impact the news would have on my father. Do less painful words exist to change the bitter truth? If so, I could not find them. I stuck the letter in my pocket and walked into the barracks. I knew that Papa had to be told. My father sat at the edge of his bunk. I walked over and, without saying a word, handed him the letter. As he began reading, his face turned pale, and his shoulders slumped. Wrenched with pain, he closed his eyes and put his hands on his face. When I saw him wring his hands, I knew that he was saying Kaddish. He finished and, in a mixture of pain and anguish, said, "If they can kill women and children, perhaps the whole world has gone mad." Though our hearts were full of tears, we had forgotten how to cry.

"Only God knows what is happening, son," Papa said to me. He hadn't called me son in years. We sat a long time in silence, our heads bowed. There was little we could say that would make sense. Then, as if my father could take it no longer, he walked out.

It was a Sunday afternoon, a day of rest for us, no doubt intended for the welfare of the guards and the SS men. I lay open-eyed, motionless, staring endlessly at the high ceiling of the barracks. A few rays of sunlight penetrated the dirt-clogged windows, and particles of dust danced in a never-ending pattern. It didn't seem possible. They could not be dead. I read the letter again and feared that it was irrevocable and final. I pulled out a few old family photographs that I had kept under my pillow. By now they were yellowed and scuffed. I looked at Mama and remembered the last words she said to us when we left: "When this nightmare is over, we will all meet back here." I felt alone. I needed to share my grief with someone. But there was no longer any intimacy. Our lives were so agonizing that each person kept things like this to himself. Everyone focused his strength on his own survival. Nor did I have the right to burden others with my pain. Didn't each of us here have his own tragedy?

Behind our bunk someone finished a silent prayer with a loud "Amen." Then another man next to him began to question his devotion to God. "How can you still believe in prayers? They won't help you," he said.

"You don't have to believe in God. I still do. Just because you're here doesn't mean that you stop believing," said the first. "What is going on is not his fault. It's the failure of men. In the end they'll have to pay for these inhuman acts, for their immorality."

"Inhuman acts, immorality—leave that nonsense out. The Germans don't believe in God and morality. They follow Hitler," the second said.

"God does things his way. You must believe that he is the Righteous Judge. He won't turn his back on his chosen people," said the first.

"Chosen?" the second interrupted. "You mean we are the chosen? Chosen for what?"

"Having been chosen does not mean that we are chosen to be different from other people or better. He chose us to accept him and his teaching without question. He, the Righteous One, is always with us," the first said insistently.

"You may be convinced of this, but I'm not. If this continues any longer, he will be left without his people to worship him. If there is solace in being one of the chosen, I don't feel it," he added.

I did not deny the existence of God, but I asked myself where the God was that my father taught me to believe in. I stopped relying on him the moment I lay bleeding outside the first aid room in Steineck. There I embarked on a genesis of my own, without God. To come to terms with Jewishness in the pit of this inhumane life was very difficult. I buried my head in my pillow to close myself away from this, and I fell asleep.

I woke up in a sweat from a bad dream and realized that, in effect, my nightmares and my life now were much the same. I took a spoonful of belladonna for my excruciating stomach pains, slipped down to the floor, and left the barracks. I met Papa. We stopped and looked at one another without speaking. Our hurt could not be explained. It was a long and painful day for both of us, and that night the barracks seemed like a silent morgue.

The next night I dreamed I was home. It was Friday evening, the beginning of Shabbat. My father, my brother, and I had just returned from the synagogue. Mama closed her eyes, put her hands over the burning candles, and said a prayer. Papa raised a chalice of wine and said kiddush. Grandfather blessed the challah. Wildflowers that Pola had picked were on the table. Everything seemed so convincing, so real, as if I had never left. The next morning I was back to my bitter reality, and every German I saw seemed to me to be guilty of killing Mama and Pola.

As Nazi Germany put its plan of massive extermination of Jews into action, they chose Poland for the staging area. Perhaps this was not purely an accident. When Tadek told me of new labor camps in the area, it intrigued me. "Where are they? Are they far from here?" I asked.

"Oh no! One is only about twenty kilometers from here. That one is a camp for women," he said. I had not heard of women being forced into labor camps. Hard labor and camp conditions would not allow them to survive very long. Nonetheless, if that was so, perhaps I would find my mother and sister there. This promising thought did not give me rest. I told Grimm that I doubted that their camp would have dental care and said that, if I was allowed, I would go there to help them. Grimm liked my idea and agreed to speak with the Kommandant.

I knew that I would not be allowed to leave the camp without a guard. Since I had not implicated him in the bread debacle in Steineck, I had a good relationship with Tadek. He agreed to go with me. I knew he had a bicycle, since he rode it every day. I asked him if he could find one for me. He thought that he could.

It had been snowing for days, and more than a quarter of a meter was on the ground. When it did not snow, dark clouds covered the sky. The infirmary was filled with the sick and dying. Most prisoners survived by bare will. I hoped to escape this prison, even if for just a few hours.

Though I saw Grimm several times, he made no mention of what we had talked about. I thought he had forgotten, but one day he and the Kommandant came to the infirmary, and the subject arose. "Achtung!" Seidel yelled out when they entered. "Herr Lagerführer, sixty-five sick in bed and seven attendants. All is well." The number of inmates changed so fast in the infirmary that, at best, he could only be guessing. Seidel knew what was important to Scharführer Köhler.

The Kommandant looked like a country farmer, a bit older than the average SS man, with hair that was turning gray. But he was not heinous, and unlike his predecessors he took an interest in his prisoners. Then Grimm turned to him and said, "Herr Lagerführer, the camp for women nearby probably doesn't have a dental station. Our dentist says that he could go help the prisoners. Of course, a guard would be with him at all times."

The Kommandant looked at Grimm, stared at me, and after deliberating said, "Freilich, OK." I bit my lips to contain my exuberance.

"Thank you, Herr Lagerführer," I said as they left. Grimm later returned to tell me that the Kommandant cautioned that my entry into that camp was up to the Kommandant there. Having gotten this far, I was cautiously optimistic.

It was late in April 1943. The sun was out, giving us a deceptive taste of spring. Wherever the sun shone, winter seemed to disappear, for surrounded by the tall buildings we lived a fortresslike existence. When I told Tadek that the Old Man, as he called the Kommandant, had given me permission to go to the camp for women, he said, "Good." He added, "I talked with my brother-in-law. He'll let you use his bike."

Now I was anxious. "Tadek, when can we go?" I asked him. Wednesday was his day off, he said, and he would try to go with me then. Tadek played an important part in my life. Being a guard did not interfere with his basic good nature. In the midst of many evil guards, he was as helpful as the situation would allow. Whereas I knew that the chance of finding my sister and mother was slim, trying to find them meant a lot to me. In my heart I still had hope.

On Wednesday Tadek came to pick me up. When I was little I had watched my brother and sister on their bicycles, and riding just came to me naturally. I was too small then to reach the pedals, so I tilted the bicycle to one side and put one foot underneath the bar. Tadek's arrival with the two bicycles reminded me of those days. As we rode away from the camp, Tadek told me to remove my yellow star. "We'd better be careful," he said.

It was sunny but still quite cold. My heart pounded with excitement. The zest of life ran through me. Leaving the camp, unmarked, gave me an illusion of freedom. I didn't know which camp we would be visiting, and neither did Tadek. Not too far away we passed a village. A few peasants were working, spreading dung on their fields. Tadek asked one for directions to a village I had never heard of. "Just follow the road," the man said. Soon Tadek recognized a landmark and was certain we were going in the right direction. A few minutes later, around a curve, we saw people working on both sides of the road. As we came close, I saw guards and a hundred men grading the embankments. We were close enough to see their yellow Stars of David. Neither of us expected this.

"Just act natural," Tadek said. As we rode past, Tadek greeted the guards with "Heil Hitler!"

"Heil Hitler!" the guards replied. Then most heads raised up with curiosity. Though I wanted to see if I recognized anyone, I could not give myself away. I drove by them, stone-faced, as if I was completely disinterested. But suddenly one of them yelled out, "Look, it's Bronek, Josek's brother!" I feared their guard's reaction and put a hand over my mouth, trying to silence him. By then they all stared at me, while I remained indifferent to what the man had said. As we rode by the long rows of inmates, I kept making the hush sign. Then I thought I saw a ghost. One man's posture and the color of his sweater reminded me of my brother. When he looked back at me, I was sure it was Josek. He stopped digging, rested his arms on his spade, and looked even more shocked than I. It was a miracle, to find my brother so unexpectedly. Tadek knew something had stirred me. I whispered, "Over there, Tadek, in the beige sweater, it's my brother!" We moved off the road and stopped a hundred meters from them. If the guards noticed anything, they didn't speak.

"Tadek," I asked, "would they let me talk to my brother, even if it's just for a minute?"

"Wait," he said. "I'll go over and see."

The whole group was looking at me, wondering how I could ride around without the mark of a Jew. As Tadek walked over to the nearest guard, I followed him with my eyes, waiting anxiously for the answer. It wasn't long until he returned. "Those are inmates from Lenzingen, the camp we are going to. Their barracks are just a few kilometers down the road. He'll let you see your brother for a few minutes. They are afraid that if any of the SS from the camp come by and see it, it may cost them their jobs," he said.

When we got together, Josek and I hugged, two brothers who had never thought to see one another again. Then we sat down on a patch of grass that was free of snow. I saw that Josek hadn't changed, except that he looked thinner. I had so many questions to ask him that I found it hard to begin. I knew I had to share with him what I knew about Mama and Pola. But first I asked him how he got here, and what went on in Dobra before he was arrested.

"It was inevitable," my brother said. "The situation was ominous." Seeing that he was prepared for the worst, I told him about Mama and Pola. "Pola had chances to escape, and as for Mama, I knew it was the end," he said. "Someone had offered Pola an Aryan document, but she refused to leave Mama."

We saw the guards' impatience. When I told Josek that we were going to his camp, he said, "Don't go there. If Krusche sees you, he will kill you."

He amazed me. How could he know Krusche, and my troubles with him? I had never written home about Krusche. Krusche, he said, was their Kommandant, and when he heard that Josek's name was Jakubowicz, he asked him if he was my brother. Hearing that he was, Krusche got angry. "I hope to find your brother and see him dead someday," Krusche said. Conditions at their camp were much like ours. Most of them were working on the same railroad.

Before we parted, Josek asked me if I could come back someday. "From twelve to one we are off," he said. I promised to try to be back there very soon.

I returned to Tadek. He was still scanning the road for any signs of danger. I told him that we couldn't go to the camp and why. He agreed. He wasn't anxious to see Krusche either.

It was past two by now. We had no time left to ride anywhere else, and we returned to Gutenbrunn. I told Tadek what the Old Man had told Grimm. It did not surprise him. He knew that Köhler couldn't speak for another camp's Kommandant. "Even being on the road wasn't risk-free," he said. Anyone who wanted to could cause us trouble.

Papa was returning from work as we entered the camp. I told him I had found Josek, and he could hardly believe it. Later I had to share every detail. When I told the unemotional Seidel that I had found my brother, he mumbled, "That's good."

Grimm, however, shared my joy in my good fortune. "Be careful," he cautioned. "You are on your own out there." In spite of the danger, I looked forward, blissfully, to my next day out. Grimm and I had a good relationship. He confided in me how difficult it was to minimize the harsh Nazi directives often given him and how hard it was to retain his self-respect. Working in the first aid room gave me a purpose. I could do something useful. Despite their misfortunes, some inmates here, eminently wise, affirmed their spiritual respect for life. This mitigated their sense of hopelessness.

The next Wednesday, with a few snowflakes falling, I went to the main gate and sneaked out. The young guard knew me. By now most of the guards knew me.

Then Tadek and I rode off. "It's too early to go to your brother. Let's try the women's camp first. It is only an hour away," Tadek said. With the miracle of finding Josek to boost my spirits, I had hopes of finding Pola and my mother. However remote hope is, sometimes it's stronger than logic. No matter how hard I pedaled the old bike, though, I couldn't keep up with Tadek's faster pace. Having served its usual time, my bike preferred to be in retirement.

We turned onto an unpaved road, where we saw many women working in a field. One kilometer further on was a cluster of barracks. "That," Tadek said, pointing, "is their camp." The barracks were typical single-story buildings all in rows. A fence topped with barbed wire surrounded the camp. We stopped. "Put on your patch," Tadek said. "The Kommandant here might not like seeing a camp inmate not wearing one." He left me holding the bicycles some hundred and fifty meters from the entrance, and he went alone to the gatehouse. The barracks were built of unfinished pine. It all looked like a hastily constructed job. Although I couldn't hear Tadek's conversation with the sentry, I followed their gestures. After a third joined in, I saw Tadek nodding his head. I suspected that they had reached some understanding. "The Lagerführer is not here, but they'll let you go in. However, only a few women are in the camp," Tadek said.

We leaned our bicycles against the guardhouse and entered the camp. The two Polish sentries gave us inquisitive stares and expressed particular interest in my little box. I assured them that it held only my dental tools. They looked at me with strange adulation and let me in. I followed Tadek. An eerie silence hung over the camp. So far I had not seen a single woman. My pulse raced. I didn't know what to expect. One door seemed an entrance to a kitchen. Surely someone must be there. We opened the door and saw two women in their early twenties peeling potatoes. Though I expected girls' faces, I was not prepared for their bizarre look: without hair, they looked more like young boys. Until we explained who we were and why we had come, they too were stunned. Then everything began to unfold. One of them was tall and slim, the other short and plump with a husky voice and a heavy Yiddish accent. The short one was the quicker to reply, very much the spokeswoman. They were dressed in their clothes from home and wore yellow stars. The tall one had a pleasant face, wide-open eyes, and a good figure. She wore a dark skirt and a light-colored flowered blouse. Once these clothes were fashionable, but now they were nearly rags. Had it not been for her bare head, she would have been very attractive. I asked them how long they had been here and where they were from. We found they had arrived only three weeks before. So far they had not buried any inmates. Of course, the term *Mussulman*—or, rather, *Mussulwoman*—meant nothing to them. There was not a doctor, a dentist, or even a first aid facility in their camp.

"I am Malka Rosen," the spokeswoman said in her colorless voice. "I am from Kalisz."

"Is Ruzka your sister?" I hastened to ask.

"Yes," she said. "Do you know Ruzka?"

"Did your father run a soda water business?"

"Yes," she answered.

I remembered Ruzka vividly. "Where is your sister?" I asked.

"She is here. She is now at work." I couldn't believe it! Beautiful Ruzka, here in this labor camp? We had gone to the same school, the Jewish gymnasium. I recalled a custom long forgotten. We used to promenade on the Boulevard in Kalisz for hours in the evening. Ruzka was always the most affable of company. When I calmed my surprise, I asked if anyone from Dobra was there.

"I am Chana Cimerman from Koło, not far from Dobra. I know a few girls from Dobra here," said the tall one.

"Do you know Pola Jakubowicz?"

They looked at each other, and then the spokeswoman said, "There is a Balcia Jakubowicz, from Uniejów." Balcia was my cousin, Uncle Chaim's youngest daughter. She should know more about what happened in the last days in Dobra, I thought. I knew I had to see her. I told Malka that we would be back the next Wednesday. Tadek added, "We will try to be here between ten and twelve."

"Tell my cousin about it," I added.

"I think it would be best if you came Saturday or Sunday," Malka replied. "Then all the girls will be here." I looked at Tadek, who shook his head no.

The door opened, and a broad-shouldered woman wearing a police armband came in, looking very surprised. Malka explained to her who we were. Satisfied that our visit wasn't her business, she left. Tadek reminded me that if we didn't go now, we might not get to see Josek.

It was half past twelve when we saw my brother. He and the others sat on the side of the road, resting against trees towering twelve to fifteen meters high. Tadek got off his bike and approached the same guard who had allowed me to see my brother the week before. By Josek's piercing look, I could see that he had been waiting. Since the guard had already given him permission, he came to me while the other one stared at us. The guard had told him that he could separate from his group but should remain in sight. We walked off on a path leading to some trees, about eight hundred meters away, and stopped there. We had so many things to ask one another. First he wanted to know if Papa was well. He was curious to know where he worked and what he did. Then he asked me how I found Zosia and where I got to see her. I told him in detail the miracle of our meeting. He also wondered where I had gotten the bike. Later I showed him the last letter we received from Mama and Pola and said that we had just been at a camp nearby that the Nazis had opened for Jewish women, and though many were from our area, I found neither Pola nor Mama there. After he had finished reading the letter, he shook his head and said that it had been obvious to him that the end of the ghetto was near. I also told him that I hoped to see our cousin Balcia and thought she might shed more light on the fate of our mother and sister.

I wanted to know about my friends from Dobra. "Sadly," he said, "most are in camps or dead."

When Josek had been drafted into the Polish cavalry and I had seen him dressed in his elegant uniform, I had wished I was him. When he clicked the spurs on his shiny high boots, he seemed to me the bravest man in our village. But I most liked his high-domed hat. Though it was three sizes too large for me, when I tried it on I felt like a grown-up hero. But now our six-year age difference vanished. Before we returned to the work detail, Josek asked me if I could bring Papa along with me to visit. As I left Josek and his fellow inmates, I felt embarrassed that, although we shared the same fate, I was free to go around and visit while all the others were confined to the rigorous life of hard labor.

When the inmates in Gutenbrunn heard about the women's camp, they swamped me with questions, and soon I found myself carrying notes back and forth between the camps.

One Thursday morning six inmates were brought to the camp in a now familiar scene. The SS and Gestapo henchmen had lots of experience, and the hangings seemed almost a joke to them. As the inmates returned from work, they were told to line up around the gallows. Out came the condemned, their wrists tied behind them, their flesh bulging, and their skin a grisly blue. They blinked at the bright daylight. They were led onto chairs, and their legs were tied together. After the Gestapo read their sentence, one of the condemned men raised his voice and yelled, "You will pay for this! Someday the world will take revenge for these crimes, you wretched murderers!"

A Jew's making such a threat stunned them. They probably had never heard anything like it before. "Keep your mouth shut!" a Gestapo man yelled. But the condemned man, having nothing to lose, continued to shout: "Murderers! Murderers!" We looked at one another, startled. We could see how embarrassed the Nazis were, and after a few more unsuccessful attempts to shut the man up, one scar-faced member of the Gestapo gave a signal to the hangman, and the ropes tightened. A demonic silence hung in the air. There were no more speeches, not even the reminder that this was to serve as a lesson. The six men were dead, and the hangman quickly left. Though this incident had been of no help to the condemned, their defiance was a brave act that burned itself deeply into my mind. After Dr. Seidel pronounced the men dead, the infirmary workers had the dreadful job of removing the corpses. As we carried their bodies, the echo of "Damn you, you wretched murderers!" hung in the air. Carrying our brothers' dead bodies was not easy. We didn't believe in martyrdom and looked upon every life lost as a penalty for being Jewish. That evening the turnip soup was difficult to swallow.

The following Wednesday, when Tadek and I again left the camp, I asked him if he knew of any other camps. "Yes," he said. "But they are too far away for us to go to." When we came to the women's camp, their Kommandant was away. We were told that he was only there in the afternoon. My cousin Balcia also wasn't there. One girl that needed my help, though, was glad that she had waited for me. She was in pain. I extracted one of her diseased molars. Her gums bled badly, so I brushed tincture of iodine on them and injected her with an ampoule of two cc's of vitamin C. We again passed my brother's work detail and stopped. This time I had letters from Gutenbrunn for inmates in Josek's camp. Our time quickly passed, as we spent it remembering the past.

Whereas the executioners usually came late in the afternoon, one Thursday an ambulance, followed by Gestapo and SS men, came early. Before the drama began around the gallows, our Kommandant led the visitors on an inspection. They marched through our rows, looking at us and making snide remarks. As they came slowly toward me, I saw that one, a man carrying a briefcase, was of high rank. He was a colonel, an SS Sturmbannführer. When he passed us, I was struck by his Semitic facial features. I turned to my right and unwisely remarked to some other inmates that he looked Jewish. The man following the colonel heard my comment, and he hit me in the face with his gloves, shouting, "Shut your mouth! You swine! Don't you know who this is? He is Sturmbannführer Adolf Eichmann!"

I wished I hadn't said it, but it was too late. Then the slim, tall Colonel Eichmann turned back, paused, looked at me, and grinned. Then, as if in an afterthought, he snapped open a thick oversized briefcase that he carried. "Look," he said. "Do you know what those are?"

That scared me. I saw rope tied neatly in four nooses. I couldn't say "nooses," for fear that the word would not pass through my lips. I didn't know what to do. Finally I said, "Herr Sturmbannführer, those are ropes."

"No, no. Those are zizith," he said gleefully, whereupon the whole entourage burst into laughter.

Though I had heard Eichmann's name mentioned, at that time I knew only that he was a Nazi bigwig. But that he knew what zizith were puzzled me. Soon afterward I heard that he also spoke some Hebrew. From then on, whenever I heard Eichmann's name, I was reminded of this bizarre encounter. In the end eight more Jews lost their lives that day in Gutenbrunn.

Hunger and hard labor were chipping away at our numbers bit by bit. Even the strong were now calling on their last reserves of energy. The monster had been devouring its prey with a ferocious appetite. "Organizing" had become more dangerous. Never a science, it now required connections and keen judgment. The squalor of our living conditions is hard to describe. Some claimed to have seen inmates inflicting wounds on themselves just to stay away from the unendurable work. In the infirmary I saw wounds and cuts on inmates that couldn't possibly have been accidental.

Mendele was our best source of news in those days. When he came one day to tell me what he had heard, he looked broken. "They are liquidating all the ghettos," he said. "They are gassing, burning, or machine gunning all the Jews." It was so startling, so unbelievable, that I had to stop listening to him. But when he swore by God, I believed him. I realized that we could be next. Zosia had visited only rarely, and when she came we hardly moved from the gate.

One Saturday an inmate told me that Zosia was waiting at the kitchen gate. As in times past, with no sentry near, we walked slowly toward our rendezvous place. This was unmistakably the nicest day that spring. Robins, swallows, and sparrows crisscrossed our path, chirping away. Their song was the only sound we heard. Fallen branches and trees toppled by the winter lay on the ground. Where sunshine hadn't reached, the young ferns seemed very pale. After a while we came to a clearing, and the bright sunshine invited us to sit down. We hadn't made love for some time, and sitting close to her I knew what I wanted. As I drew close, I saw that she felt the same, and soon we succumbed.

As we lay on the sun-warmed moss, she said, "We heard about the dreadful things the Germans are doing now to Jewish people. My family thought that you ought to come and stay at our house until the war is over. You'll be safe there." Then she added that the Allies had successfully landed on the Greek island of Crete, and that many Italians had turned to fight the Germans, and that the Russians were chasing the Nazis out of their land. "We have enough room for you and your father in the cellar. You'll both be comfortable there," she said.

She caught me speechless. I was overwhelmed. I realized that her family must have planned this for some time. Surely they must understand the danger to them. "Do you know what it might cost you if we were found staying in your house?" I answered. "You may not know, but harboring Jews is punished by death now."

"We live on a small street, and Germans rarely come there. You will be safe with us," she assured me.

The idea that they were ready to risk their lives for us was remarkable by itself. I thanked her and promised to discuss it with my father. She gave me bread and some more antacids for my ulcer. "Bronek," she said, "the war can't last much longer. Please think seriously about escaping from here."

Then we parted, leaving in different directions. When I came out of the forest, I saw two peasants crossing a field. I waited until they were out of sight, and then I returned to the camp. Rachmiel knew of Zosia, and when I passed him, he grinned. Inmates were waiting for the kitchen window to open so they could quickly grab some soup to still their hunger. Seeing this, I thought of Zosia's prediction. "The war won't last much longer." But for many, I thought, the end might come too late. I was bothered by guilt over my relationship with Zosia, but not because we had sex. It wasn't lust, I had rationalized. I really loved Zosia very much. I was not sure how long I would survive the camp. Still, comparing my life with those of my fellow inmates, I was the lucky one.

I walked to our block. A lone unburned log lay beside the stove. Bright rays of sunlight covered the wood floor. I began to mull over Zosia's proposal. I was in a terrible predicament. I felt that living in a cellar wasn't a good trade-off for what our life was like now. My father was still the coffee man in the Herdecke Kommando, and being the dentist made my day-to-day life bearable. Survival at this camp wasn't our foremost concern. Yet the offer Zosia put forward was simply too good not to deserve serious attention. When Papa heard about it, he was stunned. It was also the first time I mentioned Zosia's name to him. Reaching the right decision was not easy. I had my misgivings, and I was sure Papa had his. We carefully weighed everything we could think of, and in the end, Papa said it was up to me to decide. I knew that our roles had reversed. "Whatever you decide," he said, "will be all right with me." Still I was torn with uncertainties, and our dilemma remained unresolved.

The next time I went to see my brother, his work group was no longer working on the road. Though Tadek tried to find out where he was, I did not see him again there. At the same time it seemed that a plot around us had been thickening. The Nazi monster, now wounded and in convulsions, hastened his game, devouring his prey as never before. Many disturbing rumors circulated about the Jews who were still in the ghettos. New names like Majdanek and Sobibór were mentioned. Newly arrived inmates told us about the heroic uprising in the Warsaw ghetto and the battle that had followed. The few Jews who never doubted their end fought thousands of heavily armed Germans, they said, and inflicted heavy casualties on the Nazis. At first it was hard to believe, but as more Jews arrived, more stories detailed the ghetto's brave and fearless battles. They spoke of it with a pride I had never heard expressed before. We wanted to hear those stories over and over. We thought that the Jews had finally broken the long-standing myth of their being incapable of fighting back.

"The bastards are going to kill us all," Mendele angrily said. "If I had a gun, I would kill a hundred of them before they got me." A lot of us agreed. If we didn't rise up to fight here, it was for many reasons. Barely alive, we had nothing to rise up with. Killing one German would have meant retaliation on hundreds of us.

It was the end of May 1943, and though I had been to the women's camp several times, I had yet to see my cousin. Once again I asked Tadek if he could take me there on a weekend, but he again said no. When I suggested that we go there one evening, I saw him waver. He was close to saying yes. "If someone catches me," he said, "I'll end in Gutenbrunn, with you." Finally, when I insisted, he agreed, and we made plans for a Monday night visit, at half past ten. "This time we have to go on foot," he cautioned. He also warned me that no one was to know, not even my father. But first I had to find a way out of camp. I knew that Rachmiel could leave the back door of the kitchen unlocked. As I had often carried notes for him, it wasn't difficult for me to persuade him. In the evening when I left, I told my father not to worry if I came back late. It was warm that night, though clouds blocked the moon. Yet I was shivering, perhaps from fear and excitement. When I came to the kitchen, the door was unlocked, and a small package and a note were nearby. "Come on," Tadek said. "We have to get through this forest first."

Past the woods we heard the sound of a rushing river. We followed the stream, and when it narrowed, we jumped across. Then we crossed a stone fence. "We have to be careful now. We are coming to a road," he warned me. I followed him with Rachmiel's bundle under my arm. We were suddenly startled by automobile headlights. As they got closer, they suddenly swerved and sped away from us. This crisis over, we walked to the camp.

The perimeter guard must have heard us, because he came out of his guardhouse and looked around. Tadek walked slowly to him, and I remained out of sight. My heart raced with fear and anticipation. It seemed to me that I had lost all safety in being there. In any case, it was too late to go back now. When Tadek returned, he whispered that at first the guard wouldn't permit me to go in. Only after he had told him that I would slip into the camp while Tadek and he walked around the fence, so that he would not see me, had the guard agreed. "That way, if someone catches you, we will say that we didn't know." This was their condition, and I had to accept it.

As soon as they both disappeared into the dark, I sneaked inside. Except for the lights flooding some areas, which I carefully avoided, the camp was dark. As I raced to the first barracks, I felt my heart and my head pounding. How would I find my cousin at night in this mysterious place? I wished I had not come. At the barracks I slowly tested the steps, so that I would not make an unexpected noise and wake someone. I opened the door and tiptoed inside. It was dark in the room, and the air hung heavy with human sweat. The women were breathing out of rhythm. Soon my eyes got accustomed to the darkness, and I could make out a woman on a bunk. I tugged her blanket gently. She raised her head and gave me a startled look. I told her to be quiet. "Don't be afraid," I whispered. "I am the Jewish dentist who comes here weekly. I am looking for my cousin Balcia. I know she is here."

The girl was still scared. She pulled her blanket up to her chin and didn't answer me. By now I had awakened others. They moved slowly, like zombies, on their bunks. "Who is there?" I heard them ask. When they learned that I was the dentist and that I was looking for Balcia Jakubowicz, one said she knew her. "She is in Block 5," she added.

"Which is Block 5?" I asked.

The woman slid off her bunk and said she would take me there. We moved slowly, as she led me along the aisle. Curiosity brought questions from the women about their relatives and friends. "Is Shmiel with you? Do you know Hershel Mayer?" one asked. "Do you know my brother? my father? my uncle? my cousin?" I recognized one of the names, and that woman got excited. "Oh my God! He's alive." I promised to tell him about her.

As we reached the end of the aisle, my guide pointed to the door. "When you go out of here, you'll be facing another door. That's Block 5," she said, wanting to return to her bunk. I thanked her, turned the doorknob, stepped out, and found myself outside.

I moved in the dark and went inside the next block. There were the same piles of people, the same tired bodies, the same sweaty air. Their breathing was punctuated with occasional snoring. I remained unnoticed until I touched a woman's leg. She opened her eyes and looked frightened. She was about to scream. "Shh," I said, putting my finger on my mouth. When I told her who I was, she calmed down. Then I asked where Balcia was.

"Balcia? She is here somewhere," she said. Others also woke up, eager to find out what was going on. And then I heard someone quietly saying my first name. I recognized the voice. It was Rifka, a girl from Dobra.

"Is that you, Bronek? How did you get here?" she asked, keeping her voice low. "Balcia is right there."

When Balcia and I were kids, she was quite a tomboy. But when I saw her last, in 1938, she was fourteen and a good-humored teenager. I kneeled down to see her. Her head rose up, hitting against the bunk. Her wide, tawny eyes were sleepy. At first she didn't recognize me, but as she fixed her eyes on me, her face lit up. "It's you, Bronek. I had heard you were here."

As she stood up in her nightgown, I saw that she was no longer the gawky little girl I had known. Though the hair was shaved off her head, she looked like a mature woman. When she began saying things about home, I fixed myself on every word she said. Her sister Toba and her mother were taken to Chełmno, where my mother and sister were also sent. I remembered her brother Alje, a soldier killed fighting in the first days of the war. Another brother, Mayer, who was my age, was hanged by the Germans, along with Icek Lijek, Shlomo Lęczycki, Moishe Neuman, and Hamek Lewkowicz. She talked about all this in a calm voice, as if such cruelty was just commonplace now. Next she told me about what had happened to her sister Mania.

"When the war began," Balcia continued, "Mania married her long-time friend from Lodz, and Aaron, a baby boy, was born to them. When they were all driven into the Lodz ghetto, they feared for his life. Babies were not to live in the ghetto. Her husband's job was to gather the dead in the street and bring them to the Jewish cemetery," she continued. "To save the baby, her husband built a tiny compartment under the seat of his cart and kept the baby there during the day. The hearse is Aaron's crib," she said. At the time of Balcia's arrest, the baby had still been alive. A long silence followed. Then Balcia asked me about my father, her uncle Wigdor. I told her that Papa was with me. I also told her how I had found Josek.

It was unusual for the women to see a strange man in their room, especially in the middle of the night. They looked at me as if I weren't real. Then I saw the familiar face of a girl in a long flannel nightgown who was listening to us. When she saw I was staring at her, she said, "Bronek, is that you?" I knew then that it was Ruzka Rosen, sweet Ruzka whom I had once been so attracted to. Sweat began to run down my forehead, hazing over my eyes. I saw that she was also moved. But so much had changed. I knew that neither she nor I could still feel the same about one another as we had in the old days in Kalisz.

It was past midnight. I knew that Tadek was growing impatient. I left Rachmiel's package, said good-bye to Balcia and Ruzka, and began to trace my steps back. I found Tadek in a deep conversation with the sentry in front of the guardhouse. Gabbing was Tadek's forte. "Let's go," he said when he saw me coming.

If I had had any illusions about my mother and sister escaping their terrible deaths, it was now gone. I knew then that I would never see them again. As Tadek and I approached the road on the way back to our camp, we saw a convoy of German panzers and troop vehicles coming. My heart pounded, as if they were driving straight at us. We fell to the ground, flattened ourselves, and waited, absolutely motionless. The darkness was our ally. We kept our heads on the ground until all the vehicles passed. Then we cautiously crossed the road, and returned by the same route.

A half hour later we saw the outline of Gutenbrunn. I knew then of the real danger of my undertaking. I promised myself never to dare anything like that again. Papa was still awake. He looked relieved to see that I was back. Except for Tadek, Rachmiel, and I, no one at Gutenbrunn knew what had occurred that night. I couldn't sleep. My heart throbbed with pain. Why did they have to die? Why, oh God, such a horrible death? I had to stop thinking of it. I wanted to remember them as I had once known them.

The next day I told Papa where I had gone the previous night. When he heard what I had learned from Balcia, we both realized that all that we held dear was now lost.

Zosia now came to the camp weekly and often reminded me of her proposal. Although I had been seriously considering it, something inside me kept me from deciding. "You must not plunge yourself and your father into a worse hell than this," a voice told me. Escaping from Gutenbrunn was still possible, but for a Jew to pass through Poznan was extremely risky, and if we succeeded in getting to the Zasinas, we had something else to fear. We knew that in spite of their good intentions, in a crisis situation they would have to turn us over to the Germans. By comparison, we were not that bad off here. Papa still had his job brewing coffee, and I enjoyed some benefits. Small as they were, they were still very important. The next Saturday Zosia came again. She looked beautiful, in her simple Polish peasant dress. As we had done before, we walked from the camp along the path that led to the forest. As soon as we were at a distance she renewed her bid, asking me if we had made a decision. "My father urged me to ask you when you are coming," she said. The decision was a difficult one, I told her, letting her know that we had decided to stay. She showed her disappointment. When she left she asked me to reconsider.

The next time I went to the women's camp, Tadek and I encountered difficulties. The sentries said their new Kommandant had forbidden them to let us in. A few women who were expecting me looked on while Tadek pleaded with the sentries to let me in. But we were unable to persuade them and had to leave. Though Tadek promised to make an attempt to get permission from the new Kommandant, this was the end of my travels with him.

On Saturday Rachmiel came to the infirmary and whispered, "The shiksele and someone else are at the kitchen gate." Both Zosia and her father had come to try and change my mind about leaving the camp.

"There is little you have to fear being with us," her father said. "No one will ever find you." I told him that though we were humbled and grateful, we had decided that our best chance was to remain in Gutenbrunn.

In a final attempt to persuade me, Zosia said, "It's too bad, Bronek. We have made everything ready for you." Their warmheartedness overwhelmed me, but I was unable to imagine surviving any length of time in a cellar.

Everything had a value in camp. Bread was the most wanted, but potato peelings were the most traded commodity. As bed rest curfew began at eight, there was a rush to the barracks stove before then. The healthy peelings didn't smell bad, but the once-frozen ones made the barracks reek like a cow barn. All essentials had an established trading value. For example, one cigarette was worth two handfuls of potato peelings.

My most frequent dental procedure was extracting loose and diseased teeth, often with little or no anesthetic. Because of a lack of nutrients, especially vitamin C, I also saw a great deal of gingivitis and periodontitis. All I could do for the inmates suffering from these diseases was to give temporary relief with tinctures of merbromin and iodine. Within weeks those people suffered more serious gum deteriorations, and most of their teeth had to be extracted. In time I became inventive enough to scrape decayed dentine from cavities with excavators and explorers and to deaden the nerve with an arsenic paste. Meanwhile, more inmates had reached the state of Mussulmen—easily detected by edema and bulging eyes—and they were dying. That was inconsequential to the Nazis, since a telephone call or a memo brought more Jews to replace the ones who died.

The newly arrived hoped to find a semblance of humane treatment, but they soon saw that they had been brought here to work in a systematic process of destruction. They lost their strength within weeks. My stomach had been raising havoc. The antacids only relieved the throb for a half hour at best. I continually wondered, Am I condemned to this for the rest of my life? Will I ever be normal again?

By now we were on our fourth or fifth Lagerführer. It seemed that Gutenbrunn was their training camp. I don't recall this one's name. In any case, he was one of the young Nazi breed. Strict, rigid, and unyielding, he was obsessed with *Ordnung* (neatness). He, and only he, ran the camp. If Grimm was not at the gate in the morning to salute the new Kommandant, he was seriously reprimanded. The Kommandant showed his anger with his whip. Everything had to be just so, his way, the German way. Surely, he would have never allowed me to go out to another camp. His orders were always preceded by the cynical SS epithets *Faulenzer* (malingerer) and *Drückeberger* (shirker).

There was anger in the Kommandant's face as he and Grimm entered the infirmary one day. "Scheiße," he yelled. "Where is the doctor? Why did he leave that inmate saboteur in the camp? He should be out working with the others."

Dr. Seidel got scared. At first he tried to explain to the Nazi the medical problems of the sick inmates. But seeing that this did not quiet him down, Seidel told the Kommandant that he acted in the best interest of the camp. "As his wounds heal, the inmate will become productive again." Normally this would have made sense, but it didn't to this man. The Kommandant said that he wouldn't tolerate inmates whom he thought could be working being idle in the camp. As a result of this, Dr. Seidel had to send many inmates to work whom he might have otherwise exempted.

Although we had heard of the Final Solution and its significance, it was hard to accept this new hard line that threatened the life of everyone. It had become the camp's main concern. Our days in Gutenbrunn were even more troubled. A sense of catastrophe hung in the air. In more than two years of being in labor camps, I had not seen such anguish. Soon we noticed significant changes. We were told that the Russians were racing through Poland. The guards watched us like hawks. It went on like this until the beginning of August 1943, when our deportation was announced.

One day Rachmiel informed me that Zosia was outside the kitchen window waiting to talk to me. It was no longer possible for me to leave the camp grounds. I went through the kitchen, over to the iron-barred window. When she heard of the plans for our immediate deportation, she reminded me of her family's standing offer. Could I still find a way to leave Gutenbrunn? she asked. "We begged you," she said. I too had been thinking about it. Had I known earlier that we would be deported, my father and I would probably have left. Zosia and I took one last look at each other and said a final good-bye. Her parting words were "I'll find you and come to see you, wherever you are."

That day was the last time that we saw one another. I remember Zosia as a kind, loving human being. She had always been ready to help us, regardless of the hardships she had to endure or the risks she had to take. In a world of terror, in a world littered with hatred, she still regarded us as human beings. All my attempts to find her after the war were fruitless. I was told that she had died in an Allied bombardment somewhere in Germany, where she was working as a forced laborer.

A few days after Zosia's last visit, the camp leaders stopped sending us out to work, and Grimm told us that we would be leaving within a couple of days. When I went to the infirmary for the last time, I saw a few sick inmates staring at me. I knew they were being left behind. They knew that their fate had been already decided. As I gathered my instruments, I couldn't say good-bye. It would have been too painful.

I joined Papa on his bunk. It was a long, silent night. Just an occasional sigh was heard. The thought of what lay ahead gnawed at all of us. The uncertainty even overshadowed my stomach pain. I listened to my father's heart-beat and remembered when, as a young boy, I sat on his lap, feeling warm and protected. We could do little for one another here, but having someone close meant sharing traumas that the others had to endure alone.

11

ON CATTLE CARS TO AUSCHWITZ

It was early morning. I had barely fallen asleep when I heard the police shouting, "Get up! We are moving out." Our freedom was slipping further away. Instantly everyone was in motion. A half hour later the twenty-six hundred "good workers" stood in rows of fives. Papa was at my right, my instrument box was on my left, and the ubiquitous soup utensil, the *menashka,* dangled in front of me.

As the main gates opened, I had hoped to see Tadek, but our guards were gone. In their place stood an echelon of tall, stern-faced Croats wearing Waffen SS uniforms. Their green jackets were buttoned up to their chins, and heavy carbines hung over their shoulders. The black-uniformed German SS men held German shepherds on leashes. We were ordered to march.

As we rounded the corner, I took a last glance at Gutenbrunn, which had been my home for more than a year. During this time I had believed that if Papa and I could endure just a little while longer, the Soviet army would free us. We were now on a winding road, parallel to the tracks that had just been built. The tracks, once so busy, looked deserted now. Our marching raised clouds of dust that swirled around us. As we passed Herdecke's hut, he stood in the doorway looking at us. I tipped my cap, and he nodded. I saw good-bye in his eyes.

I had regarded him as my good fortune in Gutenbrunn. I was reminded of the others who had helped me, here and in Steineck: Zosia, Stasia, Witczak, and Tadek. The good people remained much longer in my mind and heart than the villains did. Someone once said, "No memorial has ever been built for bad deeds."

"Quickly! Quickly!" the guards rushed us. After an hour we came to a road. Alongside it were three tracks. About fifty cattle cars waited on one of them, and about a dozen railroad people milled around. Beyond them was the station and a couple of steam locomotives. These tracks had been built by the sweat and blood of our brothers.

The SS men rolled open the doors of the cattle cars, and the real drama unfolded. The floor of the cars was more than a meter off the ground and difficult for inmates to climb up to. The guards again yelled, "Quickly!" and then we were beaten and pushed into the cars with their rifle butts. Though the cars were nearly full, they kept shoving more in. Only when the wagons were packed to the limit were the doors rolled shut. To avoid being beaten, some inmates ran like the animals that these cars were built to carry. Eventually our turn came. Thanks to some inmate's outstretched hands, Papa and I were able to pull ourselves up. More and more inmates were forced in. The wagon door slid closed behind us, and there was no room to stand.

The old cattle cars were three meters high inside. About two and a half meters up from the splintered board floor were four twenty-by-twenty-eight-centimeter openings. Each had two iron bars across it, strung with barbed wire. Only the very tall inmates standing on their toes could reach them. The SS men were talking leisurely, which meant that we weren't leaving yet. The sound of their conversations created fear in us. Soon the heat became unbearable. Tempers wore thin. "We'll all die here. These are our coffins," someone said in panic. "Give me a little room. I can't get any air," another said. Papa and I were wedged in. People begged for a little space, but it was useless.

As the sun set, we had still not departed. Finally we heard an engine whistle. We guessed that it must have been after nine o'clock when we moved out of the station. We were a swaying mass. Each time the locomotive slowed or banked in a curve, we were jostled from side to side. My father tried to sit on the floor, which was no small feat. Although we were told that it would take two days to reach our destination, we did not know where we were headed.

It was dark. Only occasionally moonlight passed through the small air slots in the wagon. At times Papa and I reversed positions, one sitting and the other standing, the instrument box always between us. I rested my head on my bent knees and tried to sleep. The sound of the moving wheels eventually put me to sleep, and that's when my torment began. Each time the car passed over a rail joint, I heard two words, *doom* and *death,* which stayed with me, an unending morbid echo, until the trip ended. As we snaked through the countryside the train swerved and rolled. All that we had been deprived of in Steineck and Gutenbrunn was minor compared with this. There seemed no bottom to our abyss.

I tried to move to the window to get air, but it was impossible. At dawn I tried again. This time I pushed hard, and my persistence was rewarded. I was 1.7 meters, and a fellow prisoner had to give me a boost so I could look out the window. I gulped a few deep breaths, which eased my distress a little. The train had just come to a screeching halt. As I looked out, a nearby guard stared me in the face. His merciless, unconcerned look said that I was a hardened criminal. The early sunrise had just touched the window grates. One inmate seemed happy that our Lagerführer was with us. "He can tell them what good workers we are." What an absurdity to believe that the Lagerführer was there to help us. How much of an ally could the Kommandant be? He was only there to deliver his slaves.

Our biggest dilemma was satisfying our physical needs. Everything that we once did in private had to be done now in public. Our soup bowls became chamber pots. We tried to dispose of the excrement through the wired windows but were unsuccessful. Our car began to smell like an outhouse. By midday, in the heat, it got even worse.

Should I eat now or save the bread for later? This was a constant inner debate. By this time thirst parched our throats. Our cries for water did not let up. "Water! Water!" someone dared to say to a passing guard.

"Shut your mouth," he replied. It was past noon. The cars moved a few meters forward and that much back. Each time the locomotive whistled, we thought we were about to leave. Most of us were stripped to the waist.

We got under way again, and each lurch of the wagon toppled us on top of each other. Finally, when the train stopped, Papa and I made our way to a window. When I raised him up to reach the air, I realized how little he now weighed. One inmate at another window looked to see the end of our convoy. "They must have added more cars at the last stop," he observed. "We're now at least a hundred cars. Our convoy stretches all the way around the bend."

Suddenly the door to our wagon rolled open, and an SS man placed a pail of water in our car. Each man was allowed to take one ladleful, about two handfuls, and pass the ladle to the next man. Each drop of water was precious. It did a lot to quench our most pressing thirst. I promised myself then that if I ever got the chance I would immerse myself in water. The SS guard left the door open. The fetid smell was still there, but this was a definite improvement.

As we began to move again, my father thought that we had passed Nowe Miasto nad Wartą, a town southeast of Poznan. "If we continue on that route," he observed, "we will be coming by Katowice." Katowice was a well-known city in the coal mining region of Poland.

Nighttime was a bit cooler and brought some relief in the car. But as soon as I fell asleep, I heard the two words again, *doom* and *death*. Even when I awoke, I couldn't drown them out with other thoughts. While passing over bridges, the words inside my head reverberated, and I thought I was going insane.

The train came to a halt. We were at Pleszew. The wagons jerked back and forth until they stopped. We were on a side track about two hundred meters from the station. Since we were the least important cargo, we were left standing there. "You know who lived here in Pleszew?" Papa asked me. "My sister Malka and your uncle Mordechai. You remember their daughter, Jadzia, who was Pola's age?" I remembered Jadzia well. She was slim and tall and had a small cream-colored face. I remembered visiting them one time when I was very young. Papa sighed and said, "God knows where they are now." Pleszew was a fairly large city. "We are a long way from Katowice," Papa said plaintively.

We remained standing there until morning. Many trains passed during the night carrying German soldiers and civilians. We watched as their comfortable, brightly lit cars passed by. These travelers casually glanced in our direction, and we looked back at them through our barred windows.

By midmorning a few civilians had gathered around our train. Menashe, the spunky Jewish policeman from Gutenbrunn, who was now with us in our car, begged them to bring us water. "They heard me!" he suddenly shouted. "Someone is bringing us water."

We were already jockeying for positions close to the door when a loud voice outside ordered, "Halt." Then we heard the same voice yelling, "Zurück-gehen" (Turn back). A guard had seen the civilian carrying the pail of water.

One inmate moaned, "The SS made the man pour it on the ground." There was no water for us at that station.

This was our second day. This should have been the end of our trip. Our rations were gone, and our hunger and thirst had become intense. One man asked our guard where we were being taken. "I don't know," the Croat answered in his twisted German. I reached into my pockets, hoping to find some crumbs. But I only found a few bits of lint.

A little while later we began moving again. At each whistle we believed that the train would stop and we would be at our destination. My father still thought we were headed for Katowice. Finally we arrived. We were at Katowice.

The streets were lit, and the factories spewed dark smoke. It seemed that the war hadn't caused much damage here. Even the railroad station was brightly lit. As we passed through the city and kept moving, I could see my father's great disappointment. He had thought Katowice was our destination because of the many iron factories and steel foundries there. "They could use us here," he said.

We were puzzled. We hoped this traveling purgatory would soon end. The locomotive labored hard and loud, pulling the long train up a mountain. At night it slowed further, and we again stopped. After the usual tugging and screeching, we ended up stopped on a dead track. The guard slid the door open wide so we could empty our overflowing buckets. We were near Częstochowa. Częstochowa was a well-known Catholic mecca. There at Jasna Góra was the shrine to the Black Madonna. I remembered pilgrims frequently passing through our village, some walking barefoot, bound for this shrine.

It rained during the night. This was a blessing, for the rain cooled the railcar and us. At four in the morning we still idled. As the sun rose we could see the mountains. Suddenly there was excitement. "Boruch Hashem!" (Thank God), someone yelled, as vats and baskets were moved to our train. I tried to get up, but I was fused into a solid mass of bodies. My legs were cramped, and I couldn't straighten up. It took about an hour before the SS guards opened our wagon door. Understandably, when it opened, pandemonium broke out. Although we got nearly double the usual ration of bread and a ladle of coffee each, we gulped it all down at once. Why keep some for later? It would only cause a struggle.

The results were astonishing. "They want to keep us alive," we all thought. Since the heat was not excessive that day, and the door had been ajar for a while, and our thirst was quenched, as was our hunger, this was the best day of the journey. Then, all too soon, the guards slid the wagon doors shut and slammed their latches. They were ready to take us farther on.

The name of the next station was obscure. After a few more kilometers our transport took a course to the south, where we passed the peaks of Wieliczka. A while later the train stopped again. The rest of the day train men moved our cars from one track to another to let other trains go by. At evening we were about to enter our fourth day of travel. It was anybody's guess as to when and where it would end.

Time had been passing very slowly. I took advantage of the stilled wheels and fell asleep. It must have been past midnight when I heard movement. It was pitch dark. Only an occasional engine whistle broke the loud noise of the wheels. The only other sounds were the groans and moans of my fellow passengers. I looked at Papa's ashen face, and in it I saw thoughts as dark as mine.

It is I who is responsible if you must die, Papa, I thought. It was I who decided to stay in Gutenbrunn rather than accept Zosia's offer. There is no way I can express my regret to you.

The wheels continued: doom and death. I felt broken and afraid of the future. I pitied all the others that didn't know that they too were going to die. Don't you know, my brothers? You too are doomed. The train suddenly sped up as if it were in a hurry. I could not keep my eyes open any longer. The harder I tried, the heavier my lids became. Even when I was asleep, the message "doom and death" sounded with each bump. Oh God! Why are you letting them do this to us? Why are you giving them such an easy victory? Certainly our God wasn't there, or else he hadn't been listening. I dreamed on.

I woke up numb. Fear had dulled my senses. We knew it was night, but no one knew the time. We thought it was two thirty or three o'clock. I lay pressed against my father. I was certain these were my last hours. The train slowed, and the engine whistled. Smoke trickled into our car through the cracks and windows. We thought it was the smell of the locomotives. The train crept on, a centimeter at a time. We were not near a settlement. We did not know where we were. It was strange: we were not near any station either. Why did the trains move so slowly? People near the window said that they could see only bare fields.

AUSCHWITZ

Traumatized, starved, and soaked with human waste, we looked to be the inhuman, useless creatures the Nazis had characterized us as being. It was dark when the train stopped. Dawn came a few minutes later, and light began breaking through the windows. We are not at a station. Why did they stop? we wondered. A few minutes later the wheels began to roll slowly; then they stopped and rolled and stopped again, screeching.

It was light enough to see distant fences. We must be at a camp, and at least at the end of this misery. Perhaps the prophecy of our doom and death was wrong after all? The smoke, with the odor of burning flesh, that we suddenly smelled we passed off as the friction of the train's wheels on the rails. As the locomotive crept forward, we saw strangers on a ridge dressed in striped clothes with matching berets, walking like zombies and staring at our train as though they had been expecting us. We yelled, asking them to tell us where we were. But no words came back, just a sign from one of them: he slid his hand across his throat in a cutting gesture. The others that looked at our caravan twirled their fingers at the sky. We stared, frightened, in disbelief. We knew that it meant crematories. In the quiet that followed, a boy of perhaps sixteen asked what the strange gestures meant. No one answered him. No one wanted to share his grimmest thoughts. It is hard to describe our macabre mood. The meaning of the smoke was now apparent. It was not the train. My father was praying. I no longer thought that God could save us. My trust in him had ended. My genesis without him had taken place long ago, in Steineck.

The train rolled on. We passed more uniformed people. They looked on while SS men held flashlights and other prisoners gave us more strange signals. Some raised their arms up, mimicking Hercules. A constant stream of smoke spewed into the air. The train slowed and stopped.

The doors rolled open and startled us with loud bangs. "Raus! Alle raus! Alles liegen lassen!" (Out! All out! Leave everything!), the SS shouted. The cement platform was crowded with SS men, yelling and waving us impatiently out of the wagon. "Raus!" they yelled, as their dogs growled, showing menacing teeth. The word *Auschwitz* hung like a bad omen in the air. The impact shocked us. It was a ghastly sound that no one repeated. We knew that that word stood for selections and death. We knew that in Auschwitz Jews were turned to ashes. Their net was closing around us.

People began to pray. "Shma Israel Adonoi Eloheino Adonoi Aikhod. God is one. God is mighty."

"Raus! Raus! Alle raus!" they yelled with guns in hand. After being locked in the wagons for days, we had enormous difficulty in leaving the car while in a panic. Our limbs had molded to the mass of men in the cars and would not easily straighten again. "Leave everything on the platform!" the SS yelled. I only had a coat, besides the rags I wore, and I left it, but I held tightly to my life-saving dental tools. We knew things were bad. Bedlam erupted as SS men tore into us, whipping us for no reason. A whip swung across my body. "Das auch!" a contemptuous SS man shouted.

"These are a few of my dental instruments," I said, hoping he would allow me to keep them. Without another word he seized the box, snatched it off my shoulder, and flung it to the ground. The treasures that I had carried with me all this time, my fate and that of my father, lay scattered on the cement platform.

More prisoners in their zebra-striped suits gathered, watching us from behind the fence. We were ordered to undress and to leave our clothes on the platform. Carpenters, lawyers, shoemakers, businessmen, students, and professors undressed—we were just plain Jews to our captors. They ordered us into the customary rows of fives. "Rechts schwenk, vorwärts marsch."

The skies were gray and had a strange look of finality. It was a cool morning, and the stiff breeze blowing across our naked bodies chilled us deeply. We pressed together, and I held on firmly to Papa, realizing that if we were separated we would never find one another. Then the dreaded word "Selekcja!" Polish for "selection," went like lightning through our lines and sent a bolt of fear through everyone. We knew the apocalypse was near.

We thought we knew all about Auschwitz's horror, but we were soon to discover how little we actually did know. Each of us had been quietly evaluating his chance of survival. To escape from here, one would have to be

Houdini. We had barely taken ten steps forward when our line slowed to a crawl. We now crept forward, stepping on each other's heels. Some wept, and others tried to muster courage to appear strong and look healthy. Papa and I were several rows away from the bunch of SS men who, with flashlights in hand, were scrutinizing the naked men before them. I knew that each step took us closer to our doom and death, as the rails had predicted. A few more minutes and it will all be over, I surmised.

We were still moving and were soon to meet the group of SS men with the flashlights. One Nazi, who appeared to be the highest-ranking SS officer, wore a spiffy black uniform with a doctor's badge—a serpent wound around a sword. He was tall and slim, with a dark complexion. His thick black hair was cut short. He left no uncertainty that he was in charge. The procedure seemed well rehearsed. As his assistants paraded a row of prisoners before him, he made mysterious gestures. Only the guards understood, and they quickly executed his orders. A blink of his eyes, a wave of his hand, a twitch of his finger—each held a clue. Some people were ordered right and others left. It soon became apparent that one line seemed more fit than the other.

Two of the five men in the row ahead of us were ordered to join the weaker line. One of them courageously attempted to persuade his judge to let him go with the others. "Look! I am strong," he said. "I can work. I worked on laying rails for more than two years and did not skip one day." But an SS man shoved him back in his line. A daily supply of people, demand for labor, and the availability of room in the barracks were equally important factors in determining who lived and who died.

Before our turn, a fellow captive whispered, "Lift your heads. Act strong." The judges asked the first question of me. What was my age?

"Twenty-three," I said.

"Occupation?"

"Dentist," I replied.

They ordered me to the right, to join the healthier-looking group. As I stepped aside, I took my father with me.

"Halt! Nur Du!" (Only you), I heard one shout. I knew that Papa was at their mercy. They asked him his age and occupation.

"Forty-two, farmer," he said.

My father was forty-nine then. I thought it sounded good.

But "Links!" I heard them order. I saw them push him to the left.

"It's my father," I said, begging them to understand.

"Nein, nur Du geh nach rechts. Dein Vater muß nach links gehen." (No, only you to the right. Your father must go to the left.) They had condemned him to death. I tried to beg for their clemency once more. But I watched in horror as they began to select people in the next line. I was as close to tears as I could ever be in camp. They have just orphaned me, I thought.

Suddenly a commotion erupted as one man tried to escape the platform. He was quickly mowed down by gunfire. In that moment of confusion, I grabbed my father and tried to take him with me. He was frozen with fear and did not move. I tugged sharply and whispered, "Papa! Come with me." He followed. If we had been caught, it would have been death for both of us.

I still do not understand why none of them noticed me and stopped us. It all happened purely by chance. In writing about this incident I must add that survival, all else aside, was primarily luck. Sometimes more than luck was needed. Sometimes strange things had to happen, as if one's fate was guided by a mysterious hand.

We stood there, and each minute was an hour long. I felt as if I were standing on hot coals. We could hear praying: "O Lord, have mercy on thy children. We are truly thine and are pure in heart." But it didn't help. In the end, the doctors were all powerful. I held on to my father, amazed at what had happened. Seventy-five of us hopeful people were finally led away. The billows of smoke rose from the chimneys as the sky brightened. Our brothers in the other group were also led away, soon to be silenced.

After walking a hundred meters, we were loaded onto trucks and driven along a double fence, passing three-story brick buildings. We saw groups of people marching. Their clothes were dirty, and they wore striped miners' lamps on their heads. They were on their way to work. I was struck by the paradox: the coal they mined might have been used to move the trains that carried us here. Some looked lifeless, barely dragging their feet. In front of each group walked someone in the same striped clothes wearing a black armband, a Kapo.

This camp did not look like any I had seen before. The outside perimeter was fenced with heavy wire, with barbed wire on top. Along the inside ran what seemed to be an electric line. Perched above in towers were green-uniformed Waffen SS. Their guns pointed into the camp. As we were driven further, we heard an orchestra playing and people singing. "Today Poland. Tomorrow the entire world," they sang in German. Each refrain had a different verse and mentioned a different country. When the trucks stopped, we heard "We're marching on England today, and tomorrow on the entire world!"

A sign at the gate read "Stop, high voltage!" Above the gate another sign read "Auschwitz," and below it, "Arbeit Macht Frei" (Work makes you free). We knew it wasn't meant to be a promise, not even a pledge. The truth was that we were here to work until we died. In front of a small shack a conductor directed thirty musicians. The scene was grotesque. They followed his baton as if they were playing in a symphony orchestra.

Once inside, our truck turned left and stopped in front of one of the huge three-story brick buildings. A smartly dressed SS sergeant took charge of us. "Down," he shouted, as the rest of the SS began to enforce his order. I looked at my father. He was shivering, and his face was blue. We hoped, but we still didn't know what would happen to us.

Suddenly someone signaled to me. I looked and saw an inmate waving from the opposite side of a fence. He was staring at my boots. "You'll have to leave them anyhow. Throw them to me," he shouted. "I'll take care of you with some extra food when you get to the camp. I am a Blockkapo," he added. These were the first words I heard spoken by any prisoner in Auschwitz. It was a Kapo's introduction.

He wore a clean suit, a dark cap, and the Kapo's armband. I did not believe him at first. I thought he was only after my boots. But when the Scharführer ordered us to leave behind anything we still might have with us, I yielded to the inevitable. I removed the few photographs that I still had from one of my boots and threw the boots over the fence to him. In the aftermath I realized that I did not know how to find him. As it turned out, it really didn't matter. We were not allowed to mix with inmates in the main camp anyway.

I looked at my family photographs: my mother, sister, brother, and Aunt Rachel, Uncle Shlomo, and Aunt Sara. Also I looked at the picture of Uncle Izchak, whom everyone said I resembled. There was Uncle Mordechai, Uncle Chaim, cousins Toba, Balcia, Nachme, Josef, Mayer, and Mendel. Finally I looked at my grandfather's picture for the last time. Much later, when I remembered that August day in 1943, it was as if by my leaving those photographs, my relatives pictured there had also died at Auschwitz. We saw groups of inmates with their heads bowed low, and I decided that someday someone should tell the world what I saw. But, I thought, no epic drama could duplicate the sight that was before me. No one would be able to find such emaciated bodies to re-create the scene.

The morning mist remained. More trucks arrived. One group, also from our train, was from Lenzingen, the camp my brother had been in. They claimed to have seen him before the selection on the platform. Papa and I feared for him.

The Scharführer ordered us into the cell block we were facing. As we entered through a long corridor, we had to pass other SS men. They searched us once more, but this time they made us spread our legs and bend over. Further down the corridor, we walked through brackish fluid that smelled of kerosene or naphtha. Soon we had the same mixture showered on our heads and bodies. "Schnell! Schnell!" they urged. We ran like cornered sheep to avoid the German shepherds. Then we were led to the yard once again.

The sun shone. It had burned off the fog. Naked and wet, we were freezing. Scratches and scrapes on our bodies had reddened from the fluid, and these were painful. Next we were ordered into another building that had a sign: "Brause" (shower). The terrible word stared us in the face. We are not safe, I thought. We are in their concealed gas chamber. "Los machen!" they yelled, and we were pushed in the door from all sides. The large metal door locked behind us with a clang. We were in a large hall. We saw the shower heads hanging down. The prisoners who were already there stood praying, perhaps for all of us. We heard another clang, and all became quiet. My father's eyes were fixed on me. He was thinking, like me, that this might be our last moment together. My heart raced. Light rings swirled in front of my eyes. For kilometers and days the train wheels had warned me of doom and death. That promise was about to come true. I closed my eyes and stopped breathing, fearing that the deadly gas would shower down on us at any minute. A passive silence persisted.

Suddenly I felt a trickle of water. I didn't dare to look up, afraid the miracle would stop. When I looked around, I saw that we were all still on our feet—alive. Soon the water flowed steadily, and it did not smell or taste odd. I gulped down a mouthful. Water had never tasted so good or meant as much to me. With a burst of relief, we all felt that a new life had been given to us. It was our only happy moment in Auschwitz. For Papa and me, this was the second miracle of the day.

When the water stopped, an inmate nearby said he had seen my brother in the hall. The man took me by the hand, and we both elbowed our way through the mass of wet bodies until we saw Josek. We looked at each other in disbelief. It was a third miracle! We returned to Papa, who was happy to be reunited with both his sons. Josek looked considerably thinner than he had when I had last seen him. His eyes were sunken, and he slouched. His health was delicate. This was not an asset in any camp. Now that we had found one another, we vowed to stay together no matter what.

As the doors opened, we were ordered into the next room, a large hall that was now a makeshift barbershop. It was full of inmates sitting on benches. The barbers were also inmates, but they wore clean, striped prison uniforms. They had crew cuts. "Sit. Stand. Turn around." Each of the eight barbers ordered inmates about. I overheard one man telling of an episode he had witnessed at the railroad station. He was from Vienna, and he said he saw a man about forty-five years old tell an SS officer that he had been arrested by mistake. "I fought in the First World War for Austria and lost both my legs. I am exempt from any deportation," the man had argued. He showed the officer his Iron Cross and his documents. The SS man, however, ripped them out of his hand and shredded them. Then he pushed the crippled man in front of an oncoming train. Another witness corroborated this story. "We all gasped," the storyteller continued, "as the train crushed him."

My turn came, and the barber began to clip me bald. He shook his head, pondering why so many of us managed to get in alive. "Auschwitz is full. You were lucky to escape the chimney." Inmates used the word *chimney* as a metaphor for being gassed and cremated. *Konzentrationslager,* the word for concentration camp, was difficult to pronounce, so they called it KZ. "Only if there is a demand for workers does Dr. Mengele pass Jews into camp," the barber said, adding, "At times they are short of gas."

I told him that most of us were veterans of other camps, having spent as much as two years in labor camps near Poznan, where we worked building railroad tracks. Perhaps that had helped us escape death.

"I doubt it," he said. Then he went on to tell me that we were now in Stammlager, the main camp of Auschwitz. He also said that there were many satellite camps around Auschwitz. "Buna, Trzebinia, Jawiżowiec, Janinagrube, and Günthergrube, just to mention a few," he said. "Their organization will amaze you."

He stopped talking, but I wanted to know more. He answered my questions readily. "What is that number you have on your arm?"

"Everyone is known by a number here. You will get one too, and then," he said, "you'll be known only by a number. You'll have to remember it and respond to it when you're called."

I saw his number was tattooed. "Where do we get those numbers tattooed?" I asked.

"You will see where. You'll be tattooed as soon as you leave here." Then he told me that he had been in Auschwitz for a year and a half.

"How long can one survive here?" I wondered aloud. That question puzzled him.

"Auschwitz is a much different place now than it was when I came here," he said. "When we first arrived here, one sign read, 'You can expect to survive three months here, at most six. And if you don't like it, go to the fence and end it now.'" That confirmed my suspicions that deadly electricity did indeed flow in the inner fence of Auschwitz. He continued explaining that obeying was an inmate's unalterable duty. "Remember, never walk in Auschwitz. Run." He then urged me to learn the names of the SS rankings and use them correctly. "When you pass SS men, take your cap off and walk in military steps. Play by those rules regardless how ridiculous they may seem to you." Throughout it all he kept repeating to me how lucky we were. "At times you have to have luck here," he said. "Another reason that many of you passed the selection was because there were no women, children, or elderly among you." I knew he had survived eighteen months in Auschwitz, and that left me with a bit of hope. His final comments to me were "No matter how sick you are, never go to the infirmary. Working is the best recipe for not dying."

I then knew a lot more about Auschwitz and its special lingo. KZ meant concentration camp. KB (*Krankenbau*) was the infirmary. Kanada referred to the inmate groups that were gathering everything the arrivals were forced to leave on the platforms. The Kapos were inmate foremen. Bunker was a penal place. Sonderkommandos were inmates assigned to special work details. The barber, though, had dropped words that seemed strange: *horse, rack,* and others whose meanings I could not fully understand.

Naked and shaved from tip to toe, we followed one another into the next barracks. Pairs of clogs, jackets, and pants were thrown at us, regardless of the size or fit. "If these don't fit you, swap with others," the inmates behind the counters told us. The clothing reeked of the very same brew that we had been sprayed with earlier. We each received gray-striped underwear and a striped beret. The jackets were either too large or too small, and most of the pants pulled up to the chin. Papa, who had never been without a thread and needle, was helpless, for the button that was supposed to hold up his pants was missing. Josek's trousers didn't stay on his waist either. Robbing us of our names was a way to complete our dehumanization. Our names became numbers. In time we knew why. Numbers had no faces. They were much easier to deal with.

When the numbering process began, Josek, Papa, and I followed one another and received consecutive numbers. We thought that this would lessen the chance of our being separated. A prisoner with a tool similar to a fountain pen began to inject a black dye into my lower left arm. At first it wasn't painful, but as he progressed, it hurt. When I pulled my arm away, I saw a few drops of blood over the numbers he had just tattooed. He looked at me, and I knew he had to finish. Afterward we received cloth patches with our numbers and were told to sew them onto our jackets and pants. I became number 141129, my father number 141130, and Josek number 141131. The red triangle on the patch denoted a political crime. Three yellow corners were added to all patches of Jewish inmates. In time we learned even to distinguish what the alleged crime had been. Communists and former fighters of the Spanish Civil War who fought for a republic and against General Franco had a triangle pointing down, while the remaining political inmates had triangles pointing up. Green triangles denoted criminals, pink represented homosexuals, and purple stood for Seventh Day Adventists and Jehovah's Witnesses. Brown designated the gypsies. Those alleged to be escapees wore large black circles on their backs. Because a Jew was simply shot or hanged when caught escaping, there were no Jews among this last group. The first letter of one's country name in German—for example, *D* for Deutschland, *F* for Frankreich, and *P* for Polen—appeared in the center of the patch.

The Kapos were the ones we learned to fear first. Some were in charge of the blocks in camp. Others went with us to work and were in charge of us there. Nearly all were non-Jews, and most were German. They came from a wide variety of backgrounds: they were con men, desperadoes, convicted murderers, and petty criminals. Among them were also former soldiers from the International Legion. Though some of them had first been at odds with Hitler, they changed their allegiance when given the opportunity to leave the jails and become Kapos in concentration camps. All showed a certain contempt for newcomers and acted as if all Jews were their enemies. Although they faced the same life that we did, they seemed to us arrogant and harshly indifferent.

It was amazing how the Nazis had singled us out from the rest of the inmates. If there had ever been a thread of harmony between Jews and non-Jews in the camps, we did not see it in Auschwitz. In spite of our common plight, the others didn't want to associate with us. They did not have to fear selections. The gas chambers were purely for Jews and gypsies.

In assembling this time, we had to follow our numbers in consecutive order. "Los! Los!" the guards herded us through Auschwitz. We saw a group of inmates carrying stones in one direction and another doing the same going the opposite way. They looked toward us, but I was not sure that they could see us. Finally we came to the Quarantine Block. We had not eaten in two days and thought that having passed Auschwitz's symbolic baptism, our fellow inmates would find enough compassion for us to let us into the building. But the Kapo and three of his assistants marched us to the side of the building. There they chilled us with an unfriendly reception.

"Where were you all this time?" the Kapo growled. He sounded as if he was accusing us of not having come to Auschwitz sooner. Next the clerk checked to see if we were all there. He was tall, about two meters, skinny and bowlegged. He wore a red triangle with a capital *P,* which made him a political prisoner from Poland. His tattooed number was a little over 100000. One of his ears curled upward, and the other looked as if it was folded back. Of the three assistants to the Kapo in that block, he turned out to be the friendliest and the most decent.

In a hoarse, quivering voice, he encouraged us to be hopeful. "You will probably be sent to an Aussenlager [subcamp], of which there are thirty-nine here in a forty-kilometer radius." After two weeks, barring any problems, he said, we could expect to be sent out to work.

The Kapo, however, was different. When he began to speak, he demonstrated how, in Auschwitz, men became more aggressive than animals. He looked well-nourished. He laid down the rules. "Anyone who leaves this block will receive ten lashes. If anyone brings food in the barracks, ten lashes. If you leave your bunk unmade, ten lashes. Missing at a roll call, ten lashes. Stealing, twenty lashes." By the end of his tirade, we were numb with rules.

As noon neared, it was time to fetch food, and he allowed us to go into the rooms. Our pants were still loose. If we couldn't find something to keep them up, we knew we would get scolded by the Kapo. Luckily Josek had found a bit of string. Once we were in the barracks we quickly secured three adjacent bunks. For the first time since we became camp inmates, we were in a vermin-free block.

In both Steineck and Gutenbrunn we got our rations regularly. Here, however, even though we received soup morning and night, we got bread sporadically. Since no one could venture beyond the block, stealing was out of the question. Even Mendele, who had nearly always found ways to circumvent the system, had trouble. When the block orderly arrived with vats of soup, we each received two ladles of boiled water with bits of potatoes and an overcooked turnip in it. We had no spoons and had to drink from the bowl.

The roll call could last hours. One Sunday, just before noon, I heard my name being called. I didn't recognize who it was. I wondered how anyone would know my name. When I came to the door, I saw a Kapo. I didn't know why he was looking for me. After confirming that I was Bronek Jakubowicz and from Gutenbrunn, he said there was a girl outside who had asked him if he knew a Bronek Jakubowicz. After he described her briefly, I knew it could only be Zosia.

He said he had advised her to leave, after promising her that he would find me. I was curious to know how the Kapo had found me. "She told me when and from where you came, and I knew, if you were alive, you could only be here in the Quarantine Block," he said. He considered his mission completed and left. Our class distinction was such that it would have been too demeaning for him to stay and socialize with an ordinary inmate who had just come to Auschwitz. How Zosia knew where we had been sent I have never learned. Considering the extraordinarily tight security at Auschwitz, which would have discouraged her from coming back, she must have realized that she could not have met me even if she did return. What came back were my memories of our days together at Steineck and Gutenbrunn.

The Auschwitz veterans looked upon us as greenhorns. They answered all of our questions with questions of their own. When I asked a Kapo's aide where I could wash some of my clothes, he answered, "Where do you think you are, in a sanitorium?"

More people kept coming. We saw tattooed numbers upward of 150000. That meant that almost ten thousand people had been brought here since we had come. According to the normal pattern, only 25 percent actually passed into the camp. That meant that in the two weeks since we arrived, more than forty thousand people had been transported to Auschwitz. I wondered about the women's camp and the fate of Balcia and all the others.

One day a few civilian Germans, accompanied by SS men, came and looked us over. Our good-worker status, however, was apparently not known to them, and our isolation continued. We heard of Allied forces landing somewhere in Europe. One day late in the afternoon, twelve inmates went past our barracks. Usually inmates inside the camp were escorted by the Kapos, but these men were led by the SS. Their faces exuded fear. One of our room orderlies said that they were being taken to the *Strafbunker* (penalty bunker). "Few survive a long stay there," he said. "And if they do, they're physically and mentally broken for life." The Strafbunker had no light or toilet. It was barely big enough for one person to stand up in. "They would have been better off to have gone to the electric fence," the orderly said.

Another day we heard that there was no further need for inmate workers and we weren't to go anywhere. This was the worst news we could have been told. Being unneeded meant being dispensable. Passing Dr. Mengele's selection was just a temporary reprieve, we thought. We already knew that to remain alive we had to keep working. Being idle beyond a certain point was a threat to our lives. I was no longer optimistic that we would ever leave Auschwitz alive. After the years of living on the edge of existence, we were resigned to whatever fate had in store for us, and we didn't look at our lives in any long-term way.

One day the Kapo kept us outside in the cold rain for more than an hour. When we finally got back into the block, we were dripping wet. We hung our clothes around the room to dry. When the Kapo noticed, he asked us who had had that idea. Since we all did it simultaneously, no one admitted guilt. Then he ordered us to go outside naked and circle the block. As we passed by him standing at the door, he swung his whip at us. Mendele was hit badly, but even though some lashes on his back drew blood, he didn't whimper. I thought this teenager's heart was made of stone. Looking around and seeing the rain dripping off of us, I thought of cattle in a pasture. Here we were treated alike, driven, herded, and even branded like cattle. Later one of the prisoners, Moishe Chernicki, came down with a fever and was taken to the infirmary. No one ever saw or heard from him again.

We had been in this isolation for more than two weeks. The draconian rations barely kept us alive. When the sun didn't shine, the camp was draped in the black of the rising smoke. There had not been a shortage of courage before, but now we were at our lowest point ever. Reality seemed twisted and out of shape. At times we stared into space. Some wandered around the barracks in loneliness. Although we had passed Dr. Mengele's selection, we were destined to flunk life anyway. Suicides, though, were rarely heard of here. Only a few Jewish inmates succumbed in this way. Perhaps our generation's experiences had endowed us with extra ability to endure. The undaunted believers still prayed every day. It amazed me how they still remembered word-for-word the various prayers of shaharith, minhah, and maarib—the morning, afternoon, and evening liturgies.

Then a number of civilians came to the block. They were accompanied by Hauptsturmführer Rudolf Höss, the Kommandant of Auschwitz. The consensus of our block supervisors indicated that they were from I.G. Farben, a large German pharmaceutical company that already employed prisoners in the nearby Buna camp. At Buna, the I.G. Farben Company was making synthetic rubber. There, we were told, the inmate death rate was very high, and they had a continuous need for replacement workers. We believed that it could only be better than our present situation. We just wanted to get out of here.

Finally we got orders that we would leave the camp. A little after five the next morning, we were each given leather shoes with wooden soles to replace our clogs. After roll call we were given a generous portion of bread and were lined up. There were eight hundred of us who would be workers and twenty-five other prisoners, including Richard Grimm, who would take charge of us. We did not know where we were going. Except for Grimm, all the others had low prisoner numbers. The lowest I recall seeing was on Klaus Koch, who became our cook. Coincidentally, an SS man by the same name turned out to be his boss. Most of the workers wore green triangles, the color designated for criminals, but there were also political prisoners and even one homosexual bearing a pink triangle patch.

As we left, Josek and I walked on either side of our father. I looked up and saw the paradoxical Auschwitz sign, "Work makes you free." By leaving Auschwitz, I felt that we had a new lease on life. A large group of people were being led into the camp. They were gypsies, and I had to think of the contradiction, that they, people who so loved their freedom of spirit, were also chained in Auschwitz. I remembered when I was just a boy how I loved to listen to the gypsies' music. They would make the violin cry and laugh at the same time.

While still in grammar school I learned to play the mandolin and had a unique experience with a gypsy girl. She was about twelve, my age, and very beautiful. When she came to the back of our house, where I played my mandolin, she stopped and listened for a while. Then she persuaded me to come with her to their camp, which was not far from our house. At first I felt fearful, because I had been warned that they abducted dark-haired children. But I went with her anyway and later visited her a few more times. In time I came to appreciate our differences. I liked the gypsies' communal, nomadic, exciting lifestyle. By the time they moved away, the gypsy girl and I were in love. About three weeks later she returned and insisted on living with us. It was a dilemma for my parents. Finally, after finding out where her tribe was, Papa bought a railroad ticket for her and sent her back to them.

We continued marching, seventy Croats and twenty German Waffen SS with us. They were mostly *Rottenführer* (privates) and *Unterscharführer* (corporals). Ahead of us walked a statuesque and fearless-looking SS man. He was Hauptscharführer Otto Moll, our future Kommandant. Rumor had it that Moll had played an important role in Auschwitz, where in less than six months he had risen from the rank of sergeant to Hauptscharführer and Kommandant. This meteoric ascension was due to his skill in killing. He had pioneered the dropping of canisters of the poison gas Zyklon B into the phony showers, which he accompanied with his favorite saying, "Laß sie fressen" (Let them eat).

It was the late summer of 1943, and to have escaped the Quarantine Block at Auschwitz alive was a metaphor for freedom. Our fate, we thought, had changed. We had been close to being pushed off the cliff, and now we had a new lease on life. I felt resentful as we passed people who were still allowed a near-normal life. I wished I had not been born a Jew. I struggled in my wooden-soled shoes as we walked. It was noon, the sun was high, and we had just passed by a little town called Lędziny. We were ordered off the road and told to sit on the ground. There was an eerie sensation. The grass felt scorched, dead, as if just after a famine. Anyone lucky to have bread left finished it, and soon we continued our trek to the north, coming by another camp, Günthergrube. A few kilometers farther on, we came to the village of Piast. Not too far from there, visible from the road, was another camp with a strange name, Janina. In Polish this was a popular girl's name. One kilometer farther, across the road, were two more camps. One was Ostland, which housed Polish and Russian women. The second camp was Lager Nord, which had Russian war prisoners. Next we came to a place called Wesola, which means "happy" in Polish. This seemed to be a camp territory. Five kilometers farther was yet another camp. Most prisoners here worked for I.G. Farben. Finally we came to Fürstengrube, or "Noble Mine." This was to be our new home. We were only about sixteen kilometers from Auschwitz I.

FÜRSTENGRUBE

Above the gate was a sign: "Fürstengrube." Below it was a German miner's salute, "Glückauf." Fürstengrube was a subcamp of Buna, Auschwitz III. On one side the land was dotted with gnarled trees, brush, and partially dried weeds. The camp was rectangular with single-story barracks, which, unlike those in the main camp in Auschwitz, were newly constructed. The windows and doors faced the yard. In the farthest corner, squeezed between two barracks, stood two cement-slab buildings. The entire camp was surrounded by a brick wall and a mesh fence with barbed wire on top. Brick towers stood at the corners of the yard. Our entrance into Fürstengrube was not as tumultuous as our arrivals had been at the three prior camps.

Inside, the yard was still full of construction debris. We were marched to the center of the yard, arranged in a square, and made to face the Hauptscharführer and his entourage in the middle. The guards had already taken up their positions in the towers and at the gate. A roll call count confirmed that the same number had arrived that had left the main camp. Grimm ordered us to follow the Blockführers to the barracks. Before we left, Grimm reminded us to come back as soon as we were assigned to blocks and bunks.

Each barracks consisted of one room. Inside, there were five rows of three-level bunks with narrow passages between. On the bunks lay straw-filled pallets, pillows, and burlap blankets. This was home for about 140 of us. As we returned to the yard, the sun was setting. Once we were in place, Moll instructed us. "I am your Lagerführer here. Those who are willing to work hard will be safe." Then he pointed at the SS men behind him. "Raportführer Anton Lukoschek," he said, "is my assistant." Under him, he explained, were Arbeitsdienstführer Schwiętny and Blockführer Pfeiffer. Then came SS-Rottenführer Adolph Voigt, who, he said, would be in charge of the KB. Lastly, he pointed at Klaus Koch, who was to be in charge of the kitchen.

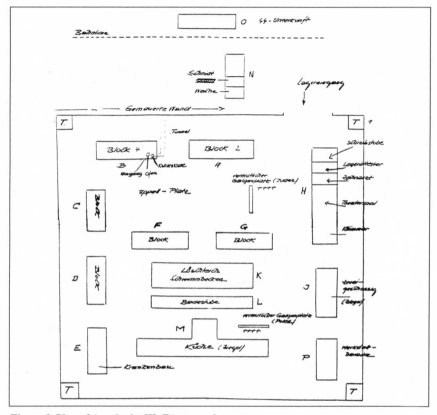

Figure 1. Plan of Auschwitz III, Fürstengrube
A–D, F, G: Barracks for inmates
E: First aid and infirmary
H: Camp offices, camp elder's quarters, dental station, theater, and penalty room
J: Practice area for shooting
K: Reservoir for fighting fires
L: Showers and washrooms
M: SS and inmates' kitchen; at right, the Polish gallows
N: Quarters for kommandant and his subordinates
O: SS quarters and railroad tracks
P: Workshops for inmate workmen: carpenters, handymen, tailors, shoemakers, and barbers
T: SS guard watch towers
The broken line between Blocks A and B shows the ill-fated escape tunnel dug by Kapos. To its right, the Jewish inmate gallows.

Source: Drawn May 11, 1965, by former camp elder Herman Josef. Translation here by Benjamin Jacobs.

Although Moll was about forty-five, weighed about 120 kilos, and was of only average height, which was odd for an SS man, he carried himself well. With his broad shoulders and muscular body, he looked youthful. His straight blond hair was cut short. In his chiseled face were set a pair of cold blue eyes. Only one of them was real, for he had lost the other fighting in France. When he spoke, only the live eye shifted. There seemed to be no real feeling in the heart beating beneath his bulging chest. All in all, in his tight uniform and knee-high boots, he looked like a Prussian warrior or the perfect Nazi poster boy. Moll announced that Richard Grimm would again be our Lagerältester and then left.

The Kapos were usually one ruling clique, but that by no means ensured a safety net for them. Even a Lagerältester might find himself out of power, as Kurt Goldberg did in Gutenbrunn. There were Kapo Michael, Kapo August, Kapo Karl, Kapo Hermann, Kapo Wilhelm, Kapo Olschewski, Kapo Jurkowicz, and others. Although they didn't like to see Grimm, a newcomer, take charge of them, they kept quiet at first. Grimm had a quiet discussion with them, and then he turned to us.

"Here we will be working in a coal mine called Fürstengrube," he said. Then he pointed at the Kapos standing behind him. "They will be taking you to and from the mine. Each block will also have a Blockkapo." Grimm then appointed Goldstein, the former first aid attendant at Steineck, to be our barber. Two more inmates were to repair shoes, two more would work as tailors, and six others would be carpenters in camp. They were to help with the remaining construction of the camp, under Kapo Josef Hermann. Though there were many medical doctors in our ranks, including Seidel from Gutenbrunn, a new doctor named Lubicz, who came with the Kapos, was assigned to the KB. The rest of us were divided into three groups, each of which would work eight-hour shifts in the mine. One shift lasted from 6:00 A.M. until 2:00 P.M. The second ran from 2:00 until 10:00 P.M., and the third began at 10:00 P.M. and ended at 6:00 A.M. Our only chance for survival seemed to lie in our being valuable to the Third Reich's war machine.

Kapo Hermann wore a red triangle without yellow corners, which marked him as a political non-Jewish prisoner. Nathan Green became the Blockkapo in Block 4, to which Papa, Josek, and I were assigned. He was the only Jewish criminal I had seen in Auschwitz and came from nearby Katowice. What crimes he had been convicted of I never learned. Green was tall, trim, and handsome. Like other Kapos, he wore better prison clothes, which distinguished him from common inmates. In this topsy-turvy world, being a criminal was not a stigma. In fact, criminals thrived in Auschwitz, because they did whatever the Nazis ordered them to do. Green's prison number was around 70000, which meant that he had been in Auschwitz for at least a year and a half. It was demeaning, being ruled by the lowest element of society.

Nothing ever escaped Green's shifty gray eyes. He systematically skimmed rations from us, not only for himself but also for his friends. Papa, Josek, and I worked the early shift, leaving camp at five in the morning. That was the most preferred shift, but unfortunately we were rotated weekly. The night shift allowed us little time to rest, because of the day's barracks activities.

On the first morning of work, Richard Grimm and Kommandant Moll arrived when it was still dark. "Raus, raus, alle raus, eintreten, schnell!" Grimm bellowed. Nathan Green yelled, "Alle aufstehen!" We were given normal rations again and miners' overalls and lamps. At five thirty Scharführer Pfeiffer, assisted by Kapo Michael Puka, marched us out of the camp. Kapo Puka, a German criminal, turned out to be cold-blooded and sadistic. As a long-time inmate, one of the first fifteen thousand, Puka enjoyed a certain status in the camp. Though only 1.7 meters tall, he nevertheless was the most fearsome of all Kapos. He spoke to us only to curse us. His insults he accompanied with grinding teeth. "Scheiss Juden" was his mildest abuse of a Jewish inmate. He was cynical and quick to ridicule.

About two hundred of us were under Puka's command. After leaving the camp, we passed a cemetery. The gravestones inside were surrounded by withering weeds. Some stones were toppled and sunken. Two and a half kilometers further on, we came to a hut with a slanted roof. At first it did not look like a mine, but when several men in overalls with lights and lunch boxes in hand came out, we knew we were there.

In prewar Poland, this was known as the Harceska Mine, and it had been inoperative for over twenty years. Rubber was crucial to the German I.G. Farben Company. In order to manufacture synthetic rubber, coal was needed. When the Germans occupied this area in 1939, they reopened the mine and renamed it Fürstengrube. Günthergrube, not far away, had a similar history. It had been renamed in honor of Günther Falkenhahn, the I.G. Farben director there.

The first thirty men, including Josek, Papa, and me, descended into the mine on a hand-operated elevator. We could smell the coal. I knew that miners worked hard and always faced danger. I respected the danger and did not know what to expect. None of us had ever seen or ever been inside a mine. When the elevator stopped and the doors opened, a thick coal fume greeted us. The air lacked oxygen and was full of coal dust. We could hardly see ahead of us. Before long our eyes adjusted, and we saw a long tunnel with a rail track and carts in the middle. One foreman took my father and me, and another led the rest of the group down the track. We followed our foreman into a cave. There lay coal lumps weighing from a few grams to fourteen kilos. Some were still lodged in the cave walls. "This cave was just blasted yesterday," said the foreman, as he handed us shovels and buckets. Our job was to fill the buckets and load the coal onto the carts.

The cave was barely big enough for both of us to fit into. The only light we had came from our lamps. We began working, on our knees with our heads bent. The smell of the coal made us dizzy. At midday a couple of inmates brought down buckets of soup—the usual turnip and water and, if we were lucky, a potato. Then we saw Josek again. He told us that he and two others moved the filled carts to the end of the mine, where a locomotive pulled them further. By then we were all weary and tired, and as black as chimney sweeps. Coal dust had settled in our mouths and noses and had covered our skin. Kapos Puka and Pfeiffer were waiting as we came up at two o'clock. "One, two, three," Puka yelled, demanding that we march back to camp. When we neared the camp, he created a real charade: "Mützen ab! Mützen auf!" (Caps on! Caps off!), he shouted. That day, in order to ingratiate himself with Pfeiffer, he beat up an inmate without reason or provocation.

Soup once a day, a little bread, and coffee twice a day was not enough nourishment to prevent the further deterioration of our health. Zosia, Stasia, and all those kind souls who had helped us in the past were far away, so hard times continued. After a week or two our arms hurt from lifting the heavy shovels. Lugging the coal lumps by hand to the carts was even more difficult, and our hands were now calloused and cracked. The coal dust gradually baked into our skins, and the fat-free soap we used could not wash it off. My eyelids looked as if they were coated with mascara. Papa and Josek didn't look any better. It won't be long before all of us are black Mussulmen, I thought.

Most *Schachtmeisters* (foremen) here were Poles. But there were also some Germans and Volksdeutsche. Most started out as reasonable and decent people, but in time they adopted the Kapo tactics and resorted to abuse and beating. We soon discovered that Hauptscharführer Moll regarded the physical punishment of inmates as his privilege. He disliked being upstaged by others. One day when Moll learned that an inmate had been beaten and disabled from work by a foreman, he ordered the foremen to stop punishing inmates and instead to report inmates' offenses to the camp. One day an inmate gave his foreman a letter to mail, as he had done many times before. This time, however, the foreman reported it to Kapo Puka. Puka in turn told Pfeiffer about it, and Pfeiffer then ordered the prisoner punished upon his return to the camp. From then on, no one dared to send out a letter.

At the beginning of December 1943 the first snow fell. Winter was coming. Our difficulties increased as the cold took its toll. At least one inmate per day was unable to make it back from work on his own. One day Papa was fortunate to be given an extra portion of bread. He kept it all day long to share with his sons in the evening. That was a day of reprieve for us: we got our first extra food since leaving Gutenbrunn.

At the end of a day's work I could hardly straighten my hands. My knuckles were bruised and oozed blood. In the meantime, our camp kept growing. Two more medical doctors were added to the KB, and Dr. Seidel finally got his old job back.

Josef Hermann's Sonderkommandos built two more barracks and an addition to the KB and also sectioned off space in Barracks 7 as an inmate penal room. Hermann, the architect, always kept his distance from the rest of the Jewish inmates. Yet he did not act like the ordinary Kapos did, often not wearing his Kapo armband. Another individual, Willy Engel, the Lagerschreiber, slowly gained importance in camp. He kept the camp's records and handled the SS men's mail. Hermann was from Nuremberg, and Willy from Prague. Willy had come to Fürstengrube with his identical twin brother a month before. Sometimes it was hard to tell them apart. Willy had a degree in accounting from Prague University, where Viky, his brother, had been a chemistry student. Willy was clear-headed and reasonable, and Viky was a bit cynical. I got to know them both and liked them. Because all mail came to the office, where Willy worked, he monitored matters concerning us. Like most camp functionaries, he received "Kapo rations" and so could help his brother, who worked in my shift in the mine.

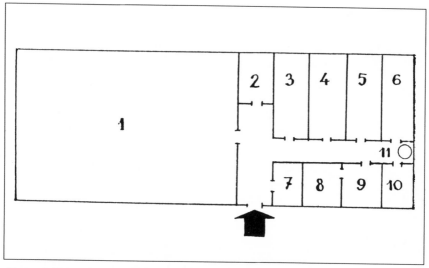

Figure 2. Plan of Inmate Infirmary at Fürstengrube
  1: Common hall, with three-tier bunks
  2: Living quarters for Dr. Lubicz and his assistants
  3: Office
  4: Room for patients with infectious diseases
  5: Room for the seriously ill
  6: Food storage
  7: Living quarters for block elder and nurses
8–9: Operating rooms
  10: Washing and toilet facilities
  11: Stove for heating water
Josef Jorkowski, a Pole, was the block elder. Caring for the ill were also Jablonski, a Polish Jew from Wroclaw, and Teintuch, from Lodz. The dental station was run by inmate #141129, Bronek Jakubowicz.

Source: 1975 drawing from Tadeusz Iwaszko, *Hefte von Auschwitz* 16 (Auschwitz: Verlag Staatliches Auschwitz-Museum, 1978): 41. Translation here by Benjamin Jacobs.

It is important to mention that an inmate could not make a complaint about a Kapo, regardless of what the Kapo did. Thus the dishonest Kapos went on cheating their charges with impunity. They had cigarettes, vodka, and real leather shoes. Some had separate rooms with furniture—even real beds. Block-kapo Michael Eschmann's room was the best example. The walls, alternately, were painted blue, strawberry red, canary yellow, and kelly green. The ceiling was purple, and the floor was a high-gloss pink. The room looked so perverse that I have never forgotten its appearance.

Srulek Lipshitz, a Jewish inmate who knew about electronics sometimes repaired radios for the SS and on those occasions heard BBC newscasts. Unlike the gossip that we heard otherwise, his bits of news were valuable. He reported that the Allies were on the assault. Everything he told us made us feel as if the arms of the Allied forces were reaching out to us. But there was also fear that the Nazis' enmity toward us was so virulent that the Allies' advance might hasten our deaths. We had real doubts that the Nazis would ever let us go. One day Srulek overheard two SS men discussing a Jewish woman who had shot a guard before going into the gas chamber. We later heard about it from other inmates as well.

We were in a constant state of hunger. Sometimes I closed my eyes just to invite a vision of food. My strength was slipping. There was not much flesh or muscle left on my body. Each day I feared the next. Papa and Josek had also deteriorated. My father had once weighed ninety-one kilos, and now he was just half that. How long could we hold on? Hope seemed to be drifting away.

| 14 |

THE DENTIST OF AUSCHWITZ

I usually waited until just before curfew before going to wash up. Then I didn't have to jockey to find a spout. One evening as I undressed, Richard Grimm came in, purely by chance. In Gutenbrunn we had been close: I was the dentist, and he had seen me every day. But it was different here. I was just an ordinary mine worker, and he was the Lagerältester.

When I turned around to face him, he looked at me in a strange way. "I meant to find you," he said. "The Hauptscharführer wants to install a dental station here." He continued, worried, "Look at you. You look like a Mussulman. You are in no shape to be a dentist."

I knew he was right. By then there were many dentists in Fürstengrube who were better trained than I. "Richard," I pleaded with him as he kept scrutinizing me, "if he gives me a chance, I assure you I can do it." He made no promises, but after giving me a long and hopeful look, he said he would try.

The December cold was most apparent in the mornings during roll call. One day, just as the tally of our group was completed and the number of the sick was read to Moll, Grimm yelled, "Gutenbrunn dentist! Report to the Hauptscharführer immediately!"

My heart began pounding. Could it be? I asked myself as I ran toward them with a vigor I did not know I still possessed. I stopped two meters in front of them as I was required to do, and then I staggered and almost fell. "Herr Hauptscharführer, Häftling 141129 meldet sich gehorsamst zu ihrem Befehl." (Lieutenant, prisoner 141129 obediently reports to your order.)

I was frightened. It was the first time I had seen Moll up close. He sized me up with his one cold, critical eye. Moll never addressed inmates in the first person. "Bleiben Sie stehen," he said. I stepped to one side of him, uncomfortable, with all the inmates staring at me. It took twenty minutes for the Kommandos to leave. Then Richard Grimm spoke. "This man was our dentist in Gutenbrunn, as I had mentioned to you, Herr Hauptscharführer." I followed what he said very closely, and I observed Moll's reaction, for in his response lay my hopes.

"Let me see your hands," the Kommandant said. I stretched out my arms, palms up. "My God! How can you be a dentist with these lacerated hands? Look, Grimm! Let him stay in camp until his hands heal," Moll said. I stared in disbelief as Moll's one eye stared back at me. I would not forget the human, almost tender way in which he spoke. Just when I was nearly ready to give up, this Nazi came to my rescue.

Grimm walked Moll to the gate, and when he returned, he said that Moll had ordered a dental station built in Block 7, the office barracks near the camp entrance. He wanted me to let him know when it was ready. Moll had also ordered that extra rations be given to me. This had far-reaching consequences for my father and brother. From that day on, I could share my extras with them. I began to recover quickly, as did my hands.

Any idle inmate in camp drew the Kapos' attention and their ire. In spite of what the Kommandant had ordered, they had little tolerance for an inmate not at work. I remembered the camp code: Working is the best recipe for not dying. I was unwilling to jeopardize my chances, so I volunteered to work in the first aid room, as I had done in Gutenbrunn. The KB had sixty beds.

The first time I met Oberkapo Josef Hermann was when he started building the dental station. He also built a workbench for me and seats in the waiting room. The Sanitätsdienstgefreiter, called SDG, was a low-ranked Waffen SS man with minimal first aid training. He supervised the KB and the dental station. His rank was Unterscharführer, and his name was Adolf Voigt. He was ambivalent about his duties. He came to the first aid room, looked around, and left.

Even the worst, most menial job in camp could make the difference between life and death. Because of that, many prisoners were anxious to take any camp job, even if it meant helping the Nazis. Fortunately the camp dentist did not have the same dilemma.

Josef Hermann had the dental station ready in a few days. I was given an elite camp suit, a sweater, and a pair of real leather shoes, which distinguished me from the Kommando inmates. I also continued to receive kitchen privileges. I stopped being the dumb inmate and no longer needed to fear the Kapos or the foremen. Even Kapo Puka showed me new respect. Although the station was ready, I had no equipment. Moll wasn't someone I dared to ask for equipment. I asked Grimm, and he told me that it would be coming the next day. About two thirty in the afternoon Moll rode into camp on his motorcycle with an ambulance following. He ordered the driver, an SS man, to help me unload the truck. I could not believe what I saw. Not only did they bring the most up-to-date dental equipment, instruments, and supplies, but also a complete dental laboratory.

When my brother returned from the mine, he came to help me set up an electric adjustable chair, complete with drill and overhead light. Some of the instruments looked brand-new. Among the supplies were a few ampoules of novocaine, and even textbooks and dental manuals and a patient appointment book with the name Dr. Władzimież Kamienski. Immediately I plunged into reading the manuals. As Grimm later told me, Moll had gone to nearby Sosnowiec and confiscated the equipment from a Polish dentist.

The next day during the roll call, Grimm announced the new dental station. "But you can't skip work to see the dentist," he said.

My function was only to extract teeth. Since I did not have enough novocaine, I economized, using one two-cc ampoule for two or more extractions. I also filled the cavities with silicone or phosphate cement. The inmates' main problem was bleeding gums, a result of vitamin deficiency and the complete absence of toothbrushes and dentifrice. Dabbing the gums with iodine only offered temporary relief.

Adjoining the dental station was the camp office, where Willy Engel worked. To the other side was a penal room, separated from the dental station by a thin plywood wall. I could hear shrieks when inmates were brutalized. A few days later Willy said a hanging was about to happen in Fürstengrube. I had not expected to witness any more hangings. Though hanging wasn't new to me, seeing it happen never ceased to be a numbing experience. I knew that the SS had many other ways to kill us in Auschwitz.

It was the end of December 1943, and it had become clear that the Nazis were losing the war. We expected a change in their treatment of us. One day, as the men on the day shift began to return, instead of being freed to go about their business, they were marched to the part of the camp where the gallows stood. Then a loud horn ordered all the rest of us to come out. Soon several inmates were brought into the yard. They looked baffled, almost indifferent. "Inmate [number] is guilty of sabotage to the Third Reich and is to die on the gallows," the Gestapo announced. No specific act of sabotage was voiced, for these were the verdicts routinely read before all executions. Killing people for undefined charges seemed to be the most cynical of all their heinous acts.

As the chairs were pulled from under the condemned, the men tried to gasp for air before they choked. Their tongues hung out to the side of their faces. Their eyes were open but not focused. It was the first hanging in Fürstengrube, but we feared that more would come. Following orders, the inmates began to circle the gallows. Dr. Lubicz, Dr. Seidel, Felix, one of the first aid helpers, and I were ordered to remove the bodies and take them to the *Leichenzimmer* (morgue). The faces were swollen, but the bodies were still warm. We had to fight feelings of revulsion as we carried them in a funerallike procession. That night I thought I heard their voices. Had they come back to life?

Since the dental station was near the camp entrance, when SDG Voigt came through the gate, he inspected it first. "Herr Unterscharführer, Häftling 141129 obediently reports to your orders" was how he was expected to be greeted. "Weiter machen," he usually replied. If Voigt still believed in the thousand-year Reich, he didn't seem to show it. He was here, playing his part, I thought, because he preferred this to fighting. He didn't seem to like the formality. It was my duty, however, to act out my part also. He allowed me to set up a bunk in the laboratory and sleep there. I no longer had to line up and attend the daily roll calls.

But gradually Voigt's indifference became obvious to Moll, and he was replaced by Unterscharführer Günther Hinze. While Voigt took his assignment lightly, Hinze was driven by an uncommon zeal for the job. He was a psychopath and a appalling Jew-hater. Hinze was about twenty-three years old. He had reddish straight hair and was severely cross-eyed. A large scar was visible from his hairline down to his left temple. He had an arrogance that I immediately perceived.

When he came into the dental station for the first time, he eyed me coldly. This distorted his face even more. As I continued my laboratory work, he tilted his head and began to criticize everything I was doing. When I said something, he picked my words apart and contradicted me. When he finally left, I was worried. Willy Engel told me that Hinze had been severely wounded in the head on the eastern front. After recovering from surgery, he was allocated a new function, as the SDG at Fürstengrube. The next day Hinze came to inspect the dental station. Since I knew he would pick on me for neatness, I had everything in place. After he opened the door, he cocked his head and looked at me.

Then he drew his white glove across the top of the door frame, looked at it, and said, "It's filthy." It was clear to me that he had just found an excuse to punish me. He ordered me to step onto a chair with my heels over the edge. He then made me do deep knee bends up and down while counting. Occasionally he made me stop at a most painful point, during which he maligned and slandered everything Jewish.

"You know why the Jews are punished?" he asked. "Because they are the cause of the war." I did not say anything. There was no point in my disputing him. I let him throw his trash, hoping that eventually it would end. After half an hour, as he saw that I was getting exhausted, he left. He was my worst nightmare. When I got up in the morning, I knew what to expect. Sometimes I wished he would come and just get it over with. This became such a daily routine that I thought of hiding from him. One day after I had already gone through one of those sessions in the morning, Hinze returned in the afternoon and made me do it all over. He sat near me, clapping rhythmically. After a while I was so exhausted that I only heard his thudding voice ordering me: "Up, down." When I slowed down and said that I couldn't do any more, he countered: "You have it too good here. I can't stand the smell of a Jew." Then he left. I slumped in the chair, depleted of all my strength.

One day, late in the afternoon, an ambulance arrived, and an SS officer came to the station. I had no idea who he was. "Are you the dentist?" he asked.

"Yes, Herr Hauptscharführer," I answered.

He looked around the room first, without a comment. I thought he approved of what he saw. "I am Dr. König. I will be coming here to see the *Mannschaft* [team]," he said pompously. Then he ordered me to prepare weekly reports. He said that he had informed the SS that he would be coming to Fürstengrube on Tuesdays, between four and six. Before he left, he asked me if anything was needed in the station. "Vitamin C and novocaine in any form, Herr Hauptscharführer," I answered him.

On weekdays, when most inmates were out at work, I worked in the KB. On one such day, a chauffeur-driven black Mercedes drove up, and four high-ranking SS officers came in. One of them looked familiar. Their emblems showed they were all medical people. Dr. Lubicz reported the usual: the number of sick in the KB and "all is well." Commenting to one another, they next passed Dr. Seidel, Felix, Boris, and me, as we all stood at attention. After they entered the sick ward and saw the hospitalized prisoners, one asked Dr. Lubicz what was wrong with them. At one point I heard Dr. Lubicz address one man as Dr. Mengele. In that instant I remembered having seen him on the unforgettable morning of our selection. His cool manner and his nonchalant air were unmistakable. Dr. Lubicz told me he knew him from the main camp, where he had once worked. Dr. Mengele, however, acted as if he had never seen him before. Lubicz also knew two of the other three: Dr. Fischer and Dr. Schwartz. As they passed by the bedridden inmates, Mengele asked Lubicz why each was there. Lubicz gave him a brief description of each patient and his illness and also gave an opinion on how soon the inmate could return to work. Mengele, however, made his own conclusions and ordered that the numbers of inmates he chose be recorded. In the end, of the sixty that were in the hospital at the time, twenty-two were on the list. These would be picked up and taken to Auschwitz II, Birkenau. Lubicz tried to save some of them, but his plea did not matter. The verdict for all those on the list was final. Those selected knew what awaited them. One of them said, "I know where I am going," and he twirled his finger up in the air. On the following day they were taken to a certain death. This was the beginning of selections in the camp. From then on, the doctors came to Fürstengrube every week. Mengele often had other doctors with him, most often Fischer, who later came on his own and eventually replaced Mengele. They came only to destroy lives. A German doctor's Hippocratic oath was hypocrisy.

In the meantime, the Allies were increasingly victorious. After the Soviets threw the Germans out of Russia, the British and American troops chased them out of North Africa. Our minds latched on to any news that would spell hope. We had survived this long, and we hoped that we were now living through the final darkness before the dawn. The news reports forecast a quick end to the war. But that hardly made a difference. The Germans still thought they were invincible and continued their cruelties against us. One day an inmate with a bullet wound was brought into camp on a stretcher. I watched as Max Schmidt, an Unterscharführer, bent over him and said, "Es ist vorbei" (He is gone). With this, he shot him twice in the head. He then ordered him taken to the corpse room. Another inmate told me later that when the prisoner had stepped out of line, a guard pulled the trigger that put a bullet into his chest. It may well have been true that there wasn't much anyone could do for the wounded man, but at least Schmidt should have had him brought to the KB to see if a doctor could help him. This was the first time that I saw the usually mild-mannered Schmidt kill someone. It demonstrated to me how little a Jewish life meant to any of them. Max Schmidt was not the usual SS man. He just did not fit the Nazi mold. I thought that he could not take Hitler's rubbish seriously. But evil can have many faces.

Another day Dr. König took an impression to replace the bridge of an SS man. Then he asked me if I had enough dental gold to make a new one. That surprised me. How would I have dental gold? I wondered. I said no.

"Don't you take out the gold teeth from the dead inmates?" he asked. "If you are not doing that, plenty of gold is going to waste."

I looked at him in disbelief. "Oh! Herr Hauptscharführer," I answered, stunned.

"Why don't you?" he said to me, annoyed.

"I didn't know. No one had ordered me," I said in my defense.

"Be sure that from now on you remove all the gold before they are taken to the Stammlager."

I felt revulsion. I did not think that anyone could stoop that low. Killing people was horrible enough, but tearing out teeth of the dead moved me to disgust. I did not think that I could do it. But it was inevitable. I had no choice. "Jawohl, Herr Hauptscharführer," I said, sickened and scared.

As appalled as I was at having to do it, as repulsive as the thought was, I knew that since I was the only dentist in Fürstengrube, I had to do it. It was by far the hardest thing I had to do in any camp. I often asked myself what would have befallen me if I had not complied with this order. I have never stopped wrestling with that question. When I approached the corpse room for the first time I tried to rationalize that what I was about to do was meaningless to the dead. But it never was to me.

Repugnance preceded each of my trips to the morgue. I never lost that feeling when I went to that small room—two and a half by three meters. When I opened the door, the smell of death greeted me. I shivered. Atrophied bodies lay in a mass on the cement floor. They were grotesquely misshapen, with surprise on their faces, as if they did not know why they had to die. I heard the voices of broken hearts and crushed souls. Some were still clothed. I tried to force myself to believe that they were only bodies and never were human. But as hard as I tried, and as much as I pretended not to care, I could not keep myself from trembling. So many emotions ran through me. I was sickened and unable to begin the task I had come to do. I walked out and went around the building several times. When I returned, I forced myself to approach a middle-aged man's body. His half-open eyes stared up at me, as if to accuse me of the crime I was about to commit. As I tried to pry open his mouth, I felt his ice-cold skin. When I finally forced it open, his jawbones cracked, and that frightened me. Following each turn of the mouth opener was a screeching sound. I imagined this was his way of saying "Don't!" to me. I felt as if the dead would rise up to stop me. Each piece of gold I extracted made me think how shocked they must be. Sometimes I had to pretend, in talking to myself, that what I was doing was normal. The tools I used for this grim task I kept in a red box. Why I painted the box red I didn't know. Most inmates who saw me walking to the morgue with it knew what I was doing and didn't consider it unusual. My father and my brother also knew what I was doing, though I never told them. Now I had enough gold for the SS men's bridges and caps. What I didn't use Dr. König took back with him to the main camp.

Suddenly doctors were being sent to the front, and Dr. König told me that he was making his last visit to Fürstengrube. He ordered me to care for the SS men's dental needs, an ironic request considering that Jewish dentists were not allowed to treat Germans outside the camps. The guards who came to me for treatment modified their behavior and often brought me bread, sausages, and cigarettes, while cautioning me not to tell anyone. Of course I did not ask them for anything. Nevertheless their offerings went a long way toward helping me, my father, my brother, and a number of other inmates.

A few weeks after Dr. König left, another dentist came to oversee the dental station. Dr. Schatz was in his midforties, mild-mannered, friendly, and slightly hunched over. When I recited the camp's required litany, he said that I need not say it for him. Nor did he object to my continuing to treat the guards. But one time he came in very upset. He threw his hat on the chair disgustedly and walked through the dental station, his hand clutched behind his back. "Do you know what they made me do?" he said, looking straight at me, disturbed.

My place was not to reply, but since he looked at me and waited, I said, more out of politeness than curiosity, "What, Herr Hauptscharführer?"

He held out the keys to his ambulance and said, "Go and look at the instrument panel. Then you will see what I mean." His vehicle was parked just a couple of steps from the door. I took his keys and went outside. I opened the driver's door and looked at the instrument panel, which had the usual levers: choke, lights, wipers, heater, and so on. Then I noticed a white lever below with the word *Gas* on it. Just below that was an inscription: "Achtung, nur im Betrieb gebrauchen" (Caution, use only when in motion). I knew then what it meant.

A shock went through me. I closed my eyes and stepped back. The souls of my mother and my sister were there. Though I knew that these outrageous vehicles existed, seeing one that looked so innocent evoked a new and intolerable pain. It was evidence of the most inhuman and unusual of crimes. It inflicted new and deep wounds. I stood transfixed a while until I regained my composure. The shock of this incident may be at the heart of this book.

I tried to conceal my outrage when I returned. I thought it would be best not to say that I understood what he meant. Although I thought his disgust was real, I could not allow myself to agree with him openly. "Herr Hauptscharführer, I don't know what you meant," I said.

"Did you notice the sign under a handle that says 'Gas: Use only when in motion'?"

I said that I had but claimed I did not understand. I wanted him to tell me. "I saw that lever, Herr Hauptscharführer, but I thought it was a hand accelerator."

"Don't you know what they are doing to you people?" And without waiting for an answer, he became specific. "By pulling this lever, we kill you people! With this lever the driver can divert the exhaust flow to the passenger section of the vehicle. The carbon monoxide then kills everyone in it. That is what we doctors are ordered to do." I looked at his disturbed face. It showed anger and disgust as he poured out his pent-up emotions. He then proceeded to tell me that a lot of our people had already been victims in that very vehicle.

At first I did not reply. I watched him shake his head in disgust. This encouraged me to tell him about the order of one of his predecessors: to pull the gold teeth from the dead inmates. I hoped he would tell me to stop. Instead of doing so, he replied, "You should see the gold and silver that Kanada gathers every day in Birkenau. There as many as ten inmates are pulling gold teeth from the dead at the gas chamber."

Hearing an SS doctor being that explicit about their crimes came as a great surprise to me. As he continued blasting the Führer, I still pretended to have no opinion about it, although I had lots of questions for him. What puzzled me was why a decent human being like he seemed to be would submit to the Nazis. "Dr. Schatz, was it right to see human beings trampled, just because they are different? Some, no doubt, were your friends and neighbors. Was it OK, Dr.

Schatz, to see people disinherited, so that yours would benefit? Did you approve of all this while you were winning the war? You must have known that you were placing your trust in an unscrupulous man. Did you condone Hitler's ideas at first? Did you not think that eventually there would be a price to pay?"

Although his confessions were frank and he had renounced the Führer, he still bore the disgrace of being an SS man. I liked what he said and looked forward to his weekly stops. From that day on he acted as if we were equal. I often thought that people like Dr. Schatz would bring the Nazi regime to its knees. As we know now, that did not happen. Hitler was not defeated from within. In spite of what Hitler had done, the German people continued to approve of him even when he was not victorious.

I was tempted to tell Dr. Schatz how SDG Hinze tortured me, but I knew he could not help. One day Schatz instructed me not to make dental appointments for him with the SS men. "I don't want to see them," he said as he left. From then on he came only occasionally to Fürstengrube.

One day Hauptscharführer Moll came into the station and asked me when Schatz was expected back. I told him Schatz stopped by only occasionally and that I had been caring for the dental needs of the guards. I feared his reaction, but he surprised me by saying that he might visit me someday. "I may need you to look at my teeth." He too didn't object to being treated by a Jewish prisoner. In the next few days Moll passed by the dental station several times. He must have had second thoughts. One afternoon, though, I heard his boots behind me, and there he stood. An inmate in the chair jumped up and slid past him, out the door.

"Herr Hauptscharführer, inmate 141129 reports obediently to your orders," I said.

"Will you take a look at my teeth, dentist? I think I have a cavity in one of them," he replied.

"Please sit in the chair, Herr Hauptscharführer," I said, pointing to it.

He unbuckled his belt, took off his hat, and laid both on the stool. The human skull and crossbones on his SS badge stared at me. Then, when I moved to the side where his glass eye was, he reached for his revolver and pointed it at my chest. "Don't try anything stupid, dentist," he said, half jokingly. My heart pounded. Knowing Moll's unpredictable temper, I was very uncomfortable.

"Herr Hauptscharführer," I said as I brushed his pistol aside, "you don't need to be concerned. The pistol is only in our way." He smiled awkwardly and put it back in the holster. I saw considerable decay on the lingual side of his upper right molar. The cavity was not very deep, though. I removed the diseased dentine, then cleaned and closed up the space with a phosphate cement. By then his mood had changed, and he was relaxed. That day I discovered the other Otto Moll. Unfortunately, this one made rather rare appearances.

"Dentist, I have heard that your father and brother are also here?" Moll asked.

"Yes, Herr Hauptscharführer."

"Why didn't you tell me that? Where do they work?"

"My father works at construction, with Kapo Hermann, and my brother is working in the coal mine," I said. "Herr Hauptscharführer," I added, "many fathers and sons are here. I didn't know that this mattered."

Then he asked me how old my father was.

"Forty-nine, Herr Hauptscharführer."

"Isn't construction work too hard for your father? Wouldn't he be better off doing something in the camp? Where would you like to see him working?"

"Home, where we all belong," was the reply that flashed instantly through my mind, but of course I didn't say that to him. He surprised me to no end. I had not expected to hear this from the wicked Otto Moll. I looked him in the eye. Was this a genuine offer? It sounded like compensation for my service. I paused and thought about which job would be best for Papa. Then it occurred to me: barracks orderly. "My father would make a good Stubendienst, Herr Lagerführer," I said enthusiastically.

"Good. Then it's settled. Tell Grimm to give your father a job as a Stubendienst. And your brother," he said, "can work in the KB." With that he buckled his belt, took his hat, and left.

In the past two months I had often thought of finding a way to ease my father's load. But here, asking for help had usually brought the opposite result. It was taken as an attempt to dodge work. I told Grimm about my conversation with Moll. Papa was assigned to Kapo Nathan Green's block, where the three of us had first slept, and my brother went to work in the KB. Dr. Lubicz, who always needed more help in the KB, appreciated my brother's work. Josek stayed there until we were evacuated from Fürstengrube in January 1945.

By the end of 1943 more inmates were brought to Fürstengrube, from Holland, Belgium, Morocco, and Norway. Those who spoke, or at least understood, German or Yiddish were able to follow the Kapos' orders in German. A Dutch boy, only fourteen years old, named Kopelmann, told me that he and his family were arrested because a Jewish spy was roaming the streets of Antwerp pointing Jews out to the Nazis. His family was told that they were being resettled in Poland. Because someone at their selection had liked his freckled face, he had been separated from his family and transferred to Fürstengrube. Whereas most of those who arrived with him soon became Mussulmen, Kopelmann did all right.

Fürstengrube had a mélange of Jews. The French Jews didn't like the Belgians, the Belgians didn't like the Dutch, the Dutch didn't like the Germans, and no one liked the Polish Jews. The Russians didn't even count. And as for any cooperation between Jews and non-Jews who shared the same fate, that did not exist.

The biggest priority to our oppressors in Fürstengrube was mining coal and delivering it to Buna, where it was used to make synthetic rubber. To increase production, they brought inmate specialists from our governing camp, Buna. And there were more SS men. One guard told me how he had been made a guard. He was in the army, but one day his army papers, he claimed, were replaced with those of a member of the Waffen SS. He was sent to our camp.

A former POW, a Russian by the name of Boris, whom I got to know well, told me he planned to escape. I warned him against it, but he steadfastly maintained he would find a sure way out. One Sunday afternoon Boris, counting on the laxity of our guards during the ordered bed rest, climbed up the wall and jumped to the other side. Shortly thereafter the sirens rang, and in the yard lay Boris's body on display.

On Christmas night 1943, I awoke to blowing whistles. I looked out the window and saw inmates rushing out of the barracks and into the yard. In their midst was Lagerführer Moll, Unterscharführer Schmidt, Pfeiffer, Schwientny, all the Stubenältesters and the Kapos. A recent snowfall added light to the dark yard. First, all the block elders had their prisoners count off. Then they had them rush back to the blocks, just in time to drive them out again.

I didn't know what it meant. Suddenly I saw Moll burst into the camp and begin shooting. I heard three rounds of gunshots and a loud echo. I felt cramps within me, as if I had been hit. There was turmoil outside. When I looked out again, the inmates were rushing back to the barracks. Then I saw bodies and blood-spattered snow. One of the injured inmates was trying to get up, but he staggered and fell. Other wounded men were begging for help. The macabre scene resembled a dance of the dead.

What I saw that night overshadowed all previous cruelties that I had seen. I could not bear looking out any longer. I was on the verge of breaking down. I covered my eyes, believing that my father or my brother might be out there. I felt a deep shame that my circumstances had separated me from those whose fate I shared. I learned later from Grimm that Moll had been drinking that night, and when he heard that one of our inmates had escaped, he was furious and became uncontrollable. He ordered all inmates to the yard and released a salvo of machine-gun fire into the rows of prisoners. Had it not been for Unterscharführer Schmidt, who stopped him, the massacre would have been even greater, Grimm said. The escaped inmate who enraged Moll was Gabriel Ratkopf. For his act nineteen inmates were killed that night. They suffered and died alone, since Moll forbade any help. I knew one of the murdered, Max Glazer, who was shot in the stomach. Before the war he taught German at Prague University. This incident also prompted Otto Moll to demote Richard Grimm. He brought a new Kapo from the main camp, Otto Breiten, to became Fürstengrube's new Lagerältester.

To increase the mine's productivity further, I.G. Farben introduced bonus points, which could be redeemed at an I.G. Farben stand. Jewish workers, however, were limited to a maximum of four points, which got them very little. Nonetheless, the Kapos were pleased, since they got most bonuses and could use them to enjoy the company of the Nazi-coerced prostitutes in Birkenau.

With a new transport of Jews from Austria came many talented actors from a well-known Vienna theater as well as the conductor of the Vienna State Opera, Harry Spitz, and the nephew of the popular opera singer, Richard Tauber. This undoubtedly gave Moll the idea to create an orchestra in Fürstengrube, and beginning in February 1944 our inmates went to and returned from work to the sound of German marching music. Mr. Spitz's past was shrouded in mystery. Some who knew him from Vienna claimed that he had once been married to Erna Sack, a famous German soprano. The story was that she had divorced him because of the Nazi racial laws. Staying married to a Jew would have ended her career. But Harry never spoke about it. Soon after they arrived, in an attempt to inject some light into an otherwise bleak existence, Spitz organized stage performances of Strauss, Lehár, and Kálmán operettas. The Germans liked that. A stage was constructed in the SS mess hall, and the first rows were reserved for the SS and I.G. Farben personnel. The Kapos followed, and behind them were seats for inmates. Even the sick attended. The Germans were fascinated by Tauber's tenor voice, and he was exempted from working in the mines.

One sunny day in February we saw the first Allied bomber fly over Fürstengrube. Two planes appeared, swooped down, and made a pass over us. We believed that they could distinguish who we were. We were ready to pay our price to see this nightmare end. We looked up to the sky, believing that they would drop their bombs on the camp on the next approach. To our regret they did not. We continued to be mired in our fate.

Otto Moll came to the dental station and asked me if I could make jewelry. I told him that my skills fell short of jewelry making, but I thought that there surely must be a jeweler in camp. The following day, I found an inmate, Simche Laufer, who, I was told, was an extraordinarily good jeweler. Moll relieved him of his job, and he began to work in the dental laboratory. With the limited number of jewelry tools I had, Simche blended down the twenty-two-carat dental gold from dead inmates' teeth into eighteen-carat jewelry gold. After hammering and chipping away at it, he created elegant pins, rings, brooches, and whatever else Moll ordered him to make. He also made Moll a pair of stunning gold cuff links. Simche's reward was an extra soup ration per day.

While the Nazis must have realized they would lose the war, Fürstengrube kept growing. A new barracks was finished. It was the end of February, and though the sun shone, it failed to warm us. The winds picked up the snow from the rooftops and blew it around into clouds. At night I could hear the wind whine and drive snow through the poorly joined wallboards.

SDG Hinze still stopped most mornings to continue his cruel routine with me, which had become an obsession with him. I heard about an instance at the construction site, where a guard had thrown away a half-smoked cigarette to provoke an inmate to pick it up. Tempted and little suspecting the outcome, one of the inmates reached for it and was riddled with the guard's bullets.

The lack of mine safety resulted in many inmate injuries. One afternoon an inmate from Dortmund, Germany, named Erich Wiltzig came to the dental station. He had been struck by a lump of coal at work. I looked at his bruised face, and when he moved his jaw, I saw that he had a fracture of the mandibular bone. I spoke with Dr. Lubicz, and he placed Erich in sick bay for two weeks—the longest time permitted. It actually took three times that long for his jaw to heal. Later, after he went back to work, he was brought back to camp dead. He had been labeled a work shirker, and a guard had shot him in another staged incident.

Winters posed greater threats to our survival, but the winter of 1944 was particularly cruel. The inmates returning from work were frozen stiff. Their coats looked like sheets of metal. For most of us, this was the third winter of captivity. It seemed that we were running out of the tenacity necessary to survive.

One day Willy Engel told me that a number of people from the International Red Cross were expected to come on Sunday to inspect the conditions in Fürstengrube. That Sunday we received a real meal: boiled potatoes, vegetables, and a slice of pork meat. Shortly thereafter, a group of distinguished civilians accompanied by Moll and the newly upgraded Scharführer Schmidt came in. Among them was also the Obersturmbannführer and Kommandant of Auschwitz I, Rudolf Höss. First they went into Willy's office. Next they came to my dental station. I heard Moll say this was a perfect example of the many kinds of health care they provided for us in Fürstengrube. I listened and wondered why not one of them asked me a thing. But what if they did? Could I tell them the truth? Dr. Lubicz said that the same thing had happened to him.

We heard stories about Polish partisans operating nearby. Our Polish inmates had been contacted by them, we were told, but they never contacted the Jews.

In May 1944 a new transport arrived. Among them were a few Norwegian Jews. One was the 1939 heavyweight boxing champ of Norway, named Boot.

Hinze kept up his routine of terror on me every day. Nothing ever softened his attitude. With no end in sight, I asked Dr. Lubicz for advice. Lubicz, I saw, feared him as well. He told me to speak with Josef Hermann, who by then had Moll's ear. But Hermann said that nothing could be done about the mistreatment of a Jewish inmate, and Hinze's streak of arrogance and misuse continued.

One day Blockkapos Maurice and Grimm and three Polish inmates were arrested while digging a tunnel from Maurice's barracks out beyond the fence. They dug the tunnel at night and carried the soil out in blankets. We did not hear how the guards found out. It was rumored that Goldstein, the camp barber, who was to go with them, betrayed them. Some blamed it on Josef Hermann. Anyhow, after they were quizzed about who else was involved and from whom they got the tools, they were sent to the gallows for the attempt to escape and join the partisans. Maurice, an always happy, good-spirited Frenchman, shouted down from the gallows at the Gestapo henchman, "You will pay for that soon!" And then to us, "Good-bye, comrades. Farewell!" Jan, one of the Polish inmates, sang "Jeszcze Polska nie zqinęla," the Polish anthem.

I knew that every morning I had to undergo Hinze's ritual. I walked around like a caged animal until he came. Some days I felt like hiding when I saw him enter the camp. Then he came to the dental station and said to me, "You know what you have to do, dentist. You know the routine." Then he proceeded with the torment. This went on for four incredible months. With no way out, I decided to speak to Otto Breiten.

Breiten said that he would look in when Hinze was there. The next time Hinze came, Otto peeked in discreetly, looking at us through the window. He saw Hinze abusing me and also saw him using dental instruments to clean his fingernails. On the latter point he based his attack. Mistreating an inmate, Breiten thought, was an SS man's privilege, but sabotage of German property was a crime. He told me that he would talk to Moll. "Of course," he added, cautioning me, "You will have to tell all this to Moll, in Hinze's presence." I knew the risk, but I couldn't go on like this any longer. Breiten was certain that the best place to talk to the Hauptscharführer would be in the kitchen, while he ate the lavish meal that Koch prepared for him every day.

It was about twelve-thirty in the afternoon one day when Breiten came to me, urging me to hurry. "Moll is in the kitchen, and he is in a good mood. I told him everything about Hinze, and he wants to see you."

Willy Engel, who also knew about our plan, followed us, anxious about the outcome. "Lay it on him," Willy encouraged me.

As we came into the kitchen, Moll was having sauerbraten for dinner. Moll hardly looked in our direction, as if we weren't there. It wasn't long until Hinze arrived. He sensed something unusual, because in reporting to Moll he seemed uneasy. Moll continued eating as if he did not notice Hinze either. Hinze stood, looking at me and at Breiten, weighing what was going on. Finally the Hauptscharführer, with his mouth still stuffed, said to me, chopping each word, "The Lagerältester tells me that the SDG, Unterscharführer Hinze, often interferes with your work. Is that true?"

I knew what was to follow. I would have to complain to the Kommandant, to one SS man about another. But I knew that I could not back out. I had to go through with it. With butterflies in my stomach, I barely answered him, "Yes, Herr Hauptscharführer."

"Is it true that the Unterscharführer cleans his fingernails with your sterilized instruments?"

"Yes, Herr Hauptscharführer," I answered clearly and continued with the details.

Moll listened intently to everything that I said. He was getting angry. Punishing inmates was his own privilege. Then he turned to Hinze and in a stern voice said, "Is it true what the dentist says? What do you have to say, Unterscharführer?"

Hinze was dumbfounded and stood there silent. He did not seem to grasp the situation or believe what was actually happening. He, a Nazi officer, was being questioned about what he did to a Jewish prisoner? Finally he mumbled that he was not going to answer. That did not sit well with the authoritative Moll. "Ich sehe zu, daß Sie versetzt werden" (I'll see to it that you are transferred), Moll said and dismissed us all.

I still could not trust that Hinze's tyranny had come to an end. "You won't have to fear him much longer," Breiten said. It was more surprising when Hinze came to see me a few hours later. Calmly he said good-bye to me as if we had once been friends. Had it not been for Lagerältester Otto Breiten's courage and, of course, Moll's inflated ego, I would never have been freed of Hinze's misuse. This day was special, one I would not ever forget.

Another time it was announced that German political inmates could volunteer for the German army. Not all were eligible, nor had all the eligible signed up. Otto Breiten did, and Josef Hermann became Fürstengrube's new Lagerältester. Josef Hermann was the son of a Jewish architect. His given name was Hermann Josef, and he came from Ansbach, Bavaria. His mother had converted to Christianity. He was married to a Christian, he said. His father had designed the first low-income housing project in Germany; it was built outside Nuremberg and called Gartenstadt. He came to Auschwitz as a Jew in 1942. When he was sick with typhus, he lay in the main camp's KB, and a doctor friend reversed his first and last names to make him sound Gentile. He was sent with us to Fürstengrube after his recovery. That is how the Jew, Hermann Josef, became the non-Jew, Josef Hermann. As camp elder, his position was precarious. He feared that the Kapos who came with us might know his real name and eventually give him away.

Nearly every week new Jews were delivered from such faraway places as Libya, Morocco, and Algeria. The Germans had arrested them in Vichy France. They were replacing the dwindling number of original inmates. Of the Jews from Dobra who had come with me here, only a few remained alive.

One day Kurt Goldberg came into the dental station. With coal dust baked into his face and his striped jacket hanging on his skeletal body, he was a bare image of the Goldberg I remembered. He was despised by his fellow inmates, who could not forget what he had done at Gutenbrunn. He now showed sensitivity that I thought he never possessed. "I am not here as your patient," he said. What he did in Gutenbrunn still haunted him, but he asked me for no pity. He just came in to unburden his soul. He regretted abandoning his Jewish heritage. Before he left me, he spoke in almost perfect Yiddish. Shunning those he once abused, he was completely resigned to the inevitable. In a sense, I thought, he didn't want to prolong his life. "I know that I deserve what I am getting. I am not going to last here much longer." I offered him some food, but he refused to take it. I had to persuade him to accept. This was the first time that I saw him at peace. He was completely resigned to death. A couple of days later I saw his shift returning. Someone was carried on a stretcher. I knew instantly that it was Goldberg. He was nearly unrecognizable. He was, at the end, a scant image of the man we had once feared.

I saw Boot, the heavyweight boxing champion, in the infirmary with a badly infected leg wound. With his large body and thick muscles, he looked every bit the boxer. The Norwegians were a small group, only five in all at Fürstengrube. They were proud of their country and spoke well of the courageous Norwegians that staved off their deportation for so long. But Boot's name ended up on a weekly selection list, and he was transferred to Birkenau. The irony of his life was that though he had been a winner in the ring, he could not win this bigger bout, and he died from undernourishment and overwork.

Hauptscharführer Moll eventually left Fürstengrube, and Max Schmidt, who had been in officer training school for three months, returned with the rank of Hauptscharführer. He was now the Kommandant. We heard that Moll went to assist in liquidations at camps in the east. Schmidt often came to have his teeth cleaned. He was easy to speak with and, unlike Moll, predictable. At times he had functioned as Lagerführer when Moll was absent.

One morning my brother slept beyond his usual time. When I shook him to wake him up, he pried his eyes open and then fell back to sleep. The next day he was well enough to open his eyes and drink water, but immediately thereafter he fell asleep again. By the third day, unsteady on his feet, he went back to work. I never learned which medication he took that made him so sick, or why he took it.

Within two weeks of Hinze's departure, a new SDG, Karol Baga, came to Fürstengrube. Baga was a Volksdeutscher and completely opposite from Hinze. He did not have Hinze's abysmal vocabulary and or his malevolence. Baga himself had once worked nearby as a coal miner. It seemed that he felt more comfortable with pick and ax than with his duty as a medic. He showed no interest in what anyone was doing. When he came to the dental station, he remained only long enough for me to say, "All is OK here," and then he left.

Finally, early in June 1944 we heard that the Americans had landed in Europe. The BBC reported their successes. This was the one step we felt would surely bring Hitler and his evil empire to an end. In July the heat of change was bearing down on the Germans. The Allies were pushing through France. The Soviets were chasing the Nazi army back through Poland and into Germany. They must have known that the end was near. We were trembling with hope. But all the SS men at the camp seemed to believe that Germany was still unconquerable.

Later in July we heard about an attempt to assassinate Hitler. It was unbelievable to hear that Hitler survived. We too thought then, as the Germans had, that he was indestructible. Dr. Lubicz expressed it best when he said, "If he is not defeated from within, this may still last a long time." He added, "The leaders of the free world met with Hitler several times before 1939, only to bargain away land piece by piece for his false promises. They knew of the widespread persecution of Jews then and failed to do anything for us."

By the end of July Greek Jews from Salonika were delivered to Fürstengrube. None of them understood German, but they proved themselves to be tougher than any of us.

One day, there were unusual lights in the sky, and columns of smoke drifted our way. We knew what the foul odor was. "The Nazis are gassing thousands of Hungarian Jews," we heard. "The crematories cannot dispose of all those bodies, so they're being burned in pits in the forest." Soon everyone in our camp knew the cause of the amber-red skies and the stench that flooded the camp. Hungary, too, was soon to be Judenfrei. I went to the morgue, and the dead bodies lay in bizarre positions. I had not been there in days, and some of the corpses were badly decomposed. They smelled so foul that I could not bear it. I decided to leave and not return. Should I be asked about it, I would say that I forgot. But no one asked, and that was the last that I saw of the morgue.

The newest transport brought Jews from the Theresienstadt concentration camp. Among them was a dentist, Dr. Grosch. When he learned that Fürstengrube had a dental station, he came to see me. A few weeks before he had still been free in Prague with his wife and daughter, he said. "We were first taken to Theresienstadt, where they still are, I hope." He crossed two of his fingers. "And I was transported here." Dr. Grosch had taught oral surgery in a dental school in Czechoslovakia. He also wrote two textbooks on the subject. I reckoned him to be fifty years of age. He was tall and slender, and his face, only slightly lined, displayed a lot of wisdom and also sadness. But most of all it expressed unusual intelligence. The prison jacket he wore seemed three sizes too small for him. The red triangle, yellow star, and number, along with a *T* for Tschechoslowakei, were at his collarbone.

For me, the concentration camp was by now a way of life, but to Grosch, new to the situation, Fürstengrube seemed very frightening. I had compassion for him. When he asked if he could help me in the dental station, I decided to ask Hermann, the Lagerältester. Dr. Grosch was allowed to work with me. Fürstengrube now had its largest number of inmates, over fifteen hundred, with more than a hundred SS men.

I now had gained a great deal of practical dental experience, perhaps enough for a full dental degree. I knew "It hurts!" in at least ten different languages. I had also learned to devise surrogate methods for helping my patients, and in spite of their novelty some cures really worked. Some of the cases I treated were rarely seen at normal times. I set mandibular fractures and cared for extreme gingiva diseases and periodontal and root infections. Because of the lack of proper medication, the newly arrived Dr. Grosch was often unsure of what to do. His professionalism meant a lot to me. He often talked about life in Prague. The welfare of his wife and daughter was his major concern. He was fond of me. Once, with a twinkle in his eye, he said, "After this is over, I want you to be my son-in-law."

Hitler kept dangling miracle weapons before the German people. It was amazing that they still believed him. "The war is not lost," his disciples said. The guards, of course, must have feared they would someday be held accountable for their actions. However discouraged we were, our hope for freedom kept us alive. Perhaps it was a perpetually inherited trait of ours, passed on through the experience of prior persecuted generations. No one wanted to die, not after we had suffered for so long. But freedom was not yet ours.

On a rainy day early in September 1944, Moniek, a Stubendienst from the barracks where my father worked, came running to tell me that my father was unconscious on the washroom floor. When I arrived, Papa was lying on the cement floor, his face cold and sweaty. His eyes were closed, and he was barely breathing. Moniek helped me carry him to the KB, and Josek and I put him on a bunk. Seeing how distraught we were, Moniek called me aside. "I'll tell you what happened," he said, "but don't tell Nathan. Your father wasn't well this morning, and after the inmates left, he went to lie down on his bunk. But Kapo Nathan ordered him get up and sweep the floor. I took the broom, because I wanted to finish sweeping for him. When Nathan saw this, he called him lazy and ordered him to go on, hitting him until he fell down, unconscious. Then Nathan ordered us to take him to the washroom and pour water on him."

I was in shock. As I listened, my stomach knotted, and I gritted my teeth. "Why didn't you call me?" I demanded to know.

"It all happened so fast," Moniek responded.

When Dr. Seidel examined Papa, he shook his head. Neither he nor Lubicz made any prediction. When Josek and I insisted on being told what was wrong, Seidel said that when Papa's fever subsided he could tell us more. Dr. Lubicz injected Papa with a stimulant but couldn't revive him. We knew that our father's condition was very serious. It seemed that he opened his eyes once, but the pupils were fixed and glassy. They were not the eyes we knew. The thought of Kapo Nathan made me shake in anger.

Josek and I took turns watching Papa day and night. "Papa, do you recognize me?" I asked him many times. If he ever knew that we were with him, he did not give us any sign. He was burning up with fever. His forehead was hot and sweaty. We knew that he had little chance of living, but we couldn't admit it to ourselves. We sat hoping for a miracle. The next day Moll came and said he knew Papa was very ill. He allowed me to stay with him. The next evening Papa stretched out his arms as if to embrace us. We thought we saw his lips move, but there was only silence. Then his hands fell to his side. Dr. Lubicz looked at him but saw no promising signs.

The third night was Erev Rosh Hashanah, the night before our New Year. Suddenly Papa's face turned gray. He sank deeper into the coma and soon died. Though we knew all along that his death was inevitable, seeing it happen and seeing his lifeless body was extremely painful to us. My father was my hero, perhaps even more so because of the anguishing years in camp. I missed him enormously. Josek and I knew that his children could not bestow the last tribute, to give him a decent burial.

But the morning after Papa died, Moll said, "When I saw your father I knew he wouldn't make it. An ambulance will be here to pick him up. I know you say some prayers at burial for the dead."

"Yes, Herr Hauptscharführer. Kaddish is what we say."

"Jawohl, tell the driver to wait and to allow you both the time to say what you want." Moll could even be that generous and understanding. I thought of an old well-known Jewish proverb: "The worst anti-Semite has one Jew that he likes."

The next day, the first day of Rosh Hashanah, Papa's body was taken to Birkenau. Before that, however, Josek and I recited Kaddish, as best as we recalled it. "Eternal One! Father of our father. Have mercy on him, as he has passed to his eternal rest. He raised us to know that salvation is achieved by believing in thee. He lived for thee and led us in thy way. He never forsook thee and thy teaching."

We were sure that Papa's death was due to Nathan's beating. I went to see him. Nathan avoided me for a time, but I found him and asked: "Nathan, what did you do to my father? You killed him! Didn't you know that he was sick and not unwilling, but unable, to work? When Moll said that my father could help in a block, I sent Papa to work in your barracks because I knew you. I thought you would have some regard for his age. But I see how wrong I was. You are a Jew, but you are no less brutal than the SS are. Have no doubt, you will pay for this someday. People like you get what they deserve."

His face afire, he glared at me. But I knew that he would not dare hit me. "I didn't know that he was sick, I swear," he said. I looked him in the eye. I had nothing to add, so I left in disgust. A few months later Nathan Green tried to escape. He was caught and hanged.

THE DENTIST OF AUSCHWITZ / 163

In October 1944 my brother told me that the doctors from Auschwitz I had not been in the KB for three weeks. "Perhaps there won't be any more selections," he said. This proved to be true, and none of the inmates, even the most ill, were sent to Birkenau any longer. Our infirmary became full. The sick were now placed two to a bunk. In November the weather went from cold to freezing. Two more men from Dobra died that month. Days later two Polish inmates were caught hiding in a construction delivery truck. They were arrested and later hanged. The remaining Poles were then transferred out of our camp.

In the infirmary one day I heard loud moaning and recognized the voice of the orchestra conductor Harry Spitz. The band he conducted had ceased playing because most of the musicians had fallen victim to the strain of working in the coal mine. Spitz was well acquainted with me. When he saw me, he stretched out his hand and in a faint voice begged for water. I looked at him. The talented ex-husband of the German nightingale lay forgotten. I asked Dr. Lubicz what was wrong. "There isn't much I can do to help him," he said. "He has typhoid fever. He'll either recover or die."

I knew that Dr. Lubicz cared and that he would help if he could. Spitz was burning up with fever. "He wants water," I told the doctor.

"You can give him some, but just a little."

"Is he allowed food?" I asked.

"Nothing to eat," the doctor said and left in a hurry.

I brought Spitz a cup of water and put it to his lips. Despite what Lubicz had said, I let him sip a little at a time for nearly a half hour. Then I gave him a few encouraging words. "Hold on, you have a lot to live for. In a few days the war will be over, and you will go back to Vienna."

"I'll try, dentist, I'll try," he murmured. His eyes closed, and he fell asleep. I watched as his chest rose and fell rapidly. This must have been the worst of his crisis, because from then on he began to improve. Sometimes it took little to turn an inmate's fate around.

The Nazis tried to whitewash their failures. They came up with new phrases for defeat. "Consolidating forces," "shortening defense lines," was doublespeak. They also claimed that the long-awaited counteroffensive was about to begin. The German people continued to swallow the lies. In the meantime, Lipshitz heard that the Allies had taken France and were moving on to Germany through Belgium and the Netherlands. The coal mined by our inmates lay in heaps, unused. There was no purpose in keeping us there, but the dying continued. Nothing would motivate our obsessed captors to stop killing us. Was it Hitler's Teutonic nonsensical idea of "super race" and "subrace"? Was it because his propaganda made us out to be *Unmenschen*? Or was it just that the Germans followed blindly in Hitler's destructive wake? We saw Allied bombers flying over Fürstengrube with increased frequency. We looked up and prayed, hoping.

In December 1944 the mean winter storms arrived. Heavy snows fell and piled up in the camp. I still had the last kilo of dental gold that no one picked up. After Christmas the last non-Jewish inmates in our camp were shipped out. Except for the Kapos, Fürstengrube was now 100 percent Jewish. The Nazis bore down even harder on us.

During the first week of January 1945, all work, even construction, stopped. We knew that something significant was about to happen. We heard that the Allies had crossed the Rhine and were deep inside Germany. In the east, the Russians had crossed the Oder and were aiming for Berlin. It was obvious that the German armies were crumbling. Just when hope arose, a rumor swept the camp that we were to be sent deeper into Germany.

By the end of that week we could hear the war closing in. Artillery shells were arcing above us, lighting the night sky with their glow. Fighting grew so intense that we could sometimes differentiate among the weapons. We learned that we were to leave Fürstengrube, but there was no clue about where we were being sent. We feared Birkenau most. Josef Hermann assured us that while he didn't know where we would be going, he knew that we were not going to Birkenau. "Whoever doesn't feel strong enough to walk can stay," he said. We didn't believe that staying behind would be a safe option. Everyone who felt remotely capable decided to leave. The warehouse was opened, and inmates took the clothes or shoes that were still there.

I took a parting look at the dental station, which had been my security and my torture chamber for nearly a year and a half. Willy and Viky Engel were outside burning the SS office records, under the watchful eye of the newly promoted Scharführer Pfeiffer. Dr. Grosch left the station and returned to his barracks.

I gathered a bagful of dental instruments. Then I saw the melted gold clusters. I packed it all up and went to my brother in the KB. "Two hundred and fifty inmates will remain in the KB," he said. They were aware of the jeopardy they faced, but they were too sick to travel. They knew that, walking, they wouldn't have survived long. They hoped that the Russians we heard were approaching might save them. What later happened was reported by a lone survivor in the book *Hefte von Auschwitz,* by Tadeusz Iwaszko.

> The SS left with the groups of inmates, and only a couple of foremen were guarding us. Hunger was our only companion. The next day we found outside the fence two dead horses. Those and potatoes we found kept us alive. We heard that the Russians were near. It almost seemed as if they were deliberately passing us by.
>
> On January 17 about twenty SS men came. At first we thought they were also retreating and would not harm us. Anyway, as they saw us, they began to shoot at our barracks. One threw a hand grenade into the KB, where we were. One of them looked in and shot whomever he saw move. I was hit with a bullet in my leg, and I faked death. The SS men then placed explosives at the barracks corners and set us afire. The roof soon caved in, and a part of it fell on me. Most in the block were dead by then. I feared moving, because if they saw me they would kill me. But I also knew that if I lay there I would burn to death. When the flames reached me I had a decision to make. I slowly crawled out on my hands and knees and hid behind a pillar. Then I saw the same SS men going into another barracks, where I knew a few inmates were hiding. This time they didn't bother to shoot them; they just burned the barracks down.
>
> The people in the nearby villages must have known what was going on, yet no one came and stopped them. Finally, after the SS men left, a few of the villagers came to extinguish the fires. German soldiers in passing looked at us and said to them, "Don't bother, those are only stinking Jews." The 239 that were killed were buried afterward in one mass grave.*

---

*Tadeusz Iwaszko, *Hefte von Auschwitz* 16 (Auschwitz: Verlag Staatliches Auschwitz-Museum, 1978): 71. Quotation translated by Benjamin Jacobs.

THE DEATH MARCH

At eight in the morning on January 11, 1945, we were each given half a kilo of bread, two squares of margarine, and a generous portion of marmalade. The guards searched each barracks and destroyed whatever they thought had any value.

It was a dry and cold day. The snow blew around, and some of the roads were partly covered. We were arranged in fives, as usual, yet for some reason we were kept standing in one place. "We are waiting to meet up with Buna and the other camps around here," Hermann said. Finally, near midnight, we were separated into units of one hundred and left Fürstengrube. One SS guard with a rifle marched about every ten meters beside us. My brother and I were in the second row. Srulek Lipshitz, the electrician, and Willy and Viky Engel were with us. The Kapos and the much-feared Oberkapo Wilhelm Henkel were just ahead of us. The sound of our boots echoed loudly in the silent night. Many military vehicles were passing us, also headed west.

Suddenly we heard a loud bang, as if a firecracker had exploded. We were puzzled. A few minutes later we passed an inmate lying dead on the road with blood trickling from his head. We had found the source of the noise. Soon Josef Hermann came along the lines with a warning: "The guards will shoot anyone who doesn't keep up with us." A few minutes later someone staggered and fell. We looked on in horror as a guard shot him. Before long so many lay dead on the road that we had to walk carefully to avoid stepping on the bodies. At about four o'clock in the morning we came to another group of inmates. They came from Buna.

It was still dark when we were ordered to stop at a big farm. The barn was open, and we were told that we would stay there the rest of the night. My brother and I dug ourselves into the straw; my dental tools lay beside me.

My eyes shut, and I quickly fell asleep. When it was barely daylight the Kapos flung their whips and yelled, "Eintreten!" The guards seemed to be in a big hurry. We took our positions in the same rows and left without being counted. Then we learned that we were going to Gleiwitz, a city about seventy kilometers further on.

It had snowed overnight. The snow was heavier and more difficult to walk in. Our shoes got wet, and our feet froze. There were more inmate executions along the road. In the light of day we could clearly see that those who had barely begun to fall behind were shot and left on the snowy road. The killers were not embarrassed. It was routine now. At midday we were ordered to stop at the side of the road. Though the sun shone brightly above us, it failed to bring warmth to our line of half frozen, hungry nomads. I had saved a few scraps of bread and ate them in very small bites. After nearly three more hours of walking I felt weak. Everything looked fuzzy, and my knees buckled. "Josek, I can't," I remember saying to my brother as I weaved and staggered. He gripped me by my arm and asked Willy, who was on my other side, also to hold on to me. The three of us slowed down, and we kept falling back until we were in the very last row.

The other inmates recognized me. "It's Bronek, the dentist. He'll be next." I was barely dragging my feet, and my head bobbed up and down. Three guards were behind us. Though fully aware of the consequences and though I tried hard, I stopped thinking about what threatened me. I just wanted to be left on the ground to rest.

"Berek," my brother kept encouraging me, "move." Josek and Willy practically carried me. "Berek, it isn't far. We'll stop behind this hill," Josek urged me on in panic. But we did not stop there, and then I really felt defeated. My brother unfolded the blanket that I had carried away from Fürstengrube and draped it around my shoulders.

"Just leave me," I begged him and Willy. But they kept holding on to me, insisting that we would surely stop at the next farm.

Suddenly Schmidt came by us on his motorcycle. "Was ist los mit dem Zahnarzt?" (What is wrong with the dentist?), he asked.

"He is too weak to walk anymore, Herr Lagerführer," my brother answered him.

"Hold on, dentist, I'll send the Lagerältester over," I heard him say as he sped away. A short time later he came back with Josef Hermann on the rear seat, and I soon felt something being pushed into my mouth. It was vodka. Although it burned my mouth and throat, I swallowed it and took a few more sips. Suddenly I felt my legs grow stronger, and this enabled me to walk until we stopped at the next farm. There I sank to the snowy ground.

"Stand up and wait a few more minutes until we're counted," my brother said. That, I sensed, was my salvation, but it was too big an effort for my buckling legs. Josek helped me up and wedged me between a wagon and its wheel that were next to us. With that support I got through the roll call, and then we got food for the first time since leaving Fürstengrube. We were to stay overnight in the barn.

I remember someone shaking me. I opened my eyes, and my brother was staring at me. "Get out, or they'll kill you," he said, tugging on me. At first I didn't know where I was. In my hazy memory I recalled the previous day. I couldn't believe that I was still alive and was petrified at having to march yet another day. But feeling remarkably stronger, as if new life had been breathed into me during the night, I left the barn.

Several inmates were missing. The guard's bayonets jabbed deep down into the piles of straw. "Raus!" they yelled, to scare them out. Soon three prisoners covered in straw emerged and were kicked into the lines. More threats followed, and when no others emerged from the straw, Pfeiffer yelled a warning: "I'll give you one more chance before I burn down the barn." That failed to bring them out. We counted and found that twelve were still missing.

That morning we got bread, butter, and coffee and left without the twelve escapees. Pfeiffer did not burn the barn down as he had threatened. That was the largest group of inmates I knew of ever to escape. It was another frosty day, and as we moved out the killing began again. It seemed as if we were on a unrelenting pilgrimage of death. At the next settlement was an old stone church with a slate roof and copper spires. In front of it were large heaps of snow. The guards grinned at pretty girls who watched us being dragged through their town. To them we probably did not look human. Outside the town one sign read twenty-eight kilometers to Gleiwitz. We hoped this death march would finally end there. Schmidt, with Josef Hermann behind him on the motorcycle, kept circling us. At noon we stopped to rest. The fields looked peaceful buried under deep snow. Because this region was now swarming with Waffen SS troops, we wondered if the twelve inmates who escaped earlier could elude them. Knowing how far we had still to go, Josek kept checking on me.

When we neared Gleiwitz, it was already dark. There the foundries, mills, and railroads were still intact. Some smokestacks emitted heavy, dark soot. We were led through the center of the town amid a large convoy of military vehicles, which passed us. Eventually we came to a large group of prisoners, who were enclosed behind an eight-meter-high wire fence covered with iron bars that was normally used to store coal. Two railroad tracks ran to the inside. The prisoners came from the Deutsche Werke, an iron foundry outside Gleiwitz. Some inmates from Fürstengrube had arrived before us. The remnants of coal were everywhere. We each received a bit of bread, coffee, and a small sausage. We remained there through the night.

Early the next morning we were ordered to board open cars ordinarily used to transport cattle. It was an inescapable irony—in the August heat we had been driven in closed cars. The cars were about two and a half meters high and about five and a half meters from front to rear. A guard was posted at each end. Only forty of us fitted into one car, but by pushing and shoving, the guards got another twenty people in. I clutched my bag against my body with barely enough room to stand. "Wie viele Stücke hast Du?" (How many pieces have you got?), a Croatian guard asked a Ukrainian guard. They could not communicate well. Counting and recounting and relaying the number in each car, they finally agreed. Then the locomotives started up, and with whistles blaring they began to move us west, away from possible liberation, deeper into Germany.

At first the cars moved slowly, bouncing and swaying. One locomotive pulled, and another pushed, as the many wagons snaked up and around the town. It had snowed again, and the skies were still heavy with winter clouds. Soon a couple of tin cans appeared, and the prisoners lowered them down with twine to scoop up some snow. "Don't eat the snow, because you'll be more thirsty," Dr. Seidel cautioned. But the thirst prevailed, and no one heeded his warning. The cans went down and came back up with snow, and everybody devoured it. My brother found enough room to lower himself and sit down. Suddenly he jumped up, for someone was urinating on him. We even lacked a pail in our car.

At night our thirst increased. After a while the locomotive slowed and pushed onto a dead track. By then one prisoner was dead, and another was close to death. A guard ordered them thrown off the cars. Then he went by the cars and asked how many more were dead. "There is no room for half dead," the Unterscharführer said. "Throw them out." Soon they were hurled out and fell to the ground with a thud. Those near death died. The men who had died while we were moving were piled up and tossed off the wagons at each stop. Sometimes we could see bodies flying out of the cars while we were moving. We were often shuttled between stations to let the priority trains move by. Then came the tugging backward and forward, after which we stopped on a track leading to nowhere. We thought that this trip would only end when all of us died.

Light snow began to fall, and then it became heavier and snowed throughout the night. The snow melted on the blankets we had carried with us, and the water froze and turned them stiff. We had not been given food or water all day, and despite Dr. Seidel's warning everyone took his turn at the snow.

As the trains slowed on the third day, Dr. Grosch, who was in our wagon, began to behave very strangely. He climbed on top of others and yelled, "Let me go to my wife and daughter. They need me now!" I urged him to calm down, but he was unstoppable and wrestled free. He had gone insane. The turmoil got an SS sergeant's attention. He came over and fired a shot at Dr. Grosch. He slumped back into the wagon dead. His body was flung out of the car. I hoped his wife and daughter would never learn of his tragic ending. Josek must have had the same thought. "Papa was lucky to have died when he did. He would never have survived this trip," he said. So many prisoners were dead by then that we had much more room in the cars.

There were two Greek Jews from Salonika on our wagon. Since none of the rest of us spoke Greek, they huddled together, strangers among us. Though the cold of the open wagons was freezing us to our very souls, there was one advantage over the closed cars. Here the smell of human waste dissipated, and we could discard the excrement.

We hadn't received food in two days. Our mouths were dry with a searing thirst. Finally, at about nine at night, each of us got 250 grams of bread and a ladle of ersatz coffee. Our train stopped again. This had become routine. Our transport halted at least four times each twenty-four hours. Dr. Seidel was now among the dead.

Before dawn we came to Buchenwald. "Jedem das seine" (To each his own), a sign above the gate proclaimed. Although the sarcasm was hard to comprehend, it hardly mattered. We no longer saw such words as an affront to our lost dignity. We hoped that this tortuous trip was at an end, even if we were to go into another camp.

We were kept in the cars another night. Then at midmorning the gates opened, and we were ordered to leave the cars and enter the camp. After the many days on the train, we could hardly walk. The guards were impatient and pushed the weak with rifle butts, as if they were shoveling coal.

Buchenwald seemed very disorganized. The inmates did not look much better than we did. Their faces were dull and gray and matched the dark stripes of their prison clothes. We were led into a huge unheated hall. We were given the usual soup of turnips with bits of potatoes in it. The food and close quarters warmed us up. The ugly structure outside the windows reminded us of Birkenau's gas chambers. Overhead, the Allies were more active here, but they had not yet dropped a single bomb.

It was rumored that in a few days we would be transferred to a satellite camp of Buchenwald, called Dora-Mittelbau. It was a terrible camp, the Buchenwald inmates said. We left Buchenwald and marched for four hours. We passed a few German towns, including the city of Blankenburg, and then we went east. Here, too, with the war near an end, the German people seemed not to be affected by our condition as we marched past them. Hauptscharführer Max Schmidt, Lagerältester Josef Hermann, and all Fürstengrube guards and Kapos came with us. After ten more kilometers we came to Dora-Mittelbau. It was like other camps, only this one stood among trees without a fence around it.

DORA-MITTELBAU

Kommandant Schmidt was explicit. "Don't be fooled by the absence of a fence around the barracks. Here the entire area is guarded," he said. It was again evident to us that the Nazi tentacles were everywhere.

Each of us found a bunk. I left my instruments on mine and quickly returned to the Appellplatz. The routine began. "Eins, zwei, drei," and so on we counted. We numbered six hundred by then. We received the usual rations. It seemed as if all the marmalade in Germany was red. Or was it just ours?

The barracks was new and temporary. The water for the washroom came from 2.5-cm pipes, with water dripping from tiny holes. The latrine was a wooden plank suspended over an open pit. "What work are you doing here?" I asked an inmate.

"Je ne parle pas allemand," he answered.

Another inmate turned to me and in broken German said, "Er vesteht kein deutsch, er spricht nur Französisch." He was also French but spoke some German.

Just then someone else turned to me and said, "Pan jest zPolski?" I knew that we could converse in Polish.

I first asked him the question whose answer we all dreaded most. "Are there any gas chambers here?"

"Not here. The Mussulmen are sent to Buchenwald," he said. Then I inquired further. I wanted to know what work they did.

"Have you heard of the German V-rockets? Since the Allied bombing destroyed Peenamunde, where they were first built, we assemble them here in the Harz mountain caves. At first we worked on the V1, then on the V2, and now," and here he began almost to whisper, "we are beginning to work on the V3. Almost thirty thousand prisoners have died so far here. The engineers are Wernher von Braun, Helmut and Magnus Grottrup, and Arthur Rudolf."

Dora-Mittelbau had several thousand inmates, but for some unexplained reason Max Schmidt kept us separate and under his and his Fürstengrube functionary's strict control. The only contact we had with the other prisoners was at work and in the washrooms.

The next morning the Appell foremen came seeking engineers, draftsmen, electricians, technicians, and machine workers from among us. But soon the familiar roar of airplanes was heard. The sound intensified as they came closer. The foremen exchanged worried looks with Schmidt and decided to halt the process. "Don't you stare up there gleefully," Kapo Karl snapped at us, to assert his allegiance to the new foremen. Nonetheless, our temptation was too great. Looking at the squadron of twenty Allied bombers glittering in the sun like silver doves sent by heaven was irresistible to us. They promised an end to this mad empire. When the planes faded beyond the horizon, the specialists were chosen and marched away.

Those of us remaining followed several foremen along a railroad track. Suddenly we heard the sound of heavy wheels rolling toward us. "Hinlegen!" (Lie down!), an SS man commanded. Then we heard whispers that stirred us all: "V-rockets." I turned my head slightly to one side and saw a huge bullet-shaped object, covered with canvas, pass by us. The mysterious objects shielded from our sight, we were led into a tunnel built into the mountainside. It was nearly dark and freezing inside. Small metal particles lay mixed into the soil. A strong smell of sulfur was everywhere. Above a water tank was a warning in German: "Nicht trinken" (Do not drink). The end of the tunnel was not visible.

As the foremen led us in deeper, we saw prisoners at work benches surrounded with bins that held strange-looking parts. Many gave us the thumbs-ups sign. We continued further into the tunnel, and a foreman ordered my brother and me to work with three prisoners already at work there. They looked frail: one of them was barely skin and bones. We asked them what we should do. As soon as the foremen passed, they stopped working and said to us, "Don't do a thing. Just act busy when a German comes by. The Americans are not far away, and it won't be long before they're here." They spoke German to us with a heavy French accent. Besides the sulfur smell, this place also reeked of ammonia. Each breath we took hurt.

When a foreman approached us, the three Frenchmen reached into a bin, picked up a few parts that were already clean, wiped them again, and tossed them into a second bin. We mimicked them for the rest of the day. I wondered

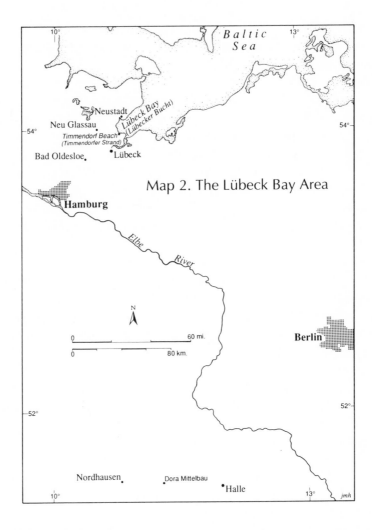

Map 2. The Lübeck Bay Area

how long they had been faking and how we would get away with this charade. Perhaps the foremen did not care any longer either.

On the first Saturday evening, as the sun was gently setting behind our barracks, I heard singing from the nearby Russian camp. Scarlet rays glided above the treetops. The song was a sad and lonely melody, full of the yearning of broken hearts. They sang of their love for their homeland. Now and then a baritone repeated the refrain: "Matushka Rossiya, how do I love thee? I love your mountains, and I love your meadows. I love your sun, and I love your steppes." I stood riveted, my heart bruised. I had no such home to yearn for. I felt like a tree without roots.

On Monday morning a fellow inmate complained about a toothache. I sat him down on my bunk and looked in his mouth. I saw a rotted wisdom tooth. I still had a few ampoules of novocaine, a syringe, and two forceps, and I used these to extract it. By the time I was finished, all the work groups had left. It surprised us that no one came looking for us. I left my instruments spread out on the bunk as an alibi for not being at work. Since no one came to check, not even Adolf Voigt, the former Sanitätsdienstgefreiter, who had come with us from Auschwitz, I had an idea. The next morning after roll call I returned to the barracks and spread my instruments out. I proclaimed myself the barracks dentist.

One day I found Nissen, my Hebrew teacher from Dobra, dead on his bunk, which was not far from mine. He was not a resourceful man. He did not beg or steal to survive. He did what was asked of him. He carried a heavy load all those years without ever complaining. How he had remained alive this long I could not understand. He never asked me for help, and I could not remember having seen him in camp during all this time.

There was ample evidence that the Allies were mounting an all-out attack on the area. They dominated the sky, and a German defense no longer seemed to exist. We were convinced that our freedom was near. The Allies appeared to be just a few kilometers away. But they could as well have been hundreds.

On the morning of April 10, 1945, no one was taken to work. Josef Hermann, on Kommandant Schmidt's orders, kept us in the barracks. Then after a swift count we left Dora. I took along my few dental tools, hoping they would still have their magical powers. After an hour of walking we came to the River Elbe. The snow had melted away, and spring had begun to stir everything to life. Max Schmidt and Josef Hermann waited for us at the river, where several empty flatbed barges stood. The Elbe, an important shipping lane, emptied into the North Sea. It broke our hearts when Hermann told us that we had left just in time: on our heels the Americans liberated Dora-Mittelbau. Our freedom had been very close, but like a shadow, it slipped away from us again. We were extremely depressed. We learned that we were to go to Max Schmidt's family estate. Where it was and why we were going there we did not know. What value could we—weak, dispirited Mussulmen—still have to them?

About sixty of us were loaded on each barge, followed by a few Kapos. We were ordered to sit down and stay in one place, so as not to upset the barge's balance. The engines came alive, black smoke rose, and we began to move. The engines huffed and puffed but could only move us slightly faster than the river's current. Bright sunshine filtered through the emerald green waters. The reflection of our tattered clothes shone in the clear waters and faded into the depths. We were a floating concentration camp—perhaps a first.

Along the banks were little houses, their windows lined with flowering plants. An occasional church came into view. Here the people seemed to be peaceful and secure. At times we could smell food cooking. The fact that such life still existed was surprising to us. Not so long ago we were like them: young, old, good, bad. We were happy, sad, foolish, vain, like all people. We were born, lived, and died together. Now we were different, the *Unmenschen.* No one came close to see who we were. Not even those at the river's edge were curious. I wondered why. Perhaps the unusual no longer seemed so strange. We looked up with disappointment, keeping our disillusioned thoughts to ourselves.

Winter's storms had just given way to springlike weather. The bushes along the shore sprouted fresh buds, and trees were covered with delicate light green leaves. Schmidt, with Josef Hermann on the rear seat of his big BMW motorcycle, rode along the river road, disappearing and reappearing on the bank. As the sun sank lower, cold air streamed across our barges. Later the barges anchored, and a few civilians brought containers of bread for us. This and coffee sustained us for the rest of the way—three and a half days in all. The waters were calmer at night, and only the passing of the barges caused ripples. Silence filled the air.

In the morning gentle breezes rustled the treetops. Allied planes were crisscrossing the skies above us all day. We still hoped at each turn that we would find freedom. As we moved north, the weather turned colder, and we could see more villages and towns. Germany was now nearly cut in two, with only a narrow corridor of land dividing the Americans from the Russians along the Elbe. In the north the British were at the outskirts of Bremen and Hamburg. In the south the French were on the upper Danube. The main roads were unusually full, with people streaming west. Women and children and army deserters were fleeing from the advancing Red Army troops. At times we also could spot groups of prisoners like us in gray striped suits guarded by the Waffen SS.

It was cold and rainy, and it felt like winter. The Schleswig Holstein region was one of the few areas still unoccupied by Allies. It was obvious now why Max Schmidt did not leave us in Dora. He decided to keep us captive on his parents' estate, because without us to guard, he would have to defend his dying fatherland. He ought to have known that his war was over. Having been the Kommandant of an Auschwitz camp, he could hardly expect to escape criminal charges if apprehended here. So why he chose to take us to his family estate was a big puzzle.

We were ordered off the barges and told to assemble beside the main road between Hamburg and Kiel. By then we numbered 540 inmates plus the Kapos. Some of us could barely move. My brother and I seriously considered escaping, but we asked ourselves, Where would we go? We knew that Hamburg was a vile Nazi nest.

As we began marching, the slaughter started again. As before, those unable to keep up were shot and left by the road. By the time we came to the Schmidt estate in a village called Neu Glassau, fifteen more prisoners were dead. We thought that by then the Kapos would end their complicity with the Nazis. They too had to know that they would be held accountable. But many of them, especially Kapo Wilhelm, remained hardened, hating his fellow Jewish inmates as much as ever.

It was late in the day when we came to the edge of Neu Glassau. From there we were led onto a dirt road, and five kilometers later we came to a large, weathered gray barn standing on a gentle incline. Hermann had told us that for the time being we would remain there. While the guards took up watch around us, we slumped down onto the bare, still-frozen ground, exhausted. A short while later Schmidt came up the road and opened the barn doors. Dusk had fallen when three women arrived with real bread, butter, and coffee. One of them was young, tall, and very beautiful. I immediately recognized her. She was Gerta, Max's fiancée. She had often visited Max in Fürstengrube. She wore her long blond hair in heavy braids.

On April 13 we were awakened by a howling Kapo Wilhelm. "The American president is dead. You haven't won the war yet, not until you all *krapiert* [croak]," he said.

"President Roosevelt dead?" echoed through the barn. We likened the president's death to our major defeat. It set back our hopes. We each had lost a friend. We were shocked and dismayed.

Fräulein Gerta came daily with two helpers, and each time we received one thick slice of bread, butter, and coffee. This was real food, and we remembered now how bread and butter once tasted. We also got potato-turnip soup at night, but since we had been deprived of food for so many years, it only quieted some of our hunger.

Behind the barn were two straw-covered mounds. Young Mendele, intrigued, kept circling them and one day decided to investigate. Keeping an eye on the guards, he walked back and forth in a cat-and-mouse game, as if he was searching for something, until he could sit inconspicuously close to the mounds. Then he casually reached into the straw and found potatoes there. He slowly stuffed his pockets with them and returned to the barn. Then he discovered that they were half frozen. He knew that eating them uncooked would cause him uncontrollable diarrhea. He started a fire using straw from the barn. Unfortunately that's where his success ended, because the guard came and stamped it out.

The emptier my stomach got, the worse my pain and cramping became. I had heard that the village of Neu Glassau did not have a dentist. I was motivated to find food, and I approached Max Schmidt to offer my services to the villagers. "Herr Hauptscharführer, I understand that there are no dentists in Neu Glassau? I still have dental instruments from Fürstengrube. If you permit me to go there, I could help those with dental problems. You know, Herr Lagerführer, that I will not escape," I pleaded.

He paused for a while, thinking over my suggestion. "I have no objection," he said, giving me the name of a family he knew there. "If you tell them that I sent you, they will let you use their house." Then he ordered the head of the guards, Scharführer Pfeiffer, to allow me to leave the barn area.

I found Schmidt's friends' place and knocked. A middle-aged woman came out and looked at me with astonishment. When I explained who I was, gave her the reason for my presence, and told her who had sent me, she invited me into her living room. She was in her midforties. Hard work was mirrored on her face. She knew that her husband was on the eastern front, but she had not heard from him in more than a year and didn't know if he was still alive. The couple was childless.

The woman was quite friendly and asked me many questions. She wanted to know about me and why we were at the Schmidt estate. I answered all of her questions except the last. I thought that responding to that one would be foolhardy and might harm my relations with the Lagerführer. She could not understand it. The Schmidts were known to be honorable people, she said. She put bread and ham before me. It was the first time I had filled my stomach since leaving Fürstengrube in January. Although she told me that she had never believed in Hitler and was not a Nazi, I had the distinct impression that she was not telling me the truth.

From then on, getting enough food for my brother and myself proved to be rather simple. The woman got her neighbors to contribute, and I was able to help some of my friends. Although the nearest dentist was thirteen kilometers away, not a single German came to see me the first week. I reduced my stay in the village, from two hours to one hour a day. One day the woman put a Holländer torte before me. The cake had more whipped cream than dough. I had not eaten anything as rich before, and I almost ate the whole cake. Then, for the first time since I had been taken from Dobra, I got sick from overeating.

In the meantime, the Allies were pounding the area with heavy artillery. It seemed as if we were only hours from freedom, but as before, it slipped away.

DISASTER ON THE BALTIC SEA

On April 27, 1945, Max Schmidt called me aside and in front of the
barn gave me a surprising message. "The director of the Swedish Red Cross,
Count Folke Bernadotte, will be here tomorrow to take some of you to
Sweden," he confided. "But he only wants prisoners who are from the West.
He won't know where any of you are from. I won't stand in your way if you
tell him you are from somewhere in the West."

"What will happen if I stay?" I asked.

"I don't know. No one can predict what will happen. The Kommandant of
Neuengamme, a concentration camp nearby, is in charge of all prisoners here
now. I know him, and I don't trust him." Then he added, "You would be safer
out of here."

What he said left me gasping. Encouraged, I dared to ask more. "Herr
Lagerführer, actually you are still in charge of us. I mean, you could order the
guards to let us go, couldn't you?" He did not respond.

After this talk with Schmidt, my fellow prisoners immediately surrounded
me. Obviously I could not tell them all that Max had said to me. I did reveal
that tomorrow the Red Cross would come to take all Western nationals to
Sweden. My brother and I conferred about Schmidt's suggestion, and we both
agreed to do as he said. Neither Josek nor I any longer considered Poland our
country. We decided to take a chance and hoped our bluff would work. I immediately began to tutor my brother in what I remembered of my limited
French. "Josek, when they ask you, 'D'où êtes-vous?' you answer them, 'Je
viens de la France.' Should they ask you, 'Quelle ville?' you answer, 'De Bordeaux, monsieur.' " I had picked Bordeaux because of Dr. Lubicz. I remembered that he came from there. We were both awake that night, full of
anticipation about what the next day would bring. We tried to envision what

Sweden would be like. Could we rebuild our shattered lives there? I wanted to see America, the land of my dreams. After our many disappointments, would this be the last day of captivity?

It was April 28, 1945, and we lay in the clothes we had not removed since we got here. At the first move of the barn doors, we dug ourselves out of the soft straw and went outside and waited. At about nine thirty, as our Lagerführer had predicted, they came. Four white paneled trucks, preceded by a black limousine with a Red Cross flag fluttering from the fender, drove up the lane to the barn and stopped. Three smartly dressed men in Red Cross outfits emerged, and we were immediately ordered by our Lagerführer to assemble.

One of the men carried an elegant baton under his arm, which made me think he must be the count. We waited, as the Lagerführer had ordered us to do, in our customary rows of fives. Before us, we thought, was our long-yearned-for freedom. Finally the "count" spoke in German: "All Western nationals step forward."*

About fifty prisoners, most from France, Holland, and Belgium, stepped out in front of us. I knew most of them well. No Englishmen or Americans were among us; the Norwegians that had been with us in Fürstengrube were all dead. I tugged my brother's jacket, and we both walked out at the same time to stand with the Westerners. Seeing this, many Eastern and Central Europeans followed, doubling the number. Everything went as we had hoped, and we were marched toward the Swedish trucks.

On their canvas tops were huge red crosses. My heart beat loud and fast. I was terrified and overjoyed. I was an imposter stealing a precious reward. We tried to mingle with the real Westerners, so as not to be detected. We were anxious. It was difficult to comprehend that all this was actually happening. Finally the four Swedish drivers lifted the canvases and dropped the truck tailgates and summoned us. "Step up," they said.

Our bluff worked. I cannot describe the feeling. We were free of scourging, beating, and thrashing. Josek and I looked at one another to be sure it was not just an unlikely dream. Afraid that someone would order us back, we

*In his book *The Curtain Falls*, Count Bernadotte makes no mention of having been in Neu Glassau. Hence I am not certain that he was one of the three Swedes. See Count Folke Bernadotte, *The Curtain Falls*, trans. Eric Lewenhaupt (New York: Alfred A. Knopf, 1945).

wanted to be the first to climb onto the trucks. Mendele had already found the right chum, the freckled, red-haired young Dutchman, Kopelmann.

The trucks drove slowly, in a gentle downward pitch to the sea, swaying on the rough gravel road. Offshore, only about one kilometer away, sat a Swedish freighter, its flags flapping in the light wind. The dinghies moved toward the shore. "We know that not all of you are from the West. Those who are not we cannot take," announced the count. Then he looked around and waited. My brother leaned on my arm. I heard my heart beating and felt my knees about to buckle. What now? The memory of Schmidt's predictions nourished my fears. A minute of silence followed, but it seemed endless. When he got no response, the count came close and looked each of us in the face. My lie covered my face like a mask. My stomach cramped, and a lump grew in my throat. The count kept walking and darting his eyes at each of us, his face expressing his thoughts: Which of you has the audacity? But he was not sure who. Not one was willing to go back to the camp. He grew impatient, and spearing us with his anger, he spoke. "As long as no one is willing to admit it, we will take you all back." Still, no one gave us away, and not one of us talked. Could he not understand why? Could he not understand that one would do anything to be free of this suffering? After years of degradation, dehumanization, after years of living with death, we yearned for freedom.

The three Swedes conferred, and after a while the count spoke again. "For the last time, we warn you. Whoever really is a national of a Western country, step out. The rest please stay back." That got the results they wanted. The real Westerners stepped forward. The rest of us no longer dared.

Only we prisoners and the Swedes were there. Not a single German was present. Even if rescuing the Westerners had been their initial objective, could they not bend a little? I approached the count and pleaded with him. "Can't you take us? We are condemned. Look at the condition of some of these people. If you return us, they will be dead tomorrow."

"I don't have enough room on the ship," he said. Looking at the huge ship, I could hardly believe that it would sink with the addition of a few more passengers.

"It's only a short trip. We will stand on deck. Please take us," I pleaded. I looked at the rest of the Swedes, asking them for help. But this did little to ease their rigidity. If they agreed, they did not say so. They remained unmoved. More desperate inmates, their limbs swollen and their bodies numb, also pleaded with them. They remained indifferent and just ordered the drivers to take us back. Liberty and freedom were gone; it all seemed like a dream, like a beautiful dream, and we had had such a brief taste of freedom. The Swedes, however polite, lacked mercy. We felt condemned and were bitterly devastated. I never learned who gave us away. Count Bernadotte had reached an agreement with Reichsführer Heinrich Himmler that allowed him to take all prisoners except Germans. To this day I still don't know why they did not take us.

With heavy hearts we had to board the truck that would take us back. It was one o'clock when we returned to Neu Glassau. Schmidt and Hermann were gone. Scharführer Pfeiffer and his guards were now in charge. I tried to talk my way out to the village, but Pfeiffer would not let me go, nor did Gerta come with food. We made a pathetic picture as we lay in a state of lethargy, in an existential emptiness, without hope. Starved, we raided the straw-covered mounds for the few half-frozen potatoes that might sustain us for a few more days.

On May 1 we learned that Hitler had committed suicide. But Kapo Wilhelm still proclaimed, "The war will yet be won!" We knew he meant by the Nazis. Despair shrouded us like a fog. Early on May 2 we were awakened while it was still dark. Gunfire was all around us, but once again we had to leave. I looked at the tools that had saved my life, which I kept hidden in the straw. "You can't help me any longer," I thought. I took the dental gold. "Only this is worth saving." After counting us, Pfeiffer insisted that six prisoners were still missing. But in the rush there was no time for a recount. Several shots filled the barn as we left.

These were the last days of the Reich. Hitler had clearly failed. But the Nazis still carried on the war against the Jews. We dragged ourselves on with our last ounce of strength. After marching for one hour we came to Neustadt and were ordered to turn left toward the Baltic Sea. There we found rafts and a dozen SS men standing by. Although the morning sun had begun to creep over the horizon, a heavy fog obscured our vision. We could see less than nine meters in front of us. Each dinghy took thirty people. We were puzzled. We did not know where we were being taken or what they planned to do with us. Everyone feared the worst. About fifteen minutes later something emerged in the fog. As the dinghy drew closer, we saw the stern of a ship. Painted on its side was its name, *Cap Arcona*.

We soon heard someone shouting down from above with a bullhorn: "Are you bringing me more prisoners?"

"Yes," the SS men replied.

"I can't take them. I have over four thousand already on the ship. I have no more room."

"We are overloaded," another man yelled. "Why don't you try the *Thielbek* or the *Deutschland*?"

"Our orders are to bring them to you," the SS men yelled back.

The sailor refused. "I am the captain of this ship, and I will not take them. That is final," he yelled down. The SS men, outranked and outmaneuvered, gave up and took us back to shore. Once there, the SS officer in charge, wearing a spiffy black uniform, stepped onto our dinghy and ordered it back to the ship. The other three dinghies followed. As if sensing the matter was not settled yet, the ship's captain was waiting when we returned. The SS man, his voice threatening, ordered the captain to take us at once. The captain insisted as before that he had no room. The exchange was heated.

Finally the captain softened and asked, "How many have you got?"

"In all about five hundred," the SS man yelled back. "Just take those sixty, and I will send the rest to the *Thielbek*." This compromise worked.

By then the fog had lifted. We saw a rope ladder come down, and we were ordered to climb up. This was risky. Balancing was difficult. We did not have much strength, and we feared that we would slip off and fall into the sea. But how could we resist? So following on each other's heels, with the rope ladder swaying and shaking, we climbed up, and somehow we made it. We followed a fair-haired, cruel-looking sailor below the deck. The stairs were covered with ornate Persian carpets, and heavy mahogany railings were anchored with shiny brass fittings. Elegant gold brocade tapestry covered the walls. One more level down, we passed a large and elegant Victorian dining room. The richness and the luxury of the *Cap Arcona* was ironic. We, the *Unmenschen,* the world's rabble, on this luxurious liner?

We followed the sailor further down and came into a long narrow corridor. Finally he stopped and unlocked a heavy metal door and ordered us to pass through it. Then he slammed the door. We were in a new concentration camp, a room about twenty-one meters long and nine meters wide, normally used to store the ship's provisions. It was barely lit and packed with prisoners from Neuengamme. We were below sea level, and the room had no portholes. A passive silence persisted there. The prisoners from Neuengamme had been there for more than a week. They were delivered to this ship by another boat, the *Athens*. In the last three days they had only had soup and water. They had no sense of time. Their isolation was so total that they didn't know whether it was night or day when we came aboard.

The *Cap Arcona* was a luxury liner of the Hamburg-Südamerika Dampf-schiffahrts-Gesellschaft. At nearly 28,000 metric tons, it was the largest and most luxurious ship of the line and was nicknamed the Queen of the South Atlantic. Ironically, the Hamburg-Amerika line, the preceding company, had been founded by a Jewish immigrant to Germany. Now the ship was to make new history.

I had hunger pains, but I resisted eating my last piece of bread, which was stuffed in my coat pocket. I lay down, squeezed between my brother and a stranger, and immediately fell asleep. Suddenly I felt a tug and woke up, aware of someone standing over me snatching my last bit of bread. I grabbed his arm, and he jerked it away. "Let go of me," he said in Russian, pushing my hand away. "You have just arrived, and I am here four days." He didn't have my sympathy. I am not sure that I then appreciated what he had gone through.

We were in the darkest gloom. Our morale was lower than at any other time I could remember. Some men were sighing, "This is our end. We won't leave this ship alive." But we were the tough and unyielding, having made it alive this far. This was the last straw for us, I thought. What will be will be. I fell asleep once more.

Suddenly we heard a loud bang, and the ship shook violently. Another and another bang followed in succession. We could hear crowds of people running by our door, shouting: "They torpedoed the ship! Just what we expected." We knew that something dreadful had happened. We found that our door was locked, and no amount of pounding, yelling, and pleading for someone to open it helped. Then another bang resounded, and the floor began tilting under our feet. Soon smoke filled the room. Without fresh air, people coughed incessantly. Shouts rose in the room. "We cannot breathe! We will all choke to death!"

We were close to asphyxiation, but no amount of screaming and pleading helped us. No one seemed to hear us. Even when we succeeded in prying a two-meter plank loose from a shelf and were hitting the door with it, no one answered. In the meantime, the sirens wailed, as we heard bang after bang. We were swaying back and forth like one body. The smoke grew heavier and so did the coughing. Suddenly the light bulb went out. The dark frightened us even more.

Finally, purely by chance, someone unlocked our door, and a wild stampede began. Everyone wanted to escape the smoky room. In this chaos I lost my brother, but we found each other while running wildly through the corridors. "Don't go that way," someone yelled, coming into our path. "You can't get out this way. The stairs are on fire." Others we encountered urged us to come with them. "There is another stairway at this end!" they shouted. We were running hard and getting nowhere. The corridor was quickly filling up with smoke, and men were coughing ceaselessly. "We want to get out of here alive," delirious people shouted. We did not know whom to follow.

It was three floors up to the top deck. We frantically ran through the narrow, slanted corridor, bouncing off oncoming people. We passed the dining room and remembered the stairs from our march down. But they were in flames, and smoke was flowing down the stairway. Nevertheless, my brother and I tried to run up. We went a few steps, but the heavy smoke and flames were impenetrable. They pushed us back. I tried again, and so did others, but again we were pushed back, our hair singed. I retreated and then tried again, and each time I had to return. I made a final desperate attempt. I closed my eyes, and sheltering my head with my arms and hands, I ran as fast as I could up the stairs. That too failed. We were terrified, fearing for our lives. We ran back into the dining room. By then it also was filled with black smoke. We ran, holding on to one another, and saw another corridor leading in a different direction. We followed it and saw daylight coming from one of the men's lavatories. The space was six meters long and three meters wide. An eight-meter shaft extended above this space, and men were lowering ropes. Some people were climbing up, but others were climbing on top of them and pushing them down. No one wanted to die, and panic reigned. Soon even more frightened men crowded the room. When one man managed to stand on another's shoulders, someone else tried to stand on his, until they all fell down.

Finally I tried the rope. Standing on my brother's shoulders, I tried to climb up, but I too was grabbed from behind and pulled down. I failed twice, and then my brother tried his luck. He was also knocked down. I can't recall how many times we tried before I was able to hold on to the rope and climb up to the point where someone from above could grab my hand and pull me up. In this man's grasp I lowered myself back down and helped my brother up. It was not a minute too soon, for the flames reached the lavatory, and others didn't make it. Clouds of dark smoke shot up into the shaft, making further rescues impossible. We heard desperate cries from below.

I looked up into the sky and pondered the reason for our survival. The sun was draped in dark clouds. "Could it be, perhaps, that the prayers of our loved ones convinced you to have mercy on us? God, you often ask us to accept the crazy things around us," I wanted to pray, but my thoughts were too painful, and I was in an emotional turmoil. In this profound chaos, I felt solace in simply being alive.

INFERNO

We were three and a half kilometers from the closest shore.
Hundreds of prisoners filled the top deck. At the stern about fifty German civilians, including a few women, and at least that many German sailors were confronted with the same dilemma that we were. Nearby were two smaller ships, the *Thielbek* and the *Deutschland*. The latter was tipped to one side and on fire. On one of its smokestacks, still visible, appeared a large red cross. A few hundred inmates were struggling in the sea, trying to swim to shore.

However fortunate we were to come out of the hell below, safety was still far away. The *Cap Arcona* was tilting, and we saw no one coming from shore to help. What's more, not a single lifeboat or life vest was on the ship.

Death stared at us. Pandemonium had erupted, and the bay was full of swimmers. Many more were jumping into the frigid water. Those near the ship were getting nowhere. The downward pull of the sinking ship created a whirlpool, and the swimmers' chances of survival were slim. Physically exhausted and no match for the elements, they struggled in vain, and one after another sank below the waves.

Suddenly from an empty sky planes appeared. We could clearly see their markings. "They're British!" we shouted, and we waved and screamed up to them. "See, we are KZ-nicks! We are concentration camp inmates!" We waved our striped caps at them and pointed at our striped clothes, but there was no mercy. They dropped fire bombs, as the *Cap Arcona* shook and burned. On their next pass they came within fifteen meters of the deck. We could see one pilot's face, and we thought we had nothing more to fear. But in that instant his plane's belly flaps opened again, and more bombs flew down. We could track each one as it fell and on impact sent sections of the deck flying about. Other bombs missed us and fell into the sea, creating fountains of water splashing over us. Machine-gun bullets sprayed us and those trying to save themselves in the sea, and then the water turned red as bodies disappeared beneath the waves.

We were terrified as the ship tilted still more. The deck surface was smooth and wet, and we could no longer stand upright. We sat at the edge and held on to the railing. The sea around us was filled with people struggling and losing their battle to survive. Escaping the turbulence of the whirlpool was nearly impossible. The few that managed to get out of the whirlpool were so weakened that they soon vanished under the churning waters as well. It was three in the afternoon. The visibility was good, and we clearly saw the shore. We hoped that someone from shore would come, perhaps to rescue the *Cap Arcona*'s crew, and we could get help. Surely they wouldn't ignore their own people.

The *Cap Arcona* was tilted about thirty-five degrees into the water. Our hope of rescue was fast fading. In spite of what everyone saw happening around us, people were still jumping overboard, expecting a miracle. Then the explosives on board ignited. My brother and I sat holding a railing post between our legs so as not to slide off the deck. Flames shot up over our heads. Fragments of the deck were breaking off after each bang. The inferno was thorough. We could no longer hang on.

Josek and I stared at one another and looked toward the shore. I knew that he could not help me, nor could I help him. Josek could not swim and knew that he would never make it, trying to swim to shore. Each of us had to make his own decision. I looked at the clear, cold, hostile sea, and every part of me shivered. We were rapidly sinking. Few people were left on deck. The sailors and some SS men were still there. Had they figured out a way to escape this nightmare? If they had, they did not share it with us. I looked to the heavens and asked why this was happening.

It was about four o'clock when I saw David Kot tie a rope to the ship's railing and slide down into the water. When I looked down at him, he shouted up, "Come on down! The rope is strong. Down here we'll have a better chance of being picked up."

I was convinced. But before I decided I thought of my brother. We had survived so much together. I tried to get Josek to come with me. I told him that the planes and explosions on the boat would surely kill us. But Josek was afraid. He shrugged his shoulders. I understood his apprehension. "Berek, you go," he said. "Perhaps you'll get help for us out there. I will stay here and wait." By then several people were hanging on to the rope, and more were eyeing it, believing it to be the miracle escape route. There was little I could do to persuade my brother. I took a last look at him, quickly turned my head, and followed Viky Engel down the rope.

I reached bottom. Seven of us were hanging on to the rope and bobbing in the water. The water temperature was cold—only about seven degrees Celsius. My jacket and shoes were soaked and heavy, and I had to take them off. Viky said that his brother, Willy, had left the ship some time ago and swum to shore. He thought that Willy was a good swimmer and that he would make it if anyone could. Desperate people seeking safety continued to slide down the rope. It was strong, but all ropes have their limits. We were nine, and more were coming. When the tenth person climbed on the rope, it stretched and crackled. "No more!" we shouted up. "The rope will tear." But there was a stampede on deck, and people kept sliding down. I knew the rope would not last much longer. I was wearing trousers, a shirt, a black short-sleeved sweater, and shoes. I untied my shoes and let them fall into the sea. I took off my trousers and let those go as well. With them went the kilo of dental gold. Now I had only my shirt, sweater, and underwear.

People still kept coming and sliding down the rope. With about fifteen holding on, the rope began to untwist. Then it snapped and tore. We all plunged down deep into the dark cold sea. It tumbled and churned, as if we were in a giant washing machine. I had no air. I struggled, my lungs bursting. Finally I surfaced and was able to stay up. David Kot was battling the sea. He couldn't stay on top. He went down, came up thrashing, and went down again with a gurgling sound. This time he vanished for good. Four others who had held the rope with me managed to stay afloat only a few minutes before they too drowned. I knew I would not get very far if I tried to swim to shore. Flinging my arms and kicking hard with my feet, I swam back to the ship. There I could escape the downward pull of the current. Then I moved along, holding onto the ship's hull, until I managed to reach the stern. There I held on and watched.

Hundreds of people were fighting death in the heartless cold waters of the sea. Then suddenly, I saw an object bobbing thirty meters from the ship. It was a small bit of wood. That gave me a new determination. I pulled off my sweater, shirt, and underwear. Naked, mustering all my strength and resolution, I began to swim for it. Every stroke was a major effort. Once I was outside the drag of the whirlpool, swimming was easier. When I came close to the wood, I could see that it was a piece of the ship that had blown free in an explosion. I grabbed it and held it tightly under my chest. "We'll both have to make it to shore, or both go down," I mumbled. "I will not let go of you until you save me."

I alternately kicked with my feet and threw my arms forward. Hard as I tried, the meter-high waves seemed to pull me up and down and keep me in the same place. I realized that I lacked the strength to make it to shore. Then I saw a small boat slicing slowly through the sea. I thought of changing direction and swimming into its path to intercept it. I redoubled my efforts. I stretched and kicked, but in spite of this I fell short. It was a four-meter boat filled with naked men. I knew it would pass before I could reach it. I wasn't the only one struggling in the water. Some others were closer to the boat's path. I feared this was the end. I heard people begging to be picked up. As a man was pulled up, I waved and yelled to get their attention. "We can't take anyone. We have no more room! We are full!" they shouted back to me. But that did not deter me. In a final effort, I lurched, throwing my arms forward to get a bit closer to them. Then I saw how low their boat was in the water, just barely above the waterline. I begged and pleaded with them until I could shout no more. "It's Bronek, the dentist. Let's try to take him," someone yelled. The motor slowed, and the boat turned and pushed in my direction. A minute later a few hands pulled me into the boat. I slumped down, barely conscious. The naked comrades and the sunburned fisherman were my archangels. As the little boat slowly plowed the waters toward the shore, many people were begging to be picked up. "If we take one more, we'll all go down," the fisherman cautioned.

The small engine pushed the heavily loaded boat, as the waves rolled it up and down. The fisherman skillfully manuevered the boat to avoid capsizing. I sat still, with my head between my pulled-up knees, and thought of my brother. I had cheated death once more, but he could not. All hope that the *Cap Arcona* would stay afloat was fading.

The fisherman's skillful hands brought the boat slowly into the shallow waters. "OK," he said and stopped. "You can make it from here." We struggled to get out. The sun was sinking into the sea. The *Cap Arcona* was barely visible. We were naked, cold, and hungry and feared capture. Was there another camp or, even worse, another *Cap Arcona* awaiting us?

Later we learned the results of the gruesome tragedy. Although the precise number of the drowned will never be known, the first estimates were that 13,000 people died in the Baltic Sea that day. Only 1,450, 10 percent of the inmates from Fürstengrube, Neuengamme, Gross-Rosen, and Stutthof camps, survived. Although no one can say how many Americans were captives on the ships, or why they were there, none survived. According to eyewitness reports, the captain of the *Cap Arcona* was the first to leave the ship. Declassified records released by the British Royal Air Force in 1975 conclusively proved that the ships were indeed sunk by the RAF. Why is still a mystery.

On January 31, 1947, the captain of the *Cap Arcona* filed the following statement:

> Captain Heinrich Bertram's Report to the Hamburg-Südamerika Dampfschiffahrts-Gesellschaft, Hamburg, Holzbrücke.
>
> On February 27, 1945, I took over the command of the 28,000-metric-ton passenger ship *Cap Arcona,* by the order of the Hamburg–South America Line, in agreement with the Navy Department.
>
> From the captain of the *Athen* I learned that the transportation of about twelve thousand prisoners from Lübeck had begun. Most of them were destined to be loaded on the *Cap Arcona.*
>
> For me it was a matter of course to refuse to accept the prisoners, since any responsible seaman knows that the risk at sea of taking on human beings without absolute necessity during wartime is dangerous enough, especially such masses.
>
> On Thursday, April 26, the SS officer, Sturmbannführer Gehrig, who was in charge of transport, appeared, accompanied by an advisory merchant marine captain and an executive Kommando, consisting of soldiers armed with machine guns. Gehrig had brought a written order to my attention that called for me to be shot at once if I further refused to take the prisoners on board.
>
> At this point it became clear to me that even my death would not prevent the boarding of the prisoners, and so I informed the SS officer that I categorically renounced any responsibility for my ship.
>
> Gehrig proceeded to order the transfer of the prisoners from the *Athen* to the *Cap Arcona.* Additional transports arrived from Lübeck, so that on April 28, 1945, I had a total of about

6,500 prisoners on board in spite of the statement of the merchant marine officer that the ship was capable of holding a limit of 2,500.

On Sunday, the twenty-ninth of April, I drove to Hamburg to request release from the order to scuttle the ship in case the enemy approached. In Hamburg I was told that Count Bernadotte had just declared that he would take all prisoners except German nationals. Swedish ships were already on their way, and I should speedily return to Neustadt.

It is worth mentioning that on Monday, April 30, 1945, the *Athen* took 2,000 German prisoners on board that were not supposed to go to Sweden, so that at the time of the sinking of the *Cap Arcona,* only about 4,500 prisoners were on board.

Signed: Heinrich Bertram, former captain of the *Cap Arcona**

Martin Gilbert, the eminent British historian, in his book *The Holocaust* describes what happened to those prisoners who were turned back from the ships:

On May 2, in Lübeck harbor, several hundred Jews who had been evacuated from Stutthof were taken out in small boats to be put on board two large ships in the harbor, the *Cap Arcona* and the *Thielbek.* The captains of these ships refused to take them, however; they already had 7,500 Jews on board. The small boats were ordered back to the shore. But, as they neared land in the early hours of May 3, and the starving Jews tried to clamber ashore, SS men, Hitler Youth and German Marines opened fire on them with machine guns. More than five hundred were killed. Only 351 survived.

That same day, May 3, the *Cap Arcona* was attacked by British aircraft in Lübeck bay. Only a few of the prisoners managed to save their lives by jumping overboard.[†]

*Joachim Völfer, *Cap Arcona: Biographie eines Schiffes* (Herford, Germany: Koehlers Verlagsgesellschaft, 1977), 120–21.

[†]Martin Gilbert, *The Holocaust: A History of the Jews of Europe during the Second World War* (New York: Holt, Rinehart and Winston, 1986), 806.

19

WHERE DO WE GO?

We asked the fisherman where we could go to find shelter. He thought a while, scratched his head, and mumbled, "Hmm." Then he directed us to a bakery. "Follow the shore until you come to a house on a hill just off the beach. That's the bakery. No one may be there, but you may find the oven still warm and even some bread." We thanked him and asked him to help those still in the sea. He did not need to be motivated. He had his boat ready to leave. A veil of darkness covered what was left of the *Cap Arcona*. A ghostlike quiet, broken only by the sound of the surf, hovered about the place where the tragedy of the last twenty-four hours had unfolded. On the shoreline the sea approached and then receded, as if nothing had happened.

As we left the boat I raised my eyes to heaven. "Dear God, my mother and my father and my sister are all dead. Please, God! Let me not mourn my brother too," I pleaded. We moved like shadows along the eerily quiet shore, trying not to be seen. Suddenly we came upon the bodies of two comrades from Fürstengrube. As we continued on, an elderly man came toward us. What if he gave us away?

The man was frightened as well. His eyes widened with each step we took toward him. The sight of ten naked men walking the beach surprised him. "What happened to you?" he asked, and we told him about our ordeal. He hadn't heard a thing, he said. We beseeched him to go and recruit people with boats to save the drowning. But he told us that most people had left the area because of the heavy fighting. "Continue moving along the shore, and you'll come to the bakery," he said, rolling his esses in the North German dialect. Then he walked off, still shaking his head. We hobbled in the deep sand, half frozen, our teeth chattering, and we discovered five more survivors. Finally we saw a faint light. It was the bakery.

Inside twenty more survivors were wrapped in scraps of burlap and rags, sitting piteously around two burning candles. They were talking about who had drowned and who had survived. The conversation was unemotional, as if they were talking about lost objects. I listened, fearing I would hear my brother's name among the dead. I still had some hope, however faint.

The ovens were ice cold. Our biggest concern was being found there and herded into another camp. We had water, and at last we could slake our thirst, but there was not a morsel of food. A few more survivors arrived. Each spoke of the miracle that had saved him. "Your friend Willy must have made it to the shore, but then he died. I saw him lying on the beach," said one. Despite the gnawing hunger, fear of another concentration camp didn't let us rest. A few more survivors trickled in throughout the night. Nearly all who were saved seemed to come to the bakery. Mendele, among the late arrivals, claimed he had seen my brother still on deck when he jumped into the water. Like most of us, he too was rescued by a fisherman.

As daylight began to filter in, a civilian came and ordered us to board two trucks. At first he did not to tell us who he was or why he was here. We feared the worst. When we asked him where he was taking us, he startled us. "We are taking you to a hospital. The British are here." Outside were two open trucks and another German civilian. There was nothing to indicate the previous day's disaster except some debris on the beach. We boarded the trucks, still stark naked. We carried those who were unable to walk. Some still refused to believe that we were free. They suspected another German trick. But there was none of the mustering of the past.

It was six in the morning when we left the bakery. The *Cap Arcona* lay on one side at a forty-five-degree angle, with part of its hull above the waterline. As the trucks followed along a shore road, we occasionally saw bodies on the beach. Then the two vehicles turned onto a paved highway. Within minutes we saw tanks roll by us painted with white stars. We thought that it was the Soviet star and that the soldiers were Russians. The uniforms and berets of the soldiers, though, convinced us that they were British. We yelled and waved, and they must have thought that we naked men were crazy.

More British tanks passed, and there was more friendly waving. We were swept away by the soldiers' warm-heartedness. Few of us spoke English, except for single words. Nonetheless, we quickly learned the victory sign. They acknowledged us, raising their fingers in a V, which said more than any words could convey. As we came to the center of Neustadt, where two- and three-story houses stood, we strained to cover our private parts.

Finally the two trucks stopped at a red brick building, a German navy hospital. We were led to a large room and shown clean bunk beds with white bedding and real linen sheets. Each of us got a blue nightshirt with a navy insignia on it. The contradiction was inescapable. Yesterday we were still useless parasites. Now we were in such an elite hospital. It was a monumental change for us.

The room was dimly lit. I lay with my eyes glued to the ceiling. So much had happened in the last forty-eight hours that I found it hard to think. If only my brother had survived. My head felt heavy. Resting on the soft, puffy pillow, I fell asleep.

It was noon when I heard voices. I opened my eyes and saw a woman, who was speaking in the distinctive German of the region. The familiar voice of Mendele answered from the bed below. The middle-aged woman had volunteered to care for us. "The doctor ordered special food for you," she said. "It will be ready very soon." Then a nurse came, raised the window shades, and began taking everyone's temperature. I did not feel feverish, but she insisted. She also spoke German. Her orders were to check everyone. Bright sunshine began to flow through the windows, washing the room with light.

At twelve thirty two women carried in a large kettle of real soup, along with bread and butter. "A doctor will be here soon. Until then you should remain in your beds," they said, sounding kind. I had freedom on my mind. Not feeling sick, I didn't need the peace and quiet of the hospital. I itched to see the world. I just wanted to leave. But how could I, without clothes? I looked at Mendele. He was only a boy, much more fit to be seen naked than I was. I did not need to insist. He offered to look for clothes. "I'll scrounge something for you," he said as he left.

I almost gave up hope of seeing him again, but he returned wearing a black tuxedo with tails that was four sizes too big for him. He didn't settle for ordinary clothes. He brought me a German naval officer's uniform with all the insignias, a pair of high laced navy boots, and an officer's hat, belt, and tie. "Where did you find this?" I asked him, surprised.

"Don't ask any questions. Just get dressed. Wait 'til you see what else I have," he said with twinkling eyes. Then he went out and came back pushing a shiny bicycle by its handlebars. "I took it away from a Nazi," he said. I was not surprised. I also felt uncharitable toward the Nazis. The law of survival in the Lodz ghetto and in concentration camps had taught him new rules, which he now followed. It was the law of the jungle.

Many of the released prisoners also wanted to leave, and those who were able walked out with us. I am closing a chapter of my life, I thought. Mendele walked with his head high, proud of this shiny bike, something he probably wanted all his life but never got. Happiness was written on his face. Then, as if in an afterthought, he exclaimed in a sudden burst, "You know what? I saw your brother, Josek."

It was as if he had hit me in the face. Josek alive? How could that be? I took him by his silk tuxedo lapels and shook him. "You saw Josek?" I said slowly, looking into his eyes. He looked back at me very seriously. I knew Mendele wouldn't tell me a lie about my brother.

"Honest to God, I saw him," he insisted.

"When did you see him?"

"Just now. I forgot to tell you."

"Are you sure that it was Josek you saw?" I said, not wanting to risk raising a false hope. "What was he wearing?"

"He still had on his camp clothes. I don't know how they survived, but there were about seventy of them. Honestly, I swear by my mother and father that I saw him." I knew it had to be true.

"Mendele! I believe you. Come with me and help me find him." We walked to the center of town, and two more survivors told me that they had also seen my brother. There could be no mistake. I was sure he was alive. I walked up the same hill we had come down two days before, with Mendele circling around me on his bike. We saw a group of fifteen of our fellows still wearing their infamous concentration camp outfits. I took a few steps forward, but Mendele was already among them. He found my brother, who was coming toward me, astounded and happy. Under his arm was a Swiss cheese the size of a bicycle wheel.

"Josek! How did you survive?" I demanded to know, as we embraced. It had been a long time since we had cried. All the tears, long held back, came pouring out. We wept like children.

"I followed you with my eyes. When you passed the stern I saw you struggle, and then I closed my eyes. When I opened them again, I saw you being pulled up into the boat. Seventy of us were still on the ship, holding on to the railing. It was dark, and I thought that was it and no one would help us then. But at daybreak, I guess about six o'clock this morning, a boat with English soldiers came alongside and took us off," Josek said, happily exuberant.

One question was always the first thing that a survivor asked another: How did you survive? No two stories were alike. Unfortunately there were few of us to ask those questions. Most of the tenacious, tough, death-resisting comrades who miraculously survived years of ghettos and concentration camps, hardened to all that the fierce enemy of ours handed us, had been devoured by the Baltic Sea. Only a small part of the *Cap Arcona* was above the water. "No one could possibly be alive out there," I thought.

The Allied soldiers who liberated the area, British and Belgian troops, could not understand how it all had happened. What we told them about the camps seemed so preposterous that they shook their heads in disbelief. It seemed as if they didn't know anything about concentration camps. We were the first inmates that they had stumbled on.

As we were saying our sorrowful good-byes to our dead comrades, those with whom we had endured the worst, a young British lieutenant asked if some of us would come with him and tell his superiors what had happened. Not many of us spoke English. I did somewhat, though not well. My brother and two others went with me and the lieutenant in an odd-looking car, a jeep. We drove west on the main road, passing hundreds of abandoned cars, trucks, and tanks until we came to a brick building, a former post office. The lieutenant told us that when the German armies pushed to the sea, they had tried to elude capture by leaving their army vehicles behind and switching to civilian vehicles.

We were taken to a major. We still felt apprehensive around authorities, especially the military. That fear continued long after the war. The major was about fifty years old, with a short haircut and a neatly trimmed mustache. He opened a package of cigarettes and offered each of us one. Then he leaned back in his chair and asked in English which one of us spoke his language. I nodded and told him that I spoke a little English. He prepared to take notes. He asked my name and where I was from.

We were concerned about being forced to repatriate to Poland. A rumor that this might happen was circulating at that time. I remembered Max Schmidt's suggestion. "We're from France," I said.

He asked how we got on the *Cap Arcona* and how it sank. When I told him in my limited English that we saw RAF planes bombing the ship, his chin dropped, and his eyebrows rose in disbelief. Intrigued, he asked more, and then it became apparent that my English was insufficient to fully describe the event. The major called an interpreter. A pretty German girl of about twenty came in and translated his questions into German for me and my answers into English for him. She was visibly moved by the account of our experiences.

The major and lieutenant listened politely. At the end of our interview, the major suggested that we leave the area because of the ongoing fighting. Of course we didn't have transportation. Having seen many abandoned vehicles on the way here, we hoped he would permit us to take one of the cars now littering the roads. He understood the connection. "I can't give you permission," he said, friendly but firm. "There are so many are out there, though. Just take any vehicle you can use. No one will stop you." As for our personal identification, he said, "Your tattoos are sufficient to identify you."

We were excited, and ten of us went to look for the right vehicle. We explored all the cars around, but one car couldn't take us all, so we decided to look for a truck. We searched until we were almost out of town. Then we saw a bus with camouflage war paint. It was a Peugeot, still in good condition. My father had once owned a Peugeot truck. I looked around inside, but the keys were nowhere to be found. It was the perfect vehicle for us, and we wondered what to do. We decided to go into the house and ask the farmer if he had the keys. He claimed that the bus wasn't his, but we thought that he had the keys nonetheless. We were determined to take that bus. When we insisted and threatened him, he went to the bedroom and returned, trembling, with the keys in his hand. He claimed he forgot his wife had put them there.

I started it up and began backing it out onto the narrow street. I had had only limited experience driving a large vehicle, and I soon got into a situation in which I could go neither forward nor backward. The engine stalled. I tried to get it going, but it kept stalling, and I finally gave up. Disappointed, we left that bus standing and went to look for another one.

We must have looked at fifty vehicles without finding a bus like the one we had just left. It was late in the afternoon. We were dulling our hunger with slices of my brother's wheel of Swiss cheese. We searched until we came upon two Italian-made Fiats that looked as if they had just come off the assembly line. The keys were in them, and we decided to take them.

My brother started one, and I the other. We were driving west, as the major had suggested, deeper into the occupied territories. We greeted the soldiers on every Allied vehicle we passed with waves. They looked at us with misgivings, wondering who the bony-faced people in striped suits and shabby

German naval uniforms were. The landscape was now free of swastikas. In their place lay the reminders of war: burned-out cars, trucks, and tanks. Among the people walking on the road was a tall, slightly hunched man carrying a bundle on a stick. He was swaying from side to side and lurching forward as if he had been on the road a long time. As we passed him someone said, "It's Ohlschläger, the SS guard from Fürstengrube." We stopped, and he continued walking calmly toward us. When he came close we asked him if he knew who we were. He acted evasive and answered no.

"Are you not Ohlschläger, the guard from Fürstengrube?"

This convinced him that it would make no sense for him to deny it. "Yes," he said, stuttering, "but I had nothing to do with the camp." We soon became accustomed to hearing this denial. "I just did my duty. I was just a tower guard." This was another excuse we would hear repeatedly. Now Ohlschläger was no longer the brazen SS trooper. He feared us as we had once feared him.

He embodied all evil to us. Our bitterness and anger were difficult to contain. Some said we should kill him. We all wished him death, but no one wanted to be the executioner. He was repeating his defense. "I was just a plain man doing my duty," he said over and over. Our positions had suddenly reversed, and he was helpless. We were unsure what we should do with him. We were intoxicated with our new freedom and found it easy to forgive. But he did not walk away scot-free. We gave him a few well-deserved kicks and slaps, and then we left him. His real punishment, we believed, was the defeat of his Führer's Nazi theory. That should bring him disgrace. Later we agonized over why we had not dealt more harshly with him.

As we continued driving, we came to Neu Glassau. By then the sun had set. We had nowhere else to go, so we decided to drive by the Schmidts' barn, take the cutoff, and go to their house. In front of their mansion was a circular driveway lined with trees. A few of our former fellow inmates who were still there were astonished to see us. They still wore striped suits, as did most of our party. They told us that they had survived by hiding in and around the barn. Unfortunately some others were not so lucky; they had been discovered and shot. Josef Hermann was also there. He preferred to be called Hermann Josef now. Schmidt, our former Kommandant, was gone.

The elder Schmidts, whom we had not seen before, came out of the house and greeted us. He was a well-to-do farmer, a dapper suntanned man of about fifty. She was a plump, well-mannered lady. Max was their only child, they said. They had one of their pigs slaughtered for dinner that night and asked us politely to stay. Whereas just days ago we were *Unmenschen* and, like cattle, had slept in and around their barn, now we were suddenly honored guests having dinner in the house of our Kommandant's parents. Had our lives taken this big a turn? No German had treated us like this before. Before dinner they served wine and schnapps. For many of us, this was our first drinking experience in years. By the time the pig was cooked and brought to the table, some of us were half drunk, or at least lightheaded. The table was festive, as if set for a joyous celebration, covered with fine china and crystal.

In this gaiety and frolicking, the time was apparently right for a surprise to be sprung on us. In walked Max Schmidt with a bright, friendly smile on his face, his hair cropped. He came up to each of us sitting around the table to shake hands. To me he stretched out his arms as if I were his closest pal. "Dentist, how nice that you survived. Too bad that Bernadotte wouldn't take you to Sweden."

Although I regarded his advice about Sweden as the best deed of his that I could remember, I asked him how he knew I was not in Sweden. "You were not around when we were returned," I said to him. He let it go by, and I did not pursue it any further.

Here we were, pampered guests in Schmidt's house eating a special meal prepared for us. The former Lagerführer sat at the same table as we did, and we all ate and drank merrily together. "Let's not talk about the past. Forget what has happened. It was a terrible time for all of us," Schmidt said. Then he rolled up the left sleeve of his shirt and showed us a number on his arm, just like the ones that all of us had. I couldn't see whether it was tattooed or painted. That seemed not to upset us. We let everything pass with laughter. The prevailing attitude was one of forgiveness.

Around midnight we all were asleep. When I woke up in the morning I saw sparkling sunshine filtering into a few small windows of the feed storage room where I had slept. Next to me were my brother and Srulek Lipshitz. My head was heavy. Something wasn't right, I knew. Weighing what had happened last night, I became troubled. I thought about Max. In the past five months, having sole command of us, he could have let us go free. Showing us a prisoner's number, to make himself seem like us, was particularly distasteful to me. This number, and the fact that his hair was cut short, convinced me that he was strenuously trying to conceal who he really was and wanted to masquerade as a camp survivor. "We cannot allow this," I thought. I could not stay there another minute.

Ten of us decided to leave immediately. Hermann Josef wanted to come with us. "We ought to turn Max over to the Allies and tell them what role he played in the camps," I said. Hermann agreed that he was not entirely innocent. Max was nowhere to be found, but his parents were there, and so, suddenly, was Gerta. It was obvious to the Schmidts that something had changed since last night. They knew that we were leaving. It was difficult to part from our brethren with whom we had shared life for several years. We had little gasoline left and thought we would stop and ask soldiers for "petrol," as the British called it. As we left we were still talking about how we were manipulated by the Schmidts and how Max's insensitive act was particularly appalling.

Five kilometers to the west we saw an British army depot. We drove in and were immediately stopped at the barrier. We explained in halting English to the two soldiers why we had stopped, but they wouldn't let us see anybody. They claimed that no one there had authority in such matters and suggested that we see British Army Intelligence. Nonetheless, we succeeded in getting a canister of gasoline for each car, twenty liters' worth, and also a box of rations. We stopped at two more depots and were told the same thing. None of the British soldiers seemed to take us seriously—as if they did not care. We were baffled and disappointed by them. Since we were not far from Westphalia, Hermann Josef suggested we stop in Lüdenscheid, where a friend of his still lived, he believed. We changed direction.

Every so often we stopped on the road and ate what the British had given us. These were American rations that included canned beef, chocolate, and powdered milk. At eight in the evening we encountered our first Americans close to the town of Münden, not far from Kassel. The road was filled with jeeps and soldiers, some wearing black armbands with the letters *MP*. They stopped us and told us to move to the side of the road. "Papers?" one of them asked. Eventually, when they saw our tattooed numbers, we managed to get them to understand that we were former prisoners of concentration camps and did not have any papers. "Where are you going?" they wanted to know.

"We are returning home," Hermann said, which was at least true for him.

"On General Eisenhower's orders, all travel by civilians is prohibited at night," they told us. "You're not allowed to drive between eight at night and seven in the morning." Hermann thought that we should turn back and drive to Lüdenscheid, which he thought might be occupied by the British. So we began turning back. "Wait!" one MP said. "We have a place for you to stay here, overnight." We thanked the "officer" (we called everyone officer at first). Among some houses behind the barrier stood a modern two-story house. We could stay there, the MPs said. They also said that there was still food left inside. Unlike the British, they seemed friendly. It did not take us long to find the essentials: enough bread, eggs, sugar, and real Nescafé coffee. It was the first time in five years we were able to cook for ourselves.

Just before we went to bed, we received a visit from a sergeant. First he seemed keenly interested in our experiences. Then he asked if we would lend him one of our automobiles for a couple of hours. We didn't need it right away, and we readily agreed. "But there isn't much gasoline in the tank," we said. Gasoline was a scarce commodity at the time.

"Don't worry," he said. "I'll bring you back all the gasoline you want." What a wonderful coincidence, we thought. We won't need to worry about gasoline in the morning. There were enough sofas and beds for everyone, and we had a sense of leisure that was hard to comprehend. To lie down in a real bed under a soft, downy comforter was an unexpected luxury.

The following morning we made two cardboard signs that read "Concentration Camp Inmates" to affix to our automobiles. But the sergeant was not there, and we began to worry. One of his squad quietly assured us that he would be back soon. "He is probably at his Fräulein's," the soldier said. The sergeant eventually arrived and signaled that the gasoline was in the trunk. He asked us not to fill our cars there, since that would get him in trouble. We checked, and indeed the cans were full. On the road to Lüdenscheid, we unscrewed one can and began pouring into the tank what we thought was gasoline. It lacked the plop, the odor, and the flow of gasoline. It was ordinary water. We could not believe that a friendly American would swindle us that way.

We were on a busy road in wartime, with some water in the tank, unable to move. For the next hour we tried to stop a passing vehicle until finally a jeep halted with army officers aboard. They gave us a canister of real gasoline. At the same time we learned that Germany had just surrendered. It was May 8. The war in Europe was over.

The engine of our Fiat sputtered and coughed but after a while began to idle. As we drove on toward Lüdenscheid, we once again returned to the British Zone. We arrived at the home of the Happes around midnight. Mr. Happe was stunned to see Hermann and even more so the ten of us with him. In spite of the late hour Frau Happe and served us food, a full meal. We were vigilant and still distrustful of all German people, but the Happes' hospitality was genuine. There must have been more like them. Where were they? Why were they just bystanders?

Lüdenscheid was a picturesque small town untouched by the ravages of the bitter conflict. It was nestled in a region called Sauerland, with lush green meadows and bountiful soil. A small river, the Volme, wound along the main road to the county seat of Hagen. Not a single house there bore the scars of war. With great fanfare, Mr. Happe introduced us to the town elders, the mayor, and the police chief. Lüdenscheid had had a small number of Jews before the war. Only one survived. The mayor, a former Nazi, made every effort to show that he had liked Jews. He said they missed the Jews who had once lived there and urged us to stay. He also promised to help find us housing and jobs. They all showed great respect for Mr. Happe's new friends.

Being the first concentration camp survivors in town made us celebrities. My brother and Srulek still wore their striped suits. I had on the navy uniform from the depot at Neustadt. The mayor offered, and we accepted, a complete set of clothing, furnishings, and an apartment. The cinemas in town issued us free passes for life, as did the dramatic theater. Suddenly everyone was our friend. No one, it seemed, had any role in our persecutions, and they all disclaimed their complicity in the Nazi regime. I could not believe that they had come full circle to see us as human again in just a few days.

Seven of our friends left to return to Poland. My brother and Srulek wanted to stay in Lüdenscheid. I was not yet ready to settle there. Hermann wanted to return to Ahlberg, in Bavaria, to his wife and children. When he asked if I would like to come, I accepted his invitation.

20

POSTWAR GERMANY

Leaving with Hermann helped me to ease the pain of the preceding five years and adapt to a new reality. When we left Lüdenscheid most roads were still impassable, especially in the larger cities in Germany. Hermann stopped in Giessen to see some of his prewar colleagues of the SPD, the Sozialdemokratische Partei Deutschland, in which he had once been active. In some cities the Americans wanted us to speak to the German functionaries about our ordeal. As if in a conspiracy of silence, they claimed to a man not to have known about any concentration camp or death camp. Hermann and I talked a lot about that. I got to know Germany's peculiarities and its diversities. Hermann knew the country well—and knew when not to believe the Germans.

When we came to his family in Ahlberg, I witnessed true joy. His wife sobbed with happiness when she saw him. The children would not let go of him the whole day. Soon his German SPD friends came, happy that he had survived. They were to rebuild the Gewerkschaften, the labor unions, which were outlawed by the Third Reich. I went with Hermann to a few of their meetings. I soon felt that it was time for me to leave. But where would I go? America always was the country of my dreams. I still wanted to reach France, from which I thought I would have a better chance of getting to the United States.

Hermann and I had only the one car, but we solved that problem by appealing to the town's mayor in Nuremberg, who was an American army captain. He called the depot where confiscated automobiles were housed and ordered the men there to give us any car we chose. I saw a 1936 Adler cabriolet. Hermann Josef agreed to keep the Fiat, and I took the Adler. An automobile registration was still unavailable, so I tied the sign to identify me as a former KZ-nick to the front grille of the Adler. The next day I began my journey to France. It was the middle of June and very warm. Mrs. Josef packed some food, and I took a few German marks with me. The real currency in Germany then, however, was nylon stockings, chocolate, and American cigarettes. The road south wound through the rolling hills of Bavaria. Driving with the top of the Adler down, I could smell the pristine country air. Along the road, set wide apart, were spacious homes, draped with wide verandas. None bore any scars of war.

Then I saw two boys on the road waving their arms. Their colorful clothes reminded me of circus clowns. Coming closer, I saw Stars of David on their shirts. I stopped and asked them who they were. At first I frightened them. They didn't know if I was a friend or a foe. But when I told them that I was Jewish, they relaxed. Akiva was from Budapest, and his companion, Yaakow, who had a slightly swollen cheek, was from Iaşi, Romania. They were both sixteen and had recently been freed from Dachau. I asked them if they had relatives. To this they twirled their index fingers unemotionally up to the sky, showing that their families had been killed at the chimneys. They feared being sent back to their countries and were not sure where else to go. They had strayed around for a month, living on what the GIs gave them and sleeping in the forests. I asked them if they would want to come with me to France, and they readily agreed.

For the next few days we lived like vagabonds, roving, rambling, not knowing where our next meal would come from. We stopped at ponds and streams and washed up amid the blossoming lily pads that covered them. On hot days we swam in the clear waters. We halted at American army depots, where we watched, fascinated, as soldiers tossed a little white ball with stitched seams while others caught it in strange-looking, big brown gloves. On some evenings we sat among them and listened to their portable radios playing the Big Band sound. All this was new to us. On cool nights we would stop at a church, a rectory, or a monastery, where we were allowed to sleep. After several days we arrived at the northern tip of Lake Constance, or the Bodensee, as the locals call it. To the south, amid green, gently rolling hills and breathtaking snowcapped mountains, were colorful chalets. In time Akiva and Yaakow felt as if I were their older brother, and to me they were "my boys."

Yaakow's cheek kept on swelling. He needed help. I only had a few marks, not enough to pay for a dentist's service. At the edge of the Black Forest, though, we came to a town called Tuttlingen. We stopped at the first dentist's sign. When the dentist learned who we were, he did the procedure free, extracting Yaakow's bicuspid. He used a brand of equipment called Simmons, which reminded me of the equipment at Fürstengrube.

The next day we were on a road in the Alps, leading to the Alsace-Lorraine region of France. It wound around the mountains like a roller coaster. Suddenly we saw two men in French army uniforms with bundles on their backs. I asked them where they were going, and they said they had been prisoners of war in Germany and were now returning home. I offered to take them with us, and they readily accepted. They were pleased not to have to struggle up the road, and we hoped that having them with us would be of benefit at the border. In the next two days we shared food, and over time we became good friends. I also managed to improve my French vocabulary.

At the border the French soldiers stopped us, and we were escorted to their quarters, in a magnificent mansion. We followed them into the driveway, and the five of us were led inside to an office. We passed a hallway lined with a light-colored mosaic marble. On the floor lay Oriental rugs. A circular staircase led to large mahogany doors. There some army officers, including some women, gathered around us, curious to know who we were. Our two French companions acted as if they were at home.

We were celebrities and were invited to dine with them and, of course, to stay the night. At dinnertime we were led into a large Louis XV–style dining room, where twenty chairs sat around a heavy mahogany table covered with a snow-white damask tablecloth. A large crystal chandelier hung over the table from a nine-meter-high ceiling. Fine china and crystal dazzled our eyes, and carafes of red wine stood spaced in the middle of the table. Soon the room filled with decorated French officers. Then a statuesque-looking gentleman entered. He was the commanding officer of the army division stationed in Alsace-Lorraine, a lieutenant general. Then all became much more formal.

As he sat down at the head of the table, everyone else also assumed places. Our two new friends translated his questions and comments into German for us. Now and then someone raised a toast, and though we didn't comprehend why, we lifted our glasses and drank the wine with everyone else. I felt nothing strange until it was too late. Even before the first dish was served, Yaakow and Akiva's heads slumped on the table. I tried to force myself to keep my eyes open, but everything around me began spinning as if I were sitting on a fast carousel. I passed out. When I awoke it was morning. I lay in a large building on straw, covered with army blankets. Next to me lay my boys. We shared the quarters with several sleeping French soldiers.

I walked out of the building and stopped a passing soldier, asking him where our interpreter friends, the two Frenchmen, were. He didn't seem to know. I looked everywhere but could not find them. It seemed as if the two former prisoners of war had disappeared. Then I asked where my car was, but no one seemed to know that either. Finally I went to the office. One soldier made a few telephone calls, and what he told me sounded incredible. "The two ex-prisoners collaborated with the Germans during their internment," he said. "They are under arrest." We were not allowed even to say adieu.

It took over an hour for us to find our car, which now had a nearly empty tank. "You have to return to the American Zone and apply for a visa there before you can go to France," a soldier said. I appealed to him, begging him to let us at least go to Strasbourg and apply there. "There aren't any French consulates in Germany," I said. This we could not do either, he said. He made it unequivocally clear that we had to go back, and so we did.

So I had to change my plans. I drove back on the same road that we had arrived on. Once more we were in the majestic Alps. I began to worry about the boys' future. They needed a home and an education, neither of which I could offer them. When I first talked to them about it, they didn't want to listen, for they preferred the gypsy life. Traveling with me was all they wanted. In Munich I heard about a Jewish American organization called HIAS, for Hebrew Immigration Aid Society, whose offices were in Frankfurt-am-Main. On the road to Frankfurt, when we stopped, I tried to reason with them. They left me and walked off into the forest. When I found them, Yaakow shyly confessed that they were praying that I would change my mind.

In Frankfurt the survivors had a new name, DPs (displaced persons), and were housed in the Olympia Hotel in a part of town close to the main railroad station. Allied bombs had severely damaged the Olympia, and only the two lower levels could be used. The staircase was rubble. We found room in a corner on the second floor and settled there. The next day Isidor Cohen, a rabbi and a U.S. Army chaplain from New York, came to the hotel.

Rabbi Cohen was stout with gray hair. He was a warm and compassionate man. He saw the boys, and he asked me to bring them to him at the airport. When we came to his office the next day, another captain, also a chaplain, was with him. They spoke a strange-sounding American Yiddish, sprinkled with English words that I did not understand. We were joined by a middle-aged woman wearing a green army uniform with a patch on one sleeve that said "UNRRA." The three discussed the fate of the boys. Then the woman turned to me and said firmly, "Leave the boys. They will go to the States as soon as we can arrange visas for them."

Though I realized that this course of action was in the boys' best interests, it was difficult for me to think of losing them. I had gotten so used to them that we had grown into a family. Akiva and Yaakow looked at me as if to accuse me of abandoning them. The rabbi read how the boys' feelings translated in my mind. "You don't have to worry. They will be well cared for here," he said. I asked the rabbi if I could also come. He said no. At my age I had to be sponsored and was advised to register with UNRRA, the United Nations Relief and Rehabilitation Administration. Knowing that I had a car, in fact the only one at the Olympia Hotel, the rabbi proposed that I come to the army kitchen every day to pick up some food for the DPs in the hotel. My Adler convertible soon carried a barrel of food to the hotel every day, and I could visit with my two boys. One day, however, I was told that they had been sent to America. That was the last I saw of Akiva and Yaakow.

More DPs arrived at the hotel, and it was soon nicknamed the Refugee Hotel. The Olympia was in fact the central meeting place for refugees arriving in Frankfurt. Many names were scribbled on the walls as people sought friends and relatives. Some succeeded in finding one another. Slowly people from partisan groups began to emerge from their hiding places. The girls began to dress in neater clothes, and the boys began to woo them. Some even learned how to smile, to frolic, and to be light again, and soon some married. Committees formed, and leaders emerged. More survivors began to arrive from the east, and the Olympia was bulging with people. We cleared the rubble from two additional floors, cleaned the rooms, and still did not have enough room. People were sleeping in the corridors and stairways. And yet more DPs kept coming.

On one day Rabbi Cohen, accompanied by a high-ranking American army officer, announced that we had to vacate the Olympia. The hotel would be renovated for American army personnel, and we would be moved forty kilometers from Frankfurt, to Salzheim. We had not heard of Salzheim before. When a few of us went there to see it, we found a camp with identical little huts neatly set in lines, which reminded me of concentration camp barracks. When we returned to the Olympia, I picked up my few things and left.

It was a nice summer afternoon. I was driving along the Mainzerland-straße, having made no decision what to do, when two girls stopped me and asked if I would take them to their hotel. I agreed. They were both Russian, about my age, and very pretty. Since they had been working in German house-holds, they spoke German well. When they heard that I had no place to stay, they offered me a sofa in their hotel room. I accepted an overnight invitation, but my stay turned into more than just a brief visit with them. I buried my lone-liness in romance. One day two Soviet secret policemen came to force them to return home to Russia. That was the beginning of a general repatriation of all Russians from Germany, and they had to leave. I decided then to go back to Lüdenscheid.

Srulek Lipschitz, helped by an electrical appliance manufacturer, had opened an electrical store. My brother also had a business selling beauty aids, perfumes, and cosmetics. The Westphalia Dental Association and the German Medical Association granted me temporary permission to practice dentistry in Germany, and I began to practice in Menden, Westphalia, in a Polish DP camp. When the camp closed, I founded the Westfälische Zahnwaren Grosshand-lung, a dental supply house that thrived even after I left Germany.

Finding Zosia was my constant thought. Short of going back to Poznan, I did everything I knew to do to find her, but it was all in vain. Her last known whereabouts, I learned, was somewhere in Germany, where she worked as a forced laborer, a Zwangsarbeiter. She did not return to Poznan.

One day I heard the name Harry Spitz mentioned on Nordwestdeutscher Rundfunk, the first German radio station broadcasting in Hamburg after the war. When I called him, he invited me to come to see him in Hamburg. The station offices, on the Oberstraße, were in good condition for that street. On the building's facade was a menorah. Inside, a Star of David hung over the staircase. Unusual, I thought, for a German radio station.

I gave the receptionist my name and told her whom I had come to see. "Do you have an appointment with the music director?" she asked. I said no but requested that she give Herr Spitz my name. "Herr Spitz, a man by the name of Bronek Jakubowicz is here to see you."

Harry came dashing down the stairs and promptly fell into my arms. Over and over again he kept repeating, "This young man saved my life in Auschwitz." Then he took me through the building. It had been built at the beginning of the eighteenth century and indeed had been a synagogue. It had several large studios, one the size of an amphitheater. It survived all the Allies' heavy bombing. We spent twenty-four hours together reminiscing.

Germany was a puzzle. In a sense the Germans were less anti-Semitic than the rest of the Europeans. Where did Hitler find the criminals to perpetrate those insane crimes on the Jews?

For the Germans life was slowly returning to normal. But we were too traumatized to live peacefully among them. In Germany we had to walk the same streets, eat the same food, and breathe the same air as they did. The sinners were suddenly saints, the guilty just bystanders. For reasons not hard to understand, even the best-known Nazis denied their complicity in the Holocaust. We had to be careful what we said and whom we trusted. All this posed an enigma. Yet we had to maintain civility and often had to bite our tongues to avoid saying how we really felt. For me the four years I lived in Germany after the war offered many lessons, about both the good and the bad in humankind. In those four years I was in and out of German hospitals seeking help for the ulcer pains that still plagued me.

The news from Poland was even grimmer. There anti-Semitism was still rampant. The spirit of Hitler's teaching was alive and well. That he chose Poland as our grave was not a coincidence. The Polish Jews were the Nazis' chief target. Many Jews who dared to return to their possessions were killed by those who had seized their property after the Germans left. Though my brother and I were heirs to property in Poland, we wanted none of it.

Josek, Srulek, and I were the only Jews living in Lüdenscheid. Though my spirituality was still undefined, having been adrift during so many years of squalid life, in darkness and away from my heritage, giving up God was still against my conscience. The spiritual vacuum in which we had been living during the past years had produced a certain void within me. I needed to confirm my faith. So when we heard that a Rosh Hashanah service would be conducted at a Jewish person's home in the nearby city of Hagen—nearly all the synagogues in Germany had been destroyed—my urge to make peace with my heritage became irresistible. I knew that the time had come for me to face God and offer my apology. When we got to the house, about thirty people were praying. When the prayers Oshamnah and Agadnah—I have sinned before thee, I transgressed against thee—were recited, all began to chant, rhythmically pounding on their chests. I too prayed, begging the Almighty for forgiveness. There and then I finally made peace with God.

When the service ended, the man who had led us through the prayers, Morris Teichmann, a handsome, well-respected, middle-aged businessman, came to shake each person's hand and wish everyone a Lashonah Tovah, a good year. Then Mr. Teichmann invited us for kiddush at his home, where we met his family. Fortunately, they had all survived the war, but their memories were no less painful than mine.

Mr. Teichmann immigrated to Germany from Poland in 1923 and settled in Westphalia. There he married a Christian woman, Herta Steinfort, who converted to Judaism. In 1938 he was arrested and sent to Poland in a mass deportation of Polish Jews. Herta was allowed a choice: to remain in Germany with their three children—Else, thirteen; Clara, ten; and Gerhard, eight—or to go with him. She and the children soon followed him. When the Germans occupied Poland, Mr. Teichmann was imprisoned in a labor camp. Herta was threatened with arrest and being sent to a camp unless she divorced her husband. She resisted at first but eventually had to give in to the pressure, as it was the only way she could save their children. The children's papers stated, "Jewish father and German mother."

Else blotted out the words "Jewish father" on her papers. To avoid being detected as a Jew, she lived a nomadic life, moving from job to job. She maintained that disguise, and the war's end found her in Prague. The Soviets, who had seized the city, did not believe her true identity, and they jailed her. Her family almost gave up finding her. One day, though, she was able to return to Germany. Mr. and Mrs. Teichmann became my second parents. Else became my fiancée.

The one object of our lives then was to try to go to the United States. But the restrictive McCarron Act prevented us. Then in 1948 the more just Refugee Act replaced it. Else and I wanted to marry, but because we had separate applications pending, we would have had to forfeit our turns and reapply. In 1949 my brother and I were called, so we went to Boston, where we met our sponsor, our great-uncle Mordechai Baily. On the first day in America we changed our names from Jakubowicz to Jacobs. My brother's name became

Joseph Jacobs, and mine became Benjamin Jacobs. A few weeks later Srulek went to his sponsor in Oregon.

I recall August 22, 1949. The tugboats were slowly pushing our troop carrier, the USS *Fletcher,* through a shroud of heavy fog into New York Harbor. Suddenly the hand and the torch of the Statue of Liberty emerged. The emotion of stepping onto America's soil after years of such struggle cannot be adequately described. It seemed as though we were leapfrogging into another age. We were grateful to the American people who opened their hearts and minds to us.

Six months later I returned to Europe, and Else and I married. The town elders honored us by arranging for our wedding on a Sunday. Afterward, we both returned to Boston to face a new land and a new life together.

POSTSCRIPT

Surviving as a prisoner of the Nazis was a hard and bitter struggle. In the face of the generous freedoms in America, our persecution was even more difficult to translate. I felt pain, lots of pain, but I had to suppress it. I envied everyone everywhere who had escaped this terrible ordeal. In America in 1949 people had already heard of Hitler and his deeds and were not eager to hear more. Only later generations wanted to know what had happened to the European Jewry. By this time a new term had arisen to identify the Nazis' mass murder and torture of millions of European Jews: *Holocaust.**

My priority, of course, was practicing dentistry. I studied English and applied for admission to Tufts Dental School. Hearing of my experiences with dentistry, the dean, Dr. Joseph Volker, said that he regretted to advise me that an act of Congress, the so-called GI Bill, offered preference to the returning soldiers and that several years might go by before my application would be acted upon. It was not realistic for me to wait, as I expected my fiancée, soon to be my wife, to come to the United States soon.

One day, while in a Boston hospital waiting room experiencing the discomfort of abdominal pains that still plagued me, I was offered a job in sales by the comptroller of an electronics firm. I held that job for two years. Then, with my brother's, my father-in-law's, and my wife's help, I established my own company. In 1953, at the time of the Korean War, Tufts Dental School encouraged me to reapply for admission. My firm grew, however, and was successful. I remained a businessman until 1987. My brother, unfortunately, died in 1965 at age fifty-one.

---

*I am the least important person in this book. It is the memories of the events that overtook us that must be remembered.

In 1972 I accompanied Else to Hamburg, where she was called to testify in a Nazi's trial. By then Germany had gone through various stages in dealing with guilt. After many denials there was slow admission. The most hopeful signs came in the 1960s, when West Germany perceived its obligation and began to help the Jewish survivors and the emerging state of Israel. Attitudes changed, but not all for the better. Some Germans remained true to Nazism's undemocratic principles, championing the idea that "enough is enough." This is not to mention the neo-Nazis, whose threats are still the most unsettling. Of course, it would be unfair not to mention the many people who committed the past to memory and supported true democracy.

After Else testified, we rented a car and drove from Hamburg to Neustadt. I wanted to know the exact place of the *Cap Arcona* catastrophe. A lot had changed there. One person directed us to a little hill in nearby Timmendorf. We walked along the shore and soon saw a sign in front of a set of stairs leading up a hill. There, tucked away, was a cemetery, overgrown and neglected, with a huge single grave of the victims who had washed ashore. The sign listed their nationalities only. Next we found another cemetery, in which the markers gave names from around the world. One placard told of the tragedy of the ships. Another listed the nationalities of all the victims. The entire area was overgrown with weeds. Compared with the crime it symbolized, it seemed rather obscure. The tragedy of many years past stared us in the face. I stood confused and bewildered. Those who perished there were not just prisoners: they were tough, tenacious, and unrelenting fighters, with hearts stubborn enough to survive all the Nazis cast upon them. Yet they died on the very doorstep of freedom.

We later stopped at a small house that seemed to be a post office. I walked in and saw a small window with an elderly man behind it. Besides him no one was there. I thought he would remember. I asked him how long he had been living here. "All my life," he answered.

I decided not to say who I was. I would just act mildly interested, as any tourist would. I said, "I noticed a cemetery up the hill. I understand that a lot of people perished here?"

He stepped away from the window and came to me. He led me to the door, pointed at the bay, and said, "Three ships sank here, and thousands of people drowned. I wasn't here when it happened, but for years bones drifted up to the shore. Many a time I found some myself on the beach." I was here on a pilgrimage, to recover all the secrets he had willingly shed. But then an elderly woman came in, and the man greeted her. I knew that our conversation was over and that this was all I would learn from him. I left with a heavy heart full of painful memories. I had revisited a nightmare.

In July 1985 I joined a group of Jewish men and women from the United States on a fact-finding mission to Eastern Europe. We went to Poland. Each site brought back more bitter memories. This is where it all began. At Auschwitz, where civilization once ceased, time and weather had rotted the structures and watchtowers of the camp. Children now played there, unconscious that they were walking on the same spot where thousands of Jewish kids took their last steps. Lawns and houses had replaced the once bare landscape. In Birkenau lay shambles of the noxious crematorium. The sign over the gate, "Arbeit Macht Frei," obscene and offensive, was still there. There were many tourists reading on a marker that four million people had been killed there. It didn't tell the real story.

The Block Smierci, the death block where I saw the showcase of inhumanity, was most poignant: stacks of clothes, shoes of all sizes—large, small, and even tiny baby shoes—suitcases with names, mounds of human hair, eyeglasses, canes, teeth, and other personal objects. I had not seen this before. It filled me with so much pain that I couldn't fathom it.

Outside the block, I stood transfixed and looked up to the sky. Where are the souls of the millions of people who rose up in ashes? Now, I thought, the guilty prosper, raise families, and are good fathers and grandfathers.

I went to the museum's archival offices. When I gave my name, Tadeusz Iwaszko, the archivist, said to me. "We know who you are. You were the dentist in Auschwitz III, Fürstengrube." Then he reached out and pulled a book from a shelf. Its title was *Hefte von Auschwitz*. "Look inside," he said. "You'll find your name and number there, and your father's and brother's." With glassy eyes I read my name, Bronek Jakubowicz, number 141129, and the numbers of my father and brother. Another note told of my posting as a dentist in Fürstengrube.

To fulfill a secret desire within me, I went to my former home, the little village of Dobra, where I was born and lived for nearly twenty-two years. When I was arrested in 1941, I left there with lots of memories. After the war, not a single Jewish person returned to Dobra, where Jews had lived for five hundred years. The gravestones from the Jewish cemetery paved the village sidewalks. I sat for a long time in silence, gripped with pain. Then I began to cry.

When I raised my head, an old woman with a weather-beaten face stared at me. "I live just a couple of houses from yours. I knew your mother very well before she and your sister, Pola, were deported. Ester said to me, 'Milka! If we are to see one another again, it will have to be in the other world.'" An irony suddenly struck me: Dobra means good in Polish.

I drove the road to Chełmno that my sister and mother were once driven along. Suddenly Dr. Schatz's confession unfolded in my mind. There Mama and Pola suffocated, and there they died.

Despite the sunny day Chełmno seemed bleak and dreary. It was a painfully morbid and desolate place. Four hundred thousand Jews were killed there, and in retaliation for the mid-1942 assassination of SS Obergruppen-führer Reinhard Heydrich, two hundred Christian children from Lidice, Czechoslovakia, were also murdered. One monument depicted the twisted faces of victims. With gut-wrenching indignation I read what was below, words written by the few Jews kept in a room to process the bodies arriving daily for the crematorium: "We are writing with our blood to let the world know that these are our last days. Here we are being killed by bullets and gassed—our bodies burned—our ashes are being spread in this forest!" Above this was a single giant word, *Pamietamy* (Remember). I will remember the images of that day forever.

Chełmno's crematorium was capable of turning 5,000 bodies each day to ashes, I also read, more even than those in Auschwitz. The maximum at Auschwitz was 4,600. Here were the souls of my mother and my sister!

Seeing Chełmno was more painful for me than being at Auschwitz. A few German students were standing there at the monument, also visibly moved. I wondered how their fathers and grandfathers would explain this to them.

I left the country where my family and my ancestors had lived for years. This was not where I wanted to live. I cut my ties with my former homeland and returned to Boston with a renewed spirit, with a sense of homecoming.

I still can't believe that all of this happened to me—in one lifetime. I have not spent much time examining the unanswered questions: Who was to blame for this? Could any of it have been prevented? If it could have been, why wasn't it? These and many other remaining questions are the assignment for the future. Perhaps more light is necessary to explain this stormy phase in our people's history.

APPENDIX A: Sinking of the *Cap Arcona*

In what is apparently the only English-language article on the *Cap Arcona* sinking, J.L. Isherwood writes in a British periodical:

> The *Cap Arcona*, launched on May 14, 1927, was probably the most luxurious ship on the Hamburg to South America route until the second World War. . . .
>
> In April 1945, with the Russian quick advance, in three of her trips, she evacuated 26,000 Germans on the Baltic from east to west. Thereafter, in April 1945, she took on 6,000 concentration camp prisoners.
>
> It was while in this capacity, lying in Travemünde bay with a number of other ships, that on May 3 British bombers attacked the port. A number of ships were sunk, the largest being the *Deutschland* and the *Cap Arcona*. Including the prisoners, guards and ship's crew, she had aboard at the time about 6,000 people.
>
> Severely damaged and set on fire by the bombs, the *Cap Arcona* eventually capsized and the appalling death toll was estimated at 5,000 people.
>
> The wreck of the charred and twisted steel of the *Cap Arcona*, the tomb of 5,000 bodies, lay for nearly five years. In 1949 it was broken up for scrap metal.

[J. L. Isherwood, "Steamers of the Past: The Hamburg-South American Liner *Cap Arcona*," *Sea Breezes*, May 1976.]

Isherwood's account is borne out by British Operations Record Books, labeled "Secret" and obtained for me by the Hamburg-Südamerika Dampfschiffahrts-Gesellschaft and the Hamburg-Amerika line.

> Detail of Work Carried Out by 197 Squadron for the Month of May 1945

[Time up, 1515; time down, 1635] DD771. Shipping strikes in Lubeck Bay. All the bombs were dropped on a motor vessel of 15/20.000 tons at 0.0208. The ship was already burning as a result of attacks by 263 Squadron and we scored two direct hits. Now left burning in five places and later seen capsized and burning, CAT. I.

[Operations Record Book, AIR 27/1109, 5822, p. 1, Public Record Office, London]

APPENDIX B: For The Record

From the Records of the Auschwitz Museum

SS-Unterscharführer Karol Baga: Baga was the Sanitätsdientsgefreiter at Auschwitz I and at Fürstengrube between May 1944 and January 1945. In light of his willingness to cooperate with the Polish investigation authorities, he served only a brief sentence in the Kraków penitentiary.

SS-Unterscharführer Gunther Hinze: His name was found in the Fürstengrube dentist reports as Sanitätsdienstgefreiter and in the records of the SS-Hygiene Institute. [Log 8, S. Kr 409, BL 87 u. 207, Microfilm 323]

SS-man Koch: A Fürstengrube kitchen chef, Koch was tried in absentia and, since no particular charges were filed, his trial was dismissed.

SS-Hauptsführer Otto Moll: Arrested in 1945, Moll was tried by the Kraków High Tribunal and found guilty of terrible crimes. He was sentenced to death and hanged the same year.

SS-man Ohlschlager: He was a guard at Auschwitz I and at Fürstengrube. He was tried in absentia but since no specific criminal acts could be established the trial dismissed. [APMO. Sign. Mat. 616a, Bd, 48, S. 71]

SS-Unterscharführer Pfeiffer: As Rapportführer at Fürstengrube, Pfeiffer's signature was found on camp records. But since accusations were not available, his trial was dismissed. [GmbH, Nr. 72829, B1.230]

SS-man Unterscharführer Erich Adolf Voigt: According to dental station reports, Voigt was a Sanitätsdienstgard at Fürstengrube beginning in May 1943 and at Dora-Mittelbau in 1945. No specific accusation could be established. His trial was dismissed. [SS trial, Sign. Mat. /589]

Many crimes at the hands of the SS men at Fürstengrube were not documented, largely because few Jewish survivors had returned to Poland after the war.

For additional records of the Fürstengrube SS team, see Tadeusz Iwaszko, *Hefte von Auschwitz* (Auschwitz: Verlag Staatliches Auschwitz-Museum, 1978).

Other Records

Adolph Eichmann: After the war Eichmann escaped to South America and eventually settled in Buenos Aires. In May 1960 he was captured by Israeli agents. In a Jerusalem court he was tried and found guilty of crimes against humanity. Sentenced to death, he was hanged on May 31, 1962. [*Encyclopedia Americana*, 1990, vol. 9]

Dr. Josef Mengele: A long-awaited U.S. government report on the case of Nazi war criminal Mengele confirms that the "Angel of Death" of Auschwitz, wanted for the murder of 400,000 innocent victims, was in fact detained by American authorities as early as 1945 in two P.O.W. camps, but was released because his true identity was unknown. Mengele fled to South America in 1949 and found asylum in numerous countries there, including Paraguay, Uruguay, Brazil, and Argentina. On February 7, 1979, he was found dead on a beach near Sao Paulo. [Gerald Posner and John Ware, *Mengele: The Complete Story* (New York: McGraw Hill, 1986).]

Walter Rauff: Rauff organized the development and production of the mobile gas vans estimated to have killed 97,000 Jews and Russians. He died of lung cancer in Santiago, Chile, in May 1983 after the failure of several attempts to secure his extradition. [Posner and Ware, *Mengele.*]

Hauptscharführer Max Hans Peter Schmidt: The case of Kommandant Schmidt is vastly more complicated than those of other Fürstengrube officials. From testimony given to the investigating attorneys from Germany, the United States, and Israel, the following facts emerged: that Schmidt (1) shot exhausted inmates; (2) killed an inmate returning from the work Kommando "Humbold-Deutz"; (3) shot a Jewish attorney from Czechoslovakia; (4) shot 20 inmates pulling a wagon loaded with rations because they were unable to continue; (5) shot inmates unable to keep up; (6) ordered the shooting of inmates he had found hidden in a barn; and (7) witnessed the shooting of inmates on marches, including the march to Dora-Mittelbau.

The defendant did not take the stand. However, his attorney entered a plea of not guilty, stating that Kommandant Schmidt was not responsible for deaths or shootings and had no knowledge of such.

On April 19, 1979, Landesgericht Kiel of Schleswig-Holstein stated in its verdict as follows:

> There was no confirmation that the accused had participated in or had any knowledge of these incidents. It is quite possible that he was not present during this part of the march. It must also be considered that the witnesses' testimonies can be considered only partially because of their weakened condition and diminished ability to remember what they saw during that time. Furthermore, after thirty years, it is possible that they may be fantasizing. Therefore, no definite conclusion can be reached that those shooting actually took place, who did the shooting, and if the accused took part in such.
>
> Based upon this, there is not sufficient evidence that the accused had participated in or had any knowledge of these incidents. Nor can the accused, Schmidt, be responsible for the shooting of inmates marching from Turmalien to Magdeburg in April 1945. Nor can he be held responsible for killing inmates hiding in the barn, or the killing of Eichler, Boot (or Booth) and the Russian inmate, name unknown.
>
> Also, the time of such trials has expired. Only for murder, manslaughter, or accessory to murder could the defendant be brought to justice.
>
> Therefore, Landgericht Kiel dismisses the trial. April 19, 1979.

[vgl. BGH St 22, 275. Mandated by Bartels Court Representative. Certified (signature illegible). Official seal of the Justiceminister des Landes Schleswig-Holstein. This quotation translated by Benjamin Jacobs]

Three survivors not present at the trial, including this author, testified to having seen Schmidt kill inmates. None of this testimony surfaced at the trial. Perhaps the verdict was predictable. The exoneration of Schmidt for all of these crimes was incomprehensible and outrages.

The Boston office of the German General Consul has urged the German Justice Department to reopen the trial. So far the department has remained silent. It is well known that the German Justice Department is still riddled with many former Nazis. It will take generations for Germany to free itself of its past.

APPENDIX C:
The Record of Prisoner 141129

May 6, 1986
1V-8521/2150/1282/86
State Museum, Auschwitz-Birkenau

Mr. Benjamin Jacobs:
The State Museum of Auschwitz acknowledges your inquiry and amiably informs you that full documentation of Bronek Jakubowicz, number 141129 as prisoner in the former concentration camp Auschwitz, has not been fully preserved.

Based on existing records, the Museum can nonetheless confirm that a prisoner with the above number 141129, name unavailable, was delivered to the concentration camp Auschwitz on August 26, 1943, with a transport from a camp in the Poznan region. It is further noted that October 25, 1944, places the named prisoner in Auschwitz III, Fürstengrube. No other data are available at the Museum.

Kazimierz Smolen, Director

[Translated by Benjamin Jacobs.]

INDEX